THE
ART TEACHER'S
DESKTOP
REFERENCE

MICHAEL E. PARKS
Buffalo State College

Prentice Hall
Englewood Cliffs, New Jersey 07632

Library of Congress Cataloging-in-Publication Data

PARKS, MICHAEL E.
    The art teacher's desktop reference / Michael E. Parks.
        p. cm.
    Includes bibliographical references and index.
    ISBN 0-13-052234-1
    1. Art--Study and teaching (Elementary)--United States--Handbooks.
    Manuals, etc. 2. Art--Study and teaching (Secondary)--United
    States--Handbooks, manuals, etc. I. Title.
    N353.P25 1994   93-8104
    707'.1'273--dc20   CIP

Acquisitions editor: *Bud Therien*
Editorial/production supervision: *Kerry Reardon/Jean Lapidus*
Interior design: *Kerry Reardon*
Electronic page layout: *Meg VanArsdale*
Cover design: *Rich Dombrowski*
Production coordinator: *Bob Anderson*

 © 1994 by Prentice Hall
A Paramount Communications Company
Englewood Cliffs, New Jersey 07632

Printed in the United States of America
10 9 8 7 6 5 4 3 2 1

ISBN 0-13-052234-1

PRENTICE-HALL INTERNATIONAL (UK) LIMITED, *London*
PRENTICE-HALL OF AUSTRALIA PTY. LIMITED, *Sydney*
PRENTICE-HALL CANADA INC., *Toronto*
PRENTICE-HALL HISPANOAMERICANA, S.A., *Mexico*
PRENTICE-HALL OF INDIA PRIVATE LIMITED, *New Delhi*
PRENTICE-HALL OF JAPAN, INC., *Tokyo*
SIMON & SCHUSTER ASIA PTE. LTD., *Singapore*
EDITORA PRENTICE-HALL DO BRASIL, LTDA., *Rio de Janeiro*

This book is dedicated to *Lisa Savage Parks,* an elementary school art teacher who has encouraged, advised, and inspired me in the writing of this book. She has always clarified my thoughts and helped me bridge the gaps between theories of art education and the realities of daily teaching in a classroom. Her approach to the art of teaching has been, and will continue to be, a model for me.

CONTENTS

PREFACE

The training of art teachers during the 1950s through the 1970s emphasized the development of creativity and self-expression as a major objective of art instruction, and it assumed that the art room was the only environment in the school where children could be free to be themselves. Many believed that art was unique from other subject areas in nurturing the growth of the affective and subjective aspects of a child's development, thus contributing to the mission of the school, which is to produce well-adjusted and productive citizens.

Artmaking was viewed as a tool to "draw out" the uniqueness of each individual, allowing the students to creatively express themselves through art materials. Teachers believed that by encouraging children to vent their feelings and emotions in art work, they were providing a healthy outlet for such experiences, thus contributing to the emotional and psychological well-being of the child. Such attitudes and practices also seemed to parallel what modern artists were doing in movements like abstract expressionism.

Art education theory during this period discouraged teachers from talking about art made by real artists out of fear that such exposure would pollute and disrupt the natural development of the child's personal expression and growth. However, measuring creativity has always been a nebulous and difficult task, and little evidence exists today that such approaches to teaching art really succeeded at developing creativity in children. Such an attitude about the role of art instruction has changed radically in recent years.

Other questions have been raised about creativity. Does creativity in art carry over into other areas of life? Does creativity really happen in a vacuum, or is it a process of "bisociation" (the synthesis of ideas) as Arthur Koestler (1949, 1964) proposed? If creativity is the product of an active synthesis of ideas, does this not suggest that the more exposure a child has to the ideas of artists, the more creative in art they are likely to be? Is not creative thinking necessary in science, mathematics, and all the other subject areas as well— and, if so, are not art educators walking on thin ice when they claim "creativity" as their primary contribution to the education of children?

Art and society are in a constant state of change; and, for education to be relevant, it, too, has to change. In an age of "back to basics," professionalism, and accountability in general education, the field of art education has shifted away from strict studio production with emphasis on creativity and self-expression (a child-centered approach) to a subject-centered emphasis. Of the subject-centered approaches, the most familiar is Discipline-Based Art Education (DBAE), which advocates incorporating the teaching of art history, art criticism, art production, and aesthetics in a sequentially arranged curriculum. A DBAE approach places emphasis on the content of art and the various ways one can experience it.

While the field of art education still acknowledges there are possible developmental benefits derived from art instruction, the primary justification for the role of art in today's school curriculum is that art is a subject worthy of study in its own right, with four disciplines, each possessing a unique body of knowledge and methods of inquiry. In other words, art is no longer viewed as a tool to be used for nurturing other areas of a child's development.

This book is divided into three parts. Part One presents a summary of the capabilities of children, including theories of child development (Chapter 1); a discussion of the methods of art instruction (Chapter 2); a summary of the history, of the field of art education and approaches to teaching history and an overview of issues in art education, such as criticism and aesthetics (Chapter 3). Each of these chapters includes accompanying lesson ideas.

Part Two is a quick reference quide with an extensive chronology of periods and styles in the history of Western art (Chapter 4) and Non-Western art (Chapter 5). Chapter 6 is an art education dictionary.

Part Three includes bibliographical listings, arranged for easy reference both alphabetically and by subject.

There are a number of assumptions about the role of art in society and in education that have guided my teaching and the writing of this book. Those assumptions are:

1. Art has been an integral activity in every known society, past and present. What we know about a society's beliefs, values, and quality of life are based on the artifacts they produced. Because art objects are cultural artifacts, such products *always* reveal the health and vitality, or sickness and deprivation of the society that produced them.

2. Art manifests itself in objects and products of thought that are the most complex forms of symbol–making produced by human beings. Such symbols are always grounded in ideas. Because of this, art has been considered a topic worthy of contemplation by philosophers since Plato.

3. Art along with science, philosophy, and religion are the primary modes through which human beings pursue truths about the human condition.

4. Psychologists identify the "aesthetic" as a need of the individual and a part of what it means to be human.

5. Because art comments on every facet of the human experience, the history of art is the history of everything.

6. Not only were visual images probably the first form of written symbol–making/notation, we are today, more than ever, a visually-oriented society. If individuals are to function intelligently in such an environment, they will need the skills, awareness, and insight to respond to the visual bombardment in reflective, critical ways.

7. Art is more than emotion or technical mastery. While there are certainly emotional aspects to making and responding to works of art, and technical skills are helpful in communicating ideas, the mental response of an educated person to a work of art is largely a cognitive experience.

Finally, *The Art Teacher's Desktop Reference* was written to fill the gaps in the limited number of publications available to art teachers in training and the seasoned professionals in the field. By providing both theoretical and practical approaches to teaching art from a subject-centered focus, quick access to basic information about art, and access to additional resources, *The Art Teacher's Desktop Reference* attempts to satisfy that need.

Michael E. Parks

1 THE CAPABILITIES OF CHILDREN

For years, art teacher training centered on the developmental research of Viktor Lowenfeld (Lowenfeld and Brittain, 1982). Lowenfeld's research identified specific stages of child development evident in the drawings of emotionally and mentally healthy children (see page 3). However, as the field of art education has moved away from a child-centered focus where art is used as a therapeutic tool, to a subject-centered emphasis which views art as a subject worthy of study, a broader view of child development is necessary. What follows are various perspectives on child development, from the cognitive approaches of Jean Piaget, to studies on developmental stages of viewing and experiencing art.

PIAGET'S THEORY OF COGNITIVE DEVELOPMENT

The Swiss psychologist, Jean Piaget, proposed a theory of cognitive development that has had an enormous impact on the study of child development. Cognition involves perception (how we take in information), conception (the formulation of ideas), the use of symbols and the understanding of abstract relationships. Piaget (1954, 1969, 1977) believed that cognitive development

1

happens in stages, as the child masters the mental operations of one stage, he is then ready to advance to the next stage of development. Piaget's stages are as follows:

Sensorimotor Operations: Birth to Age Two.

There is little at birth that is cognitive in nature. The baby functions purely with reflex responses and is incapable of understanding words or numbers, is incapable of distinguishing between herself and surrounding objects. By eighteen months, the infant starts to possess problem-solving skills—for example, the infant consistently recognizes a particular object, can figure out how to get a toy, can lift a blanket off her face if it is not wanted, and can adapt some of the newly learned skills to different situations.

Preconceptual Thought: Ages Two to Four.

As the child learns to associate objects with words, speech develops. The child sees things but imagines them as something else, creating a world of objects for mental exercise. A blanket or towel becomes a cape, he or she becomes Batman or Supergirl, and a stick or toy car can be substituted for a toy gun. A stuffed toy becomes an imaginary friend. At this stage, the child cannot yet think in terms of ideas or generalities, which require abstract thinking.

Intuitive Thought: Ages Four to Seven.

Between the ages of four and seven, the child begins to recognize simple generalities. For instance, he recognizes that the plastic building blocks can be sorted into four distinct groups based on color and that the green blocks have in common the color green. The child is intuitively perceiving the green blocks as a group, not because he has knowledge of the concept of color.

At this stage, the child can sit down in front of two glass containers, one of which is tall and slender with water in it, and the other of which is short and wide in diameter. One can pour the water from the tall, slender container into the short, fat container in front of the child, yet the child will think the tall, slender container had more water in it because the water was higher up that container's side than it was in the short, wide container. Piaget referred to the ability to perceive the same amount, mass, weight, or volume when transferred from one state to another as the principle of *invariance*, or *conservation*. Children at this stage are incapable of perceiving such things, nor are they able to apply their own thoughts within another person's frame of reference.

Concrete Operations: Ages Seven to Eleven.

At this stage, the child is able to deal with concrete problems that involve physical objects and processes, sequential developments such as progressive size increases, and can understand and perceive points of view other than her own. She can also understand the concept of conservation, and she may recognize and understand the elements of an abstract problem, but she is unable to produce a solution to the problem.

Formal Operations: Ages Eleven to Fifteen.

Now the child is able to begin thinking abstractly and logically. The child can see a problem, recognize several potential solutions, and test them until a reasonable solution is found. At this age, structures and approaches to problem solving should be introduced if continued cognitive growth—growth that can continue throughout adulthood—is to take place.

DEVELOPMENTAL THEORIES IN ART EDUCATION

Children As Artists: Lowenfeld's Stages

After years of studying drawings by children ranging in age from preschool to high school, Viktor Lowenfeld (1947) identified six general stages of emotional and mental development reflected in their drawings. The following stages are summarized from Lowenfeld and Brittain (1982):

The Scribbling Stage, Ages Two to Four: The Beginnings of Self-Expression.

Disordered Scribbling: Initially, the young child scribbles randomly using the whole drawing surface, sometimes running off the page. He uses his whole arm and shoulder to draw, frequently looking away from the paper, enjoying the experience for the kinesthetic pleasure it gives. The child at this substage makes no attempt at representation.

Controlled Scribble: As the child matures, the scribbles become smaller and tighter, and he often repeats motions. Staying within the boundaries of the paper, the child watches the scribbles while he draws them, and circles, lines, loops, and so on, are repeated.

Named Scribble: While the drawing is still composed of scribbles, the child is now pointing to them and identifying them as a particular subject (which may change during the process of drawing). Lines now become edges of shapes, and the child relates the marks to things he knows. He purposefully places scribbles on the paper.

The Preschematic Stage, Ages Four to Seven: First Representational Attempts

The child is now drawing objects on the paper, although they will not have any relationship to each other. The picture becomes a form of communication with the self. The placement and size of objects is subjective, in part because the child may rotate the paper while drawing. Objects seem to float around the paper, and are distorted to fit the available space. People are represented by a circle with feet growing out of it. Gradually, the child adds more and more details to the body, although distortion and the omission of body parts is expected. Toward the end of this stage, the child includes clothes, hair, and other details.

The Schematic Stage, Ages Seven to Nine: The Achievement of a Form Concept

At this stage, the child's drawing demonstrates her knowledge of the environment. The child has also developed a schema, or form concept—for example, a symbol for a person—which she repeats over and over again. Drawings are not based on what she perceives, but on a concept. Objects are now anchored to a baseline, often with a skyline above and air in between. There is little overlapping or sense of depth, and space is subjective through the inclusion of both plan and elevation, x-ray images, and the fusion of time and space. The human figure is a repeated schema with appendages correctly placed and with volume added. Proportions of the various objects depend on their emotional value.

The "Gang Age," Ages Nine to Twelve: The Dawning Realism.

Now the child's drawing begins to show attempts at depth and distance as the baseline disappears, a plane emerges, and the sky touches the horizon line. Objects begin to overlap and diminish in size as they recede into space. The child is becoming more self-conscious, and this is reflected in the child's drawing in that human figures are no longer represented by rigid schema and greater detail is present in clothing. However, the figure is stiffer and shows that the child has no understanding of shading and shadowing.

The Pseudonaturalistic Stage, Ages Twelve to Fourteen: The Age of Reasoning

By now, the child has become very self-conscious and critically aware of his shortcomings in drawing, causing spontaneous art activity to end. The proportions of human figures are more correct, and joints and body action are more realistic. Facial expressions vary for meaning, and sexual characteristics of the body are overemphasized. The visually minded child who draws as a spectator attempts to render his drawings in perspective at this stage. This demonstrates his awareness of the environment, but the child draws only the important elements in detail. The haptically minded child who draws as a participant uses space more subjectively.

Adolescent Art, Ages Fourteen to Seventeen: The Period of Decision

Now the child possesses an extended attention span and can control purposeful expression. If she has an interest in art, she begins consciously to develop artistic skills. If she does not have an interest in art, without further instruction she will tend to produce drawings that resemble work at the twelve-year level. The visually minded student can learn how to draw in perspective, and she can exhibit an awareness of atmosphere in her art work, thereby demonstrating pleasure in visual details, light, and shade. The haptically minded student draws more subjectively, and her drawings are nonnaturalistic in representation, moody, and use distortion for purposeful emphasis. The child at this age can use the human figure imaginatively for satire.

Children Viewing Art: Research Results

For decades, Lowenfeld's theories and developmental stages were standard content in art teacher preparation courses. However, his ideas were limited to the process of making art. In recent years, several groups of researchers have examined the capabilities of students when they are looking at works of art. Among these researchers are Gardner and Winner, Rosenstiel and others, Parsons, and Koroscik. The results of their research have provided essential insights for the practice of a Discipline-Based approach to Art Education (DBAE). A DBAE approach to art includes not only the making of art but the study of art history, art criticism, and aesthetics as well.

Gardner and Winner: Understanding Art

Howard Gardner and Ellen Winner (1976) conducted interviews with 121 children to identify developmental stages of understanding art. They concluded that children pass through three distinct developmental phases in their understanding, regardless of social status. In identifying these three phases, they asked questions that focused on the following topics:

- The source of art.
- The production of art.
- The medium.
- Style.
- Art and the outside world.
- Formal properties of art.
- Evaluation.

Gardner and Winner identified the following three developmental stages of understanding art:

Four to Seven Years: Very young children have a simplistic understanding of art: the making of art is an easy, mechanical activity and judgments about the artistic quality of a work are all equally acceptable. Some children will concede that authorities determine what is good (authorities such as moms and dads). Children in this age group tend to emphasize the technical aspects of a work of art, often initially denying that art is made by people, saying instead that it comes from materials, for example. Most of these children believe that anyone can make art, not realizing that a special group of people makes art and that it takes talent and training.

Because they view art making as a mechanical activity, many of these young children believe that animals can make art too, if they have the physical ability and the right appendages to hold the brushes or pencils. Because they lack an understanding of formal properties, they believe art-making decisions are governed by physical limitations rather than aesthetic concerns—for example, they would say the picture is finished when the paper is filled.

At this age, children generally confuse the subject matter in a picture with the actual object itself, admitting only when pressed that the object is also a picture. Many are incapable of distinguishing between a photograph and a painting and were just as likely to have difficulty distinguishing artistic styles.

The youngest children in this age group often prefer abstract paintings to representational images because of their design, bright colors, or subject matter that the child imagines is there. However, by the time the child begins formal schooling, preferences shift to more realistic kinds of pictures, reflecting their interest in the real world.

Ten Years: In the middle elementary years, children believe art should be a precise rendering of reality, reflecting the literal way they think about things. They believe there are criteria for judging quality in works of art; the more real it looks, the better it is.

Adolescence: Teenagers are more sophisticated in their understanding of art, and they are not as narrow as younger children in their views about art. They realize that peoples' opinions and values vary, but they have often regressed to the position that judgments in art are relative and any opinion is valid. Gardner and Winner (1976) argue that children will remain in an arrested state of development in their understanding of art unless their naive opinions about art are confronted.

Rosenstiel and Others: Critical Judgment.

Rosenstiel, Morison, Silverman, and Gardner (1978) sought to identify developmental stages of critical judgment in art. They interviewed children ranging in age from six to sixteen, seeking information concerning three issues:

1. What are the general characteristics of responses at each age level? This information served both as a corroboration of earlier studies and as a necessary background for the remaining questions.
2. To what extent can children of different ages distinguish among standards of personal preference, community values, and technical competence?
3. What is the course of development through which children pass as they become increasingly able to take into account each of these standards of critical judgment? (p. 96)

Rosenstiel and others identified the following developmental characteristics in children's critical judgment:

First-Graders: Children in this age group are limited to identifying subject matter and colors. They also make comments such as "it's good" or "it's pretty," reflecting the very general nature of their responses.

Third-Graders: Subject matter and color are still frequent topics, but now the children comment on the details, designs, and shapes in the work and occasionally refer to painterly surface qualities. Third graders consider realism "good" because it is hard to do, and they consider sketch work "messy." Although they still make generalized statements, unlike the first graders they add explanations for such comments.

Sixth-Graders: Sixth-grader responses parallel those of third-graders, with a few exceptions. Sixth-graders tend to use a few more terms from art history in their comments and have a tendency to mention painterly surface elements with greater frequency.

Tenth-Graders: Adolescents are far less likely than children in the other three age groups to make contentless statements. They tend to cite a variety of factors when selecting and justifying their responses to works of art. They will not be inclined to believe that a work of art is better because it is "hard to paint" or because it is in one particular medium versus another. They will tend to mention formal properties, use terminology from art criticism, and mention and recognize work from certain periods in history and specific artists' names.

Rosenstiel and colleagues concluded that younger children might be able to make finer aesthetic distinctions when viewing works of art but that their verbal responses were confined to their limited vocabulary.

Parsons: A Theory of Cognitive Development.

Parsons (1987) presented a theory of cognitive development that pertains to how people understand paintings. "The theory analyzes the interpretive frameworks with which people think about paintings, the understandings that structure the virtues they find worth looking for aesthetically" (p. 37). In presenting his ideas, Parsons was sensitive to the concern that "developmental stages" are often perceived as ways of labeling or predicting people, and he emphasized that he did not view the stages as describing people but as "...ways of thinking about art" (p. 38). He also addressed the supposition that a strictly cognitive approach to the development of artistic sensibility was inadequate because it fails to consider the subjective and affective responses one has toward works of art. Parsons argued that cognition influences the feelings one has for a work of art and that feelings, in turn, affect how one thinks about a picture.

Parsons' theory of aesthetic development is described in five stages:

Stage I: This stage is characterized by spontaneous, idiosyncratic responses to art. The individual is egocentric and does not identify strongly with the subject in a painting. The individual responds as much to color as to subject matter and tends to find satisfaction in perceiving individual objects in the image instead of in seeing them as parts to a whole. The individual likes or dislikes works that appeal to him personally and does not seem to expect others to hold the same opinion.

Stage II: This stage is characterized by structured ideas about beauty and ugliness, and "...the kind of social understanding they imply" (p. 41). An individual at this stage will view the purpose of a painting as the depiction of an object, and the quality of the image, therefore, depends on the quality of the object pictured. The individual will immediately like or dislike a painting and assume that her opinion is shared by others, that her opinion is a statement of fact. This attitude is not a result of reflecting on the opinions of others but of projecting her feelings on them. The individual at this stage depends largely on the subject for her understanding of a painting.

Stage III: At the stage, the individual is aware that a painting requires interpretation, a search for meaning, and that meaning is found "...in the subjective experience of individuals, either of herself or others, and this expectation structures her emotional response" (p. 47). She now realizes that people have their own personal way of responding subjectively to experience, and she is aware of her own self. She is aware that meaning in art is not public, but personal. Beauty and ugliness are no longer criteria for judging the quality of a painting; rather, the power of expression and a work's ability to provide significant and meaningful experience are. The individual is now capable of empathizing with a work of art but still relies primarily on subject matter for her understanding of the experience.

Stage IV: At this level of aesthetic development, the individual has a growing awareness of the importance of a painting having meaning within the context of the art world itself and an understanding of the medium in which the work is executed. "In a sense the medium *is* the painting, and its significance *must* reside there" (p. 48). When assessing the quality of a painting, he looks closely at the colors, textures, contrasts, forms, techniques, and so on, and considers what they contribute to the whole. The medium is viewed as a collaborator, an active partner with the artist. Aesthetic judgment becomes a matter of objectivity and not simply personal, subjective experience. The individual is now a part of the artistic community with an insider's understanding of art, hearing his own opinions and ideas reflected in the community's conversation about art. The public discussion enlarges his own understanding, and a work of art takes on public meaning, "...part of a complex historical web of meanings that constitutes an art tradition" (p. 50).

Stage V: The fifth stage is based on three assumptions: (1) One must constantly reinterpret one's inner self—one's thoughts, feelings, and experiences. When an individual responds aesthetically to a work of art, he is self-consciously questioning his own experience through the painting. (2) A work of art is the product of a cultural tradition and may express more than the artist intended or the viewer perceived. The individual may or may not be perceptive to the work's subtlety and may have to work hard to grasp it. (3) While art expresses one's internal life and one judges it by assessing one's own experience, "judgments about art are capable of objectivity" (p. 52). One interprets and judges paintings by presenting reasons for holding such opinions to others. At this stage, the individual is constantly aware of the question of whether his experience of a painting is public and universal or private and irrelevant. He realizes that art often questions the way we see things and, in turn, questions one's experience and the foundation on which it is based. "The essence of stage five is the seeking of reasons for interpretations and judgments, reasons which must in principle be available to anyone" (p. 54).

Koroscik: The Role of Cognition.

Koroscik (1982, 1984) examined the role of cognition in viewing and talking about art. She began with the premise that knowledge cannot be acquired without the perception, transformation, interpretation, retention, and application of information. Koroscik appropriated from learning theory an information-processing model that views learning as a continuum of successive levels or stages. In her model, the following levels apply to the processing of art:

Stage I: The analysis of the sensory or structural features of a stimulus (p. 330).

(a) encoding an artwork's physical properties (e.g., its size, surface qualities, and media).
(b) discerning visual elements that appear within the work (e.g., colors, shapes, lines, and values).
(c) observing relationships as they occur among those elements. (p. 331)

Stage II: The application of previously acquired knowledge in the interpretation of meanings that characterize semantic dimensions of stimuli (p. 330).

(a) identifying representational features and expressive qualities.
(b) recognizing instances of symbolic denotation.
(c) determining underlying religious, social, economic, philosophical, or political principles exemplified by a work. (p. 331)

The ability of the individual to remember in depth a work of art will correspond with the depth to which the work was processed. In addition to the model for processing structural and semantic information, Koroscik acknowledged the problems with deriving meaning from a work of art if the viewer lacks prior knowledge or a contextual framework for understanding or interpreting what he is looking at.

With this problem in mind, Koroscik examined the effects of verbalization on the abilities of individuals to process structural and semantic information about works of art. She examined two models and their relationship to processing art. The *dual-encoding model* argues that "...sensory features of pictures are stored in imagery codes, while the products of verbalization are retained as verbal or linguistic codes....Simply stated, two codes are better than one" (p. 331).

In the *sensory-semantic model*, "pictures and their verbal descriptions are assumed to evoke distinctive sensory representations in memory but access a common semantic system" (pp. 331–332). Subsequent investigations based on these models produced the following conclusions about the role of verbalization in the processing of art:

- Processing and the ability to remember visual art was generally higher when task instructions required the verbalization of semantic characteristics rather than structural characteristics.

- When verbal tasks required students to consider an artwork holistically and generate a title that characterized the work, retention of both structural and semantic features was better than with any other verbal or nonverbal processing task.

- The more abstract the visual art work, the more difficulty students have remembering the work. When representational features are difficult to distinguish, structural information is difficult to retain. Retention of abstract works of art is dependent on the verbal contextual information provided.

The presentation of verbal contexts ensured that meaning was processed to some extent, thus facilitating the retention of semantic information which in turn promoted the retention of structural features....Even more sophisticated viewers with prior knowledge of art benefited from the presentation of verbal contextual information. (pg. 333).

A THEORY ABOUT THE COGNITIVE AND AFFECTIVE DOMAINS OF LEARNING

In 1956, Bloom, Engelhart, Furst, Hill, and Krathwohl published *The Taxonomy of Educational Objectives.* The taxonomy provided a framework for organizing and measuring educational objectives. They identified three major domains of learning—the cognitive, affective, and psychomotor—arguing that for learning to take place, all three domains have to be engaged. The cognitive domain, for which the handbook appeared in the original 1956 publication, has played a prominent role in both curriculum and test development over the past thirty years. The hierarchical categories of behavior in the cognitive domain are relatively distinct and objectively identifiable (See Figure 1–1).

The handbook for the affective domain was published in 1964 by Krathwohl, Bloom, and Masia. Behavior categories of this domain are also hierarchically arranged from the simple to the complex. However, the affective domain deals with attitudes and values, making it more difficult to clearly identify precise categories of behavior, or the kinds of classroom activities that nurture higher levels of affective responses in students. The affective domain is also difficult, if not impossible, to measure because when children's (and adults') values, attitudes, and beliefs are questioned, they tend to

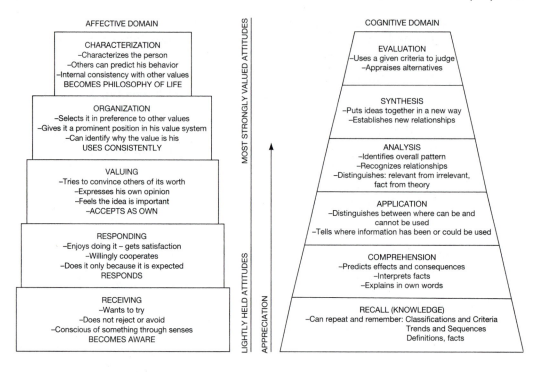

FIGURE 1–1. The affective and cognitive domains.

say what they think the teacher wants to hear, not what they actually feel or believe.

The psychomotor domain, although relevant to the teaching of art, has never been categorized in a handbook such as the two handbooks mentioned above.

The illustrations of the cognitive and affective domains in Figure 1–1 are adapted from Bloom and others (1956) and Krathwohl and others (1964), respectively. Both hierarchies begin at the bottom (simple), and build toward the top (complex), each level requiring an extension of previous levels. In Discipline-Based Art Education, quality learning experiences in all four disciplines can operate at the highest levels within the cognitive domain. For instance, when students are asked to formally analyze a work of art and discuss its composition, they are operating at the fourth level of the hierarchy. When students are required to produce a work of art that appropriates subject matter from well-known historical works of art and to use that subject matter as a metaphor for a contemporary social problem, they are "synthesizing." And, when the works are completed and hung on the bulletin board for a class critique and students are asked to identify the most successful works based on established criteria for the lesson, past experience, knowledge, and exposure to art, the students are operating at the highest level of the hierarchy, "evaluation." (For an art criticism questioning strategy based on Bloom's *Taxonomy*, see Hamblen, Questioning Strategies, p. 40).

While affective responses are important to any kind of learning if the students are to be operating in the higher levels of the cognitive domain, there is no other subject area where the relationship between the cognitive and affective is more apparent than in art. Works of art are sensory objects and they require us to respond with our intellect, values, and emotions. As objects, there is much that is factual and objective that we can learn about them—the materials they are made from, the dates of their creation, who their creators were, and so on. Yet, such information is relatively meaningless to the experiencing of the work itself.

Works of art require an empathic response from the viewer, and empathic responses require nurturing in a classroom setting. For valuing—the beginnings of appreciation—to take place, Krathwohl, and others state that conditions must be in place for the students to express their opinions and defend them. If students are to develop empathy and appreciation for art, they must do more in class than just make art. They must be looking at and talking about art, artists, and ideas if valuing, organization, and characterization are ultimate affective objectives of the art program.

ATTITUDES TOWARD ART AND LEARNING

The attitudes that students hold will determine their willingness to expose themselves to new ideas, to alter the things they value in life, and their eagerness to know more. This is true in terms of knowledge and learning in general (see Krathwohl and others, 1964, *Taxonomy*); but it is particularly true for the art educator who is dealing with beliefs about the significance of art to life, the relationship of artist to culture, and the value structures of individuals that affect their ability to make qualitative, aesthetic decisions. Aestheticians have long contemplated the idea that to have an aesthetic experience, one must possess an aesthetic attitude:

> For at least two centuries it has been a dominant view in aesthetic theory that, when we appreciate objects in nature and works of art, we are in some special frame of mind, or in some "mental set" or attitude, and that if we are not, we cannot appreciate whatever beauties may lie waiting for us in the world of nature or of art. (Hospers, 1982, p. 335)

Unlike many other subject areas, art is subjectively laden and requires evaluative-qualitative kinds of thinking. To teach art well is demanding in and of itself, and the difficulty is compounded by the preconceived attitudes about art that students bring with them to the classroom.

The Study and Measurement of Attitudes toward Art

Eisner (1969) conducted a study to determine if a federally funded Title III program in the arts for elementary school children was having any kind of impact on those involved. An instrument was devised to measure the attitudes of parents and teachers toward the overall school program. Not surprisingly, he found that the attitudes of both parents and teachers were similar, reflecting their middle-class values. Interesting discoveries were made when specific items were examined:

> When it came to questions dealing with contributions of various subject areas to the good life....Both parents and teachers appear to recognize the contribution that the arts make to a gratifying and personally meaningful life. Yet, when it came to questions such as "more instructional time should be devoted to some subject areas in school than to others"...art, music, and foreign languages were rated lowest. (p. 20)

Earlier, Eisner (1966) had also administered to high school students a sixty-item multiple-choice instrument, the *Eisner Art Attitude Inventory.* He found that:

> ...Thirty-five percent were either uncertain or disagreed with the statement, "Advances in the field of art are important for a country's progress." To the statement, "An artist's contribution to society is not as important as that of a scientist," almost 30 percent agreed. But the statement that received the highest percentage of agreement—two out of every three of the 1,488 students agreed—was, "Good art is a matter of personal taste." (p. 50)

A disturbing aspect of Eisner's study was that the majority of students participating were high school students who had an interest in art and took art classes as electives.

In 1977, Morris and Stuckhardt sought to clarify the conceptual meaning of attitudes as it applies to the field of art education and to delineate the qualities implicit in that definition. They recognized six major characteristics of attitudes that had been identified by authorities within the realm of attitude research and demonstrated the relevancy of those characteristics to the teaching of art:

1. Attitudes are affective, evaluative concepts that give rise to motivated behavior.
2. Attitudes are learned.
3. Attitudes have specific social referents.
4. Attitudes are relatively stable and enduring.
5. Attitudes vary in quality and intensity.
6. Attitudes are interrelated. (p. 22)

An important contribution of this study was the operational definition of art attitudes which incorporated the fundamental characteristics of attitudes. Morris and Stuckhardt suggested that an art attitude is "A learned and relatively enduring evaluative system of affective predispositions held toward art referents" (1977, p. 21).

A number of studies have been conducted over the years that examine various populations' attitudes toward various aspects of art and art education. Whitesel (1975) constructed a scale for measuring women art students' career commitments. Miller (1980) surveyed the attitudes concerning art education held by school board presidents, superintendents, and principals in the state of Missouri. Pum (1971) and Hall (1978) conducted studies to identify various art attitudes held by elementary-education majors, while Adams (1980) examined the attitudes of Alabama primary teachers toward selected concepts of Viktor Lowenfeld. Public school children's attitudes about selected art concepts were surveyed by Crabbe (1978) at the elementary level and by Savuto (1977) at the high school level.

CHILDREN WITH SPECIAL NEEDS

As a result of the passage of Public Law 94-142 in the mid-1970s, school districts must provide evidence that whenever possible they are educating handicapped students in regular classrooms with those who are not handicapped. The only time a school district can segregate a handicapped child in a special classroom is when the child's handicaps are so severe that they prevent the child from obtaining an appropriate education in a normal educational setting. A frequent administrative remedy for meeting the legal requirements of the law is *mainstreaming,* or *inclusion,* in which the handicapped child is placed in a subject-area classroom deemed appropriate for his or her developmental level.

A variety of conditions and handicaps can be associated with "special-needs" children, many of whom exhibit more than one of the following conditions:

- Cognitive/intellectual distinctions
- *Mental retardation*
- *Learning disabilities (for example, dyslexia, brain damage, and so forth)*
- *Giftedness (see Public Law 95-561, The Gifted and Talented Children's Act)*
- Physically impaired
- *Orthopedically handicapped*
- *Chronically ill*
- *Hearing- and sight-impaired*
- Communication difficulties
- *Speech-impaired*
- Psychosocial Problems
- *Emotionally troubled*
- *Socially maladjusted*
- Cultural differences
- *Learning disadvantages*
- *Second-language difficulties*

Art teachers who work with special-needs children should have access to, if not input in, the child's Individual Educational Plan (IEP), which establishes educational objectives and goals for the individual child. For additional reading on the characteristics of special-needs children, considerations when teaching them, and adaptive teaching techniques see Anderson, 1978; Anderson and Morreau, 1984; Art Educators of New Jersey, 1984; Blandy, 1985; Clark, 1983; Clements and Clements, 1984; Copeland, 1984; Hurwitz, 1983; Sherrill, 1979; Smith, 1983; and Uhlin, 1979.

2 ∥ METHODS OF ART INSTRUCTION

For a teacher to effectively instill in students an understanding of art content and a mindset open to learning, instruction must be organized in a way that achieves positive results. The teacher is the facilitator and the catalyst for learning in the art classroom. If a DBAE approach to art instruction is to be effective, lessons and units of instruction must be well thought out in advance, an environment conducive to productive discussions about art must be established, and forms of assessment must be implemented that encourage mastery of art content.

WRITING INSTRUCTIONAL OBJECTIVES, UNIT PLANS, AND LESSON PLANS

Instructional Objectives

When planning for instruction, a good teacher designs lesson and unit activities around the objectives to be achieved. The objectives, in turn, are based on broader goals and objectives established within a curriculum and which are appropriate for the age level of the children being instructed. Too often art teachers begin with a particular medium or project in mind and then seek out objectives that will justify the activity; this is backwards and, in all likelihood, reflects an art program that lacks continuity, sequencing, and direction. Lessons within a unit of study and in an entire curriculum should build from the simple to the complex.

Mager (1984), a noted authority on writing instructional objectives, stresses that "...the drafting of objectives causes one to think seriously and deeply about what is worth teaching, about what is worth spending time and effort to accomplish" (p. 6). He advocates thinking about objectives in performance terms—for example, what will the student be able to do as a result of instruction that he or she was not able to do before? "An objective describes an intended result of instruction, rather than the process of instruction itself" (p. 3).

Mager (1984) breaks instructional objectives down into three parts: (1) *performance*, or what the student will be expected to do to demonstrate learning has taken place; (2) *conditions*, or the limitations and restraints (if any) under which the student will be working; and (3) *criteria*, or the statement of how well the student will have to perform for that performance to be considered acceptable. For example:

- Performance: As a result of instruction, the student will demonstrate his knowledge of one-point perspective in a drawing.
- Conditions: The student will be given an 11" x 18" sheet of white drawing paper, a straight edge, and a pencil. The drawing must be completed within a 45-minute class period.
- Criterion: The final product must have a horizon line, a vanishing point, a minimum of three buildings correctly drawn on the surface plane at varying distances from the viewer, and at least one of the buildings must have a gabled roof. Extra points will be given for correctly drawn details on buildings—for example, windows, doors, brick, shingles, and siding drawn to scale.

There are advantages to stating the objectives using the three distinct components above in that it allows the writer to think concisely about what and how the objectives are to be accomplished. However, it is quite acceptable to state all three in one combined statement:

Given an 11" x 18" sheet of white drawing paper, a straight edge, and a pencil, the student will demonstrate her knowledge of one-point perspective in a drawing executed within a 45-minute class period. The final product must have a horizon line, a vanishing point, a minimum of three buildings correctly drawn on the surface plane at varying distants from the viewer, and at least one of the buildings must have a gabled roof. Extra points will be given for correctly drawn details on buildings—for example, windows, doors, brick, shingles, and siding drawn to scale.

Mager (1984) and others (Hunter and Gee, 1988) stress the importance of informing the students of the unit and lesson objectives. Students need to understand why they are learning something, and, if they know in advance what will be expected of them in terms of performance and quality, they are better able to adjust their personal learning styles to the demands of the experience and maximize their potential for success.

Lesson Plans

Strong, concise statements of objectives are always an essential component of any lesson plan. Once the objectives have been determined, the lesson and unit plan design follows. New teachers should develop thorough lesson plans, in part to ensure that important details and concerns have not been overlooked, but also because it provides a disciplined and structured way to think about the art of teaching. As one acquires more experience and expertise, the need for detailed lesson plans decreases. However, well-stated objectives should still be a primary concern for the veteran as well as the novice teacher. In general, a good lesson plan will contain variations of the following items:[*]

Title and Brief Introduction: *What* are the concepts to be addressed? Which of the domains are involved (productive, historical, critical, aesthetic)?

Goal(s): *What* is the relationship of the lesson to the purposes of art education? These are broad, general goals and may reflect national, state, or local curricular goals.

Rationale: *Why* are the students learning this? Is it relevant to the real art world? Is their understanding of art enhanced by the lesson? (For example: Do real artists glue cotton-ball tails on dittoed bunnies?).

Instructional Objectives: See the description above. How will students be informed of the objectives?

Resources: List books, articles, and references to be used, as well as the necessary art reproductions, slides, and films. List all vocabulary and definitions of art terms relevant to the lesson.

---

[*]Adapted from a lesson-plan format by Vincent Arnone.

Presentation of Lesson:

1. Introduction/Motivation—*How* will the lesson be introduced? *How* will you get the students focused on the lesson at hand? This is often referred to as the Anticipatory Set or Introduction to Set.

2. List step-by-step *how* you will demonstrate, explain, question, and discuss the ideas and concepts being taught. *How* will you help your students to understand *how* to achieve the objectives of the lesson successfully?

3. *How* will you remotivate the students should the lesson span more than one class session? What new pieces of information or perspectives might you provide them with so that each day they are in class they are learning something new and building on what they already know?

Management of the Classroom:

1. What materials, tools, and equipment will be needed for the lesson presentation and for the execution of the lesson activity itself?

2. What needs to be prepared in advance? How will materials be distributed? How will clean up and collection be handled? Storage? Traffic patterns?

Evaluation of Student Performance: *How* will you evaluate student performance? Will you use an exam, a quiz, or a critique? What procedures will you follow? How will equity be ensured?

Evaluation of Teacher Performance: *How* will you determine if the lesson was a success? What went well and what would you change should you want to use this lesson again? Was your own preparation adequate? On what teaching skills, knowledge, or attitudes were you personally focusing, and how can they be improved?

Unit Plans

A unit plan is a grouping of lesson plans—usually three or four—whose objectives are more broadly based and encompass bigger ideas than can be accomplished in only one lesson. Lesson plans within the unit are organized sequentially from simple to complex, building toward achievement of the unit goals. For example, if the theme of a unit plan were prehistoric art, lessons might be sequentially organized as follows:

1. An art history presentation on what life must have been like for prehistoric peoples, their struggle for survival, their evolving superstitions and beliefs, their need to communicate, and other aspects of their lives.

2. A lesson on the cave paintings at Lascaux and Altimira, how they were discovered, speculation about the functions the images served, and the methods used by anthropologists and art historians to arrive at such conclusions.

3. A lesson involving collecting the same primitive materials and pigments used by the cave painters and replicating the images on a wall or mural, such as may be available in the school or community.

4. A lesson requiring students to design and produce a wall mural for the school that focuses on the images and icons valued by contemporary society, emphasizing and reinforcing the notion that for at least thirty thousand years human beings have been driven to leave their mark, to say "this is what we valued, this is what we believed and felt."

RESEARCH FINDINGS ABOUT TEACHING AND LEARNING

In 1986, the U.S. Department of Education published a booklet entitled *What Works: Research about Teaching and Learning.* The publication contained research findings about effective methods of educating children. The following are some of the findings that art teachers may find useful:

Parental Involvement.

Research Finding: Parents are their children's first and most influential teachers. What parents do to help their children learn is more important to academic success than how well-off the family is. (DiPrete, 1981; Gray, 1984; Walberg, 1984).

Research Finding: Parental involvement helps children learn more effectively. Teachers who are successful at involving parents in their children's schoolwork are successful because they work at it. (Becker and Epstein, 1982; Cattermole and Robinson, 1985; Rich, 1985; Walberg, 1984).

Reading to Children.

Research Finding: The best way for parents to help their children become better readers is to read to them—even when they are very young. Children benefit most from reading aloud when they discuss stories, learn to identify letters and words, and talk about the meaning of words. (Anderson and others, 1985; Chomsky, 1972; Dunn, 1981; Heath, 1983).

Independent Reading.

Research Finding: Children improve their reading ability by reading a lot. Reading achievement is directly related to the amount of reading children do in school and outside. (Allington, 1984; Anderson and others, 1985)

Phonics.

Research Finding: Children get a better start in reading if they are taught phonics. Learning phonics helps them to understand the relationship between letters and sounds and to "break the code" that links the words they hear with the words they see in print. (Anderson and others 1985; Becker and Gersten, 1982; Chall, 1983; Perfetti and Lesgold, 1979).

Reading Comprehension.

Research Finding: Children get more out of a reading assignment when the teacher precedes the lesson with background information and follows it with discussion. (Beck, McCaslin, and McKeown, 1981; Durkin, 1983; Hansen, 1981; Mason, 1983; Mason and Osborn, 1983).

Storytelling.

Research Finding: Telling young children stories can motivate them to read. Storytelling also introduces them to cultural values and literary traditions before they can read, write, and talk about stories by themselves. (Applebee, 1978; Baker and Greene, 1977; Bettelheim, 1975; Cook, 1969; Sawyer, 1969).

Teaching Writing.

Research Finding: The most effective way to teach writing is to teach it as a process of brainstorming, composing, revising, and editing. (Elbow, 1981; Graves, 1978, 1983; Hilcocks, 1984).

Early Writing.

Research Finding: Children who are encouraged to draw and scribble "stories" at an early age will later learn to compose more easily, more effectively, and with greater confidence than children who do not have this encouragement. (Applebee, 1980, 1984; Graves, 1983).

Speaking and Listening.

Research Finding: A good foundation in speaking and listening helps children become better readers. (Anderson and others, 1985; Bagford, 1968; Humphreys and Davey, 1983).

Developing Talent.

Research Finding: Many highly successful individuals have above-average but not extraordinary intelligence. Accomplishment in a particular activity is often more dependent on hard work and self-discipline than on innate ability. (Bloom, 1985; Bloom and Sosniak, 1981; Walberg, 1969).

Ideals.

Research Finding: Belief in the value of hard work, the importance of personal responsibility, and the importance of education itself contributes to greater success in school. (Alexander and Campbell, 1964; Etzioni, 1984; Ginsburg and Hanson, 1985; Hanson and Ginsburg, 1985; Walberg, 1984).

Science Experiments.

Research Finding: Children learn science best when they are able to do experiments, so they can witness "science in action." (Champagne and Klopfer, 1984; Gentner and Stevens, 1983).

Estimating.

Research Finding: Although students need to learn how to find exact answers to arithmetic problems, good math students also learn the helpful skill of estimating answers. This skill can be taught. (Reed, 1984; Reys, 1982; Schoen, 1981; Trafton, 1978).

Teacher Expectations.

Research Finding: Teachers who set and communicate high expectations to all their students obtain greater academic performance from those students than teachers who set low expectations. (Brophy, 1981; Good, 1982; Good and Brophy, 1984; Morine-Dershimer, 1983; Purkey and Smith, 1983).

Student Ability and Effort.

Research Finding: Children's understanding of the relationship between being smart and hard work changes as they grow. (Doyle, 1983; Harari and Covington, 1981; Stipek, 1981; Weiner, 1979; Weinstein and others, 1982).

Managing Classroom Time.

Research Finding: How much time students are actively engaged in learning contributes strongly to their achievement. The amount of time available for learning is determined by the instructional and management skills of the teacher and the priorities set by the school administration. (Berliner, 1983; Brophy, 1979; Hawley, Rosenholtz, Goodstein, and Hasselbring, 1984; Stallings, 1980; Walberg, 1984).

Direct Instruction.

Research Finding: When teachers explain exactly what students are expected to learn and demonstrate the steps needed to accomplish a particular academic task, students learn more. (Berliner and Rosenshine, 1976; Doyle, 1985; Rosenshine, 1983).

Tutoring.

Research Finding: Students tutoring other students can lead to improved academic achievement for both student and tutor and to positive attitudes toward coursework. (Devin-Sheehan, Feldman and Allen, 1976; Mohan, 1972).

Questioning.

Research Finding: Student achievement rises when teachers ask questions that require students to apply, analyze, synthesize, and evaluate information in addition to simply recalling facts. (Berliner, 1984; Brophy and Evertson, 1976; Redfield and Rousseau, 1981).

Study Skills.

Research Finding: The ways in which children study influence strongly how much they learn. Teachers can often help children develop better study skills. (Bransford, 1979; Brown & Smiley, 1978; Craik and Watkins, 1973; Hayes-Roth and Goldin, 1980; Segal, Chipman, and Glaser, 1985).

Homework: Quantity.

Research Finding: Student achievement rises significantly when teachers regularly assign homework and students conscientiously do it. (Colemna, Hoffer, and Kilgore, 1982; Keith, 1982; National Center for Education Statistics, 1983; Rohlen, 1983; Walberg, 1984).

Homework: Quality.

Research Finding: Well-designed homework assignments relate directly to classwork and extend students' learning beyond the classroom. Homework is most useful when teachers carefully prepare the assignment, thoroughly explain it, and give prompt comments and criticism when the work is completed. (Featherstone, 1985; Walberg, 1985).

Assessment.

Research Finding: Frequent systematic monitoring of students' progress helps students, parents, teachers, administrators, and policymakers identify strengths and weaknesses in learning and instruction. (Rosenshine, 1983; Rutter, 1983).

Effective Schools.

Research Finding: The most important characteristics of effective schools are strong instructional leadership, a safe and orderly climate, school-wide emphasis on basic skills, high teacher expectations for student achievement, and continuous assessment of pupil progress. (Bossert, 1985; Corcoran, 1985; Doyle, 1985; Finn, 1984; Purkey and Smith, 1983).

School Climate.

Research Finding: Schools that encourage academic achievement focus on the importance of scholastic success and on maintaining order and discipline. (Basualdo and Basualdo, 1980; Brookover, 1979; Coleman, Hoffer, and Kilgore, 1982; Grant, 1981, 1985).

Discipline.

Research Finding: Schools contribute to their students' academic achievement by establishing, communicating, and enforcing fair and consistent discipline policies. (Brodinsky, 1980; DiPrete, 1981; Goldsmith, 1982).

Effective Principals.

Research Finding: Successful principals establish policies that create an orderly environment and support effective instruction. (Bird and Little, 1985; Bossert, 1985; Carnine, Gersten, and Green, 1982; Corcoran, 1985; Morris, 1984).

Collegiality.

Research Finding: Students benefit academically when their teachers share ideas, cooperate in activities, and assist one another's intellectual growth. (Glidewell, 1983; Little, 1982; Lortie, 1975; Phi Delta Kappa, 1980; Tye and Tye, 1984).

Teacher Supervision.

Research Finding: Teachers welcome professional suggestions about improving their work, but they rarely receive them. (Bird and Little, 1985; Fielding and Schalock, 1985; Natriello, 1984; Natriello and Dornbusch, 1981; Wise, 1984).

Cultural Literacy.

Research Finding: Students read more fluently and with greater understanding if they have background knowledge of the past and present. Such knowledge and understanding is called *cultural literacy.* (Anderson, Soiro, and Montague, 1977; Finn, Ravitch, and Roberts, 1985; Hirsch, 1983; Hirsch, 1985; Levine, 1980; Resnick and Resnick, 1977).

History.

Research Finding: Skimpy requirements and declining enrollments in history classes are contributing to a decline in students' knowledge of the past. (Fitzgerald, 1979; Ravitch, 1985; Ravitch, 1985b; Thernstrom, 1985).

Foreign Language.

Research Finding: The best way to learn a foreign language in school is to start early and to study it intensively over many years. (Hortas, 1984).

Rigorous Courses.

Research Finding: The stronger the emphasis on academic courses, the more advanced the subject matter, and the more rigorous the textbooks, the more high school students learn. Subjects that are learned mainly in school rather than at home, such as science and math, are most influenced by the number and kind of courses taken. (Chall, Conard, and Harris, 1977; Pallas and Alexander, 1983; Walberg and Shanahan, 1983).

Acceleration.

Research Finding: Advancing gifted students at a faster pace results in their achieving more than similarly gifted students who are taught at a normal rate. (Cohn, George, and Stanley, 1979; Getzels and Dillon, 1973; Goldberg, 1958; Gowan and Demos, 1964; Kulik and Kulik, 1984).

Extracurricular Activities.

Research Finding: High school students who complement their academic studies with extracurricular activities gain experience that contributes to their success in college. (Braddock, 1981; Purdy, Eitzen, and Hufnagel, 1982; Spady, 1971; Willingham, 1985).

Preparation for Work.

Research Finding: Business leaders report that students with solid basic skills and positive work attitudes are more likely to find and keep jobs than students with vocational skills alone. (Center for Public Resources, 1982; Committee for Economic Development, 1985; National Academy of Science, National Academy of Engineering, Institute of Medicine, and Committee on Science, Engineering and Public Policy, 1984; National Advisory Council on Vocational Education, 1984; Zemsky and Meyerson, 1986).

Nurturing Positive Attitudes toward Art

Studies in art education that have attempted to measure the effects of specific teaching methods or learning tasks on art attitudes are few in number (Dallis, 1975; Davis, 1966; Neale, 1973; Suggs, 1976). However, there have been some significant studies in the area of art attitude change. Mittler (1972, 1976) applied the concept of counterattitudinal role playing to the teaching of art.

The concept of role playing is believed to facilitate attitude change. When an individual is required to publicly argue for or defend something that they do not like or believe in, dissonance is created within the individual (Festinger, 1957). To relieve the discomfort of the dissonance they are feeling, individuals modify their attitude toward the object or concept. In Mittler's studies, the object was a work of art for which the student had originally expressed a dislike. When forced to defend the importance and value of the work they disliked to others, his or her attitude toward the work changed significantly.

An adaptation of Mittler's study was performed by Gilliatt (1980). Gilliatt examined the effectiveness of three different teaching methods on expanding the art preferences of elementary school students. The three methods tested were: (1) traditional studio activities; (2) *habituation*, the belief that a person will overcome a dislike for a work of art if they are merely exposed to it in their own environment over a period of time; and (3) the Feldman-Mittler methodology.[*] For the non-art-trained elementary teacher, the most effective method was the combined habituation-studio approach. The most successful approach was the combined habituation and Feldman-Mittler method, but it required a highly trained teacher to use it effectively. With habituation and studio activities representing rather traditional approaches to the teaching of art, Gilliatt's results supported the effectiveness of Mittler's adaptation of cognitive dissonance theory to art education.

In a similar study, Hollingsworth (1983) tested the combined effect of mere exposure, counterattitudinal advocacy, and art criticism on the art preferences of upper elementary school and junior high school students. Her major premise was that the combination of the three methods would be more effective in increasing potential learning or information acquisition than any of the methods used singly. Hollingsworth's findings, when applied to elementary students, seemed to contradict both the Gilliatt and the Mittler studies. She speculated that this may reflect the minimal amount of research that had been done in the area of counterattitudinal advocacy with children and that elementary school–age children may need more time to process information cognitively than do adolescents or young adults. In a separate analysis of the data from the junior high school students, her results did seem to confirm the data from both Gilliatt and Mittler. Hollingsworth suggested that:

1. Art criticism treatment, rather than the combination treatment, should be used with elementary school students.

2. The combination treatment, rather than the mere exposure treatment or the counterattitudinal advocacy treatment singly, should be used with junior high school students.

3. The counterattitudinal advocacy treatment may be useful as a means to

[*]See Feldman, *The Critical Performance,* in the Bibliography "Teaching Criticism and Aesthetics."

bring about a specific affective change toward a particular work of art. (pp. 108-9)

Parks (1986) conducted a content analysis of seven art education textbooks for attitude formation and change concepts. He found that the textbook authors were in general agreement that student-held attitudes are a crucial factor in the learning process in the field of art, yet few of them suggested ways for art teachers to alter poor student attitudes or nurture positive ones, representing a breakdown between theory and practice. In his analysis of the texts, Parks appropriated four fundamental concepts of attitude change from the field of social psychology (Berscheid and Walster, 1969) that had direct application to the teaching of art.

1. Characteristics of a compelling communicator.
   a. Credibility—expertness and trustworthiness. (Hovland, Janis, and Kelly, 1953)
   b. Attractiveness—"…who says what seems to be as important as what is said…." (Halloran, 1967, p. 63)
   c. Similarity—the perception that the speaker is "one of us." (Burnstein, Stotland, and Zander, 1961; Mills and Jellison, 1968)
   d. Intention to persuade—awareness of…(Mills, 1966)
2. Characteristics of a convincing communication.
   a. Primacy—individuals who publicly announce their position on a topic are far less likely to be persuaded by a subsequent communication than individuals who thought their initial positions were anonymous. (Mittler, 1976; Hovland, Campbell and Brock, 1957)
   b. Recency—memory and lapse of time influence whether a communication is convincing. (Miller and Campbell, 1959; Insko, 1964)
   c. One-sided vs. two-sided appeals—Should a teacher present only one side of an issue, or both sides of an issue? (Lumsdaine and Janis, 1953)
   d. Counterarguments—Should a teacher provide counterarguments that refute a particular point of view? (Papgeoris and McGuire, 1962; McGuire, 1961)
3. Characteristics of a facilitative environment.
   a. Rewards and punishments—behavioral approach. (Skinner, 1938, 1968; Scott, 1957)
   b. Freedom of choice—cognitive approach. (Aronson, 1966; Linder, Cooper, and Jones, 1967)
4. Characteristics of a receptive communicatee
   a. self-esteem (Gollob & Dittes, 1965; Lowin, 1967)

The Use of Art to Alter Attitudes and Performance in Other Educational Disciplines

Over the years, many studies have examined the value of using art as a vehicle for improving student attitudes and performances in other academic disciplines. Forseth (1976) examined the effects of art activities on the attitudes of fourth-grade children in relation to learning in mathematics and art. Popowicz (1975) saw potential in using art with biology as a vehicle for changing student attitudes about science. Delaney (1965) performed a comparison study of eighth-grade students' attitudes toward specific art activities and their attitudes toward creative activities in English and science. While related to art education, these studies were conducted by researchers in the respective disciplines to which the studies pertained.

The positive relationship of art to reading has been examined by Sinatra (1986) and Eisner (1978), and to American history and social studies by Corwin (1990) and Derylak (1989). While interdisciplinary studies relating art to other subject areas has generally proved successful, too often such studies place art in a handmaiden relationship to the other disciplines, rather than as a subject of study worthy of equal value within the general curriculum. If one examines these studies in a holistic manner, the implications are more far-reaching. The fact that art improves student performance in most other areas of schooling suggests two things: (1) that the fragmentation and compartmentalization of subject matter in schools today may not be an accurate reflection of reality; and (2) that art is indeed the essence of what many people think education should be—experiences with ideas and inquiry processes that stimulate children to think and feel.

DISCUSSIONS ABOUT ART IN THE CLASSROOM

How can one nurture in students the desire, insights, and skills to extract meaning from the visual images they encounter? How does one sensitize students to the diverse ways in which works of art can communicate? How does one move students beyond mere literal interpretation of works to grasp metaphor, irony, expressiveness, concept, or theme? What should all children know about art, why should they know it, and how can they best learn it? Such questions, so essential to the teaching of art, cannot be addressed in a traditional, studio-only curriculum. Such questions require the art teacher to adopt approaches to teaching that might be didactic (lecturing) at times, but in most cases are conducive to discussion activities.

Why are class discussions important? Looking at and discussing works of art requires the highest levels of activity in the cognitive domain (Bloom and others, 1956). However, Bloom and his coauthors emphasized that cognition should not be thought of in isolation from the affective domain. They argued that for significant learning to take place, students must respond affectively as well as cognitively to the ideas they are encountering. In other words, they must value what they are experiencing. This seems like a reasonable objective for the art teacher who wants to nurture an appreciation of art in students. However, Krathwohl and others (1964) noted that for valuing to take place, students must express their opinions about a topic and defend it. This can be difficult for students when dealing with works of art, for their maturity and their knowledge of art is limited, and the subject of art is vast and often ambiguous. The problem can also be compounded by the very nature of classroom discussions; children, adolescents in particular, may be very reluctant to express personal opinions in front of their peers. For meaningful and productive discussions about art to take place in class, the teacher needs to be organized, and some rules and patterns of behavior for student (and teacher) participation need to be established. The dynamics of a good discussion will be examined from the role of the teacher, the role of the students, the objects of discussion, and the classroom environment.

THE ROLE OF THE TEACHER

As the teacher, you exert an extraordinary amount of influence, both positive and negative, over the ideas, values, and attitudes that your students hold toward the subject of art. Organizing and leading discussions about art require a great deal of teaching artistry (pedagogy), a sensitivity to the subtle nuances that occur in class discussions, an ability to nudge and nurture the discussion in productive directions, and a serendipitous tolerance for good ideas that are worth talking about but had not been anticipated beforehand.

As the primary agent for learning in the classroom, the teacher serves as a role model, the most important factor in any learning situation (Gagne, 1977). If the teacher has stopped learning and growing, he is a deadening influence in the classroom (Adler, 1982). For example, parents who value reading act as positive role models for the child. If parents read to their young children, the children gain a feeling for the written language and the treasures that await them once they, too, have developed the skills of reading. The ability to read the words on a page, however, does not guarantee comprehension of what is read. Without the thoughtful and appreciative guidance of the parent and teacher, the child will never grasp the subtlety of irony, metaphor, or analogy—the very things that give language its power and richness.

The ability to acquire meaningful experiences from discussions about art requires the same nurturing process that guided experiences in reading does. The teacher must set the example of one who enjoys art, values it, finds it challenging, and, above all, gains meaning from it.

When planning a class discussion of art works, Hurwitz and Madeja (1977) suggest the following:

- In selecting works for study, respect the natural preferences of children. Research can provide cues for selection. Williams and others have noted brightness, realism, and familiarity with subject matter as bases for preference (see Chapter 1).
- Select the work with care: The point of the discussion should be embedded in the specific character of the painting, the sculpture, or the building.
- Two or three examples are more effective than one, as all of us learn more quickly through contrasting images. Three Rouaults will tell us one thing; a Rouault next to a Wesselman next to a Wyeth has something else to tell us (see section later in this chapter on the compare-and-contrast method).
- Reorganize the class for viewing: Remember that each child is entitled to a "front-row" seat. Children should learn early that seeing is a positive act involving intense visual concentration. Therefore the relation of viewer to object is an important consideration.
- When in a museum, encourage each child to discover her own "viewing space," a distance that is determined in part by the object and in part by her own feeling of comfort.
- Always honor the child's vocabulary and, when appropriate, write the correct art terminology down so the entire group can study it.
- Periodically, have a student come to the picture to point to the passage or object under discussion.
- Avoid reproductions that are too small (usually under 12" x 18") or that are of poor quality. You may even want to show more than one reproduction of the same painting in order to stress the unreliability of the reproduction process.
- When possible, use an art object you, the teacher, feel positively about. If you feel warmly about it yourself, it will show and that is all to the good.
- The larger the projected image, the better. Large-scale images make stronger responses. (pgs. 52–54)

In the *dialogical method*, the role of the teacher in preparing and leading class discussions has been defined by Shor and Freire (1987) as being both an artist and a politician:

The creative disruption of passive education is an aesthetic moment as well as a political one, because it asks the students to reperceive their prior understandings and to practice new perceptions as creative learners with the teacher....(p. 28)

Shor and Freire argue that dialogue transforms communication, that it makes the students democratic participants in their own learning by decentralizing the source of knowledge (instead of the teacher as authoritarian, the teacher becomes a participant in the dialogue by relearning and reexperiencing the material), and that the dialogue builds within the students intrinsic rewards for their learning.

Such an approach has its risks for teachers. It does mean relinquishing some control in the classroom. Adler (1982) refers to the role of the teacher in such discussions as "a first among equals," one who leads the discussion through *Socratic questioning* techniques. By beginning the discussion by asking questions and following up responses with more questions, the teacher using such techniques guides and nurtures the discussion so that students come to perceive, deduce, and realize answers and truths for themselves. Such revelations give students a sense of empowerment and ownership over the ideas they are dealing with, which, in turn, builds self-esteem and appreciation. For the teacher, such guidance again implies both artistry and politics.

In preparing for a discussion, the teacher should begin by first outlining in detail the concepts she wants to cover, then outline questions that parallel the concept outline. If works of art are to be the focal point of discussion, reproductions should be carefully selected to ensure they serve as exemplars for the concepts to be discussed.

When formulating the questions to guide the discussion, the teacher should generally work sequentially from the simple to the complex (see Bloom and others and Hamblen's [1984] questioning strategy on p. 41), helping students to understand the concepts and experience the works, building on their perceptions and insights. The teacher has to be able to think on her feet, listen to responses and the exchange of ideas, and formulate new questions that do not stifle the free flow of ideas—all the while encouraging some focus in the discussion.

I like to think of the discussion process as a set of concepts that the discussion circles around, gets an understanding of from one angle, moves away from for a while, and then returns to from another angle—certainly not a linear process. (Welty, 1989, p. 47)

There are several objectives to keep in mind when formulating discussion questions:

- Questions can encourage or limit and inhibit discussion; be careful that the wording of a question doesn't set arbitrary restrictions on discussion. For example, don't so narrowly define the style of Impressionism that students fail to recognize its place in the discussion's focus, which might be the idea that realism is a relative concept.
- Open-ended questions can be used to draw more reserved students into the discussion. To participate in discussions requires a great deal of courage, and questions that do not require a right or wrong answer can be less intimidating for students and may aid in getting a discussion started.
- Descriptive questions can also draw students into a discussion. Questions that initially ask students to describe what they see in a work of art or describe what they perceive as the general public's response to a particular issue can serve to reduce anxiety at the beginning of a discussion and get students talking.
- Questions whose answers have become obvious can be repeated periodically if their answers reinforce concepts that are important for the students to know.

Another important concept for the teacher to introduce and adhere to is distinguishing for students the difference between a *value statement* and an *attitude statement* (Wilson, 1967), or what Ecker (1967) calls a *psychological report*. A value statement contains an evaluative word like good, bad, exquisite, atrocious, and so on, and is intended to commend, praise, or criticize. A value statement is based on criteria that supports the judgment of value. For instance, art critics base their judgments on criteria rooted in their philosophies of what makes a good work of art.

Attitude statements or psychological reports express the speaker's hopes and aspirations, their likes and dislikes, and can often contain evaluative words as well. The difference between the two kinds of statements—value and attitude—are that value statements can be justified because they are based on criteria (this does not mean that everyone will be in agreement with a value statement because individuals may hold different criteria of value), whereas attitude statements or psychological reports are rooted purely in personal feelings and intuition.

There can be essentially four points of view one can hold toward an idea or a work of art (Ecker, 1967). In each of these four points of view, the first portion of the statement is one of value, and the second part is an attitude statement or psychological report:

- X is a good painting for Y reasons, and I like it.
- X is a good painting for Y reasons, but I don't like it.

- X is a bad painting for Y reasons, and I don't like it.
- X is a bad painting for Y reasons, but I like it.

As the first among equals, the teacher must ensure that what is being said by participants in a discussion is clear, sensible, and constructive. *The teacher must listen.* Value statements require supporting criteria, and participants in the discussion deserve to know exactly what is being said; otherwise, critical and productive thinking cannot take place. The teacher (and, it is hoped, the students) should ask for clarification or restate what was said to communicate that the meaning *and* context of the statement is understood. Value statements without supporting criteria should always be questioned, for if they are not, the teacher is failing her function as a role model.

An effective discussion is a complex process. Not only must the teacher periodically respond, question, synthesize ideas, summarize what has been said, and be thinking ahead in order to formulate questions that will guide discussion, he must also be conscious of the students who are puzzled, lost, out of touch with the direction of the discussion, are dominating it, or are intimidated by it.

On occasion, individual students may dominate a discussion. In this event, the teacher needs to determine if the student's actions are inhibiting others from participating or if the other students are becoming annoyed with the lack of substance in what the dominating student is saying. If such is the case, you need to take action. It might be done simply by avoiding eye contact with the student, or by directing questions to other students in the class. Welty (1989) suggests that the blackboard is a powerful tool in discussion, giving added weight and importance to what is being said. By writing down what a more reserved student has said and in turn, ignoring the comments of the dominating student, the teacher can often reestablish some balance in the discussion.

THE ROLE OF THE STUDENTS

The teacher cannot force a student to participate in an open discussion. To try and do so would likely be counterproductive. However, there are some reasonable guidelines that students should be expected to follow.

- Under no circumstances should discussions or debates become personalized. Name calling, insinuating remarks, and intimidation should not be tolerated.
- Questions and responses should be addressed to discussion participants, not to the teacher (the teacher can encourage this by avoiding eye contact with students while they are speaking).

- Participants in the discussion should be respectful of others and not interrupt individuals when they are speaking. Students have a right to not participate; on the other hand, they do not have a right to be disruptive or obstructive.

THE OBJECTS OF DISCUSSION

Works of art are symbolic objects created to embody and communicate ideas and values. The best works from a given period in history are so because they incorporated the ideas and values that were at the cutting edge of society when they were created. Such works live on in history because they best characterize the highest aspirations and levels of quality that the society or culture had achieved during a particular point in time.

To maximize the potential for quality discussions, it is essential to select topics and reproductions (or actual works of art) carefully. There are a number of different ideas that can be approached through discussion using works of art. A *few* examples are:

- Issues related to form.
  Elements of design.
  Principles of design.
- Issues related to content.
  Subject matter.
  Theme.
  Style.
  Metaphor, allegory, irony, context.
- Issues related to how we perceive art.
  Gestalt: figure-ground, closure, balance, and so on.
  Public vs. private perceptions.
  Obstacles to clear perception.
  Cultural influences on our perception.
  Do we really see what is in front of us?
  Is perceiving a work of art a creative act?
- Issues related to aesthetics and criticism.
  What is an aesthetic experience?
  What is an aesthetic attitude?
  What is art?
  How do you judge quality?

Why do human beings create works of art?

What is there about the aesthetic experience that is common to all human beings?

Why do art objects and definitions of art differ from culture to culture?

Does a picture have to be "pretty" to be aesthetic?

Does aesthetic experience reside in form alone, or in content, too?

Does monetary value reflect aesthetic value? Social value?

Should the artist's intentions be considered when viewing a work of art?

Is it possible to use the same critical methods and criteria with every work of art?

What is artistic inquiry?

- Issues related to art history (in addition to relevant topics from above).

  Why was a particular painting or style produced at a particular period in history?

  In what sequence do you think the following works were created? Why?

  How might the paintings of ___ have influenced the ___?

CREATING AN ENVIRONMENT FOR DISCUSSION

The classroom environment is crucial to effective discussions. How the space is physical arranged, the psychological environment, and the political atmosphere all have a tremendous impact on the success or failure of attempts at discussion in the classroom.

The Physical Environment

Traditional arrangements of desks and tables in a classroom are not conducive to good classroom discussions. Ideally, if space is plentiful, an area for studio activities and an area for discussion-oriented activities is best. However, most art rooms are anything but spacious.

Discussion implies communication, and communication implies listening, questioning, and responding. For a good discussion to take place, participants must be able to make eye contact with each other, and if images or artifacts are the objects of discussion, all participants must be able to see them. Here are some suggestions:

- Arrange the tables or desks in a U-shape with the teacher centered at the open end of the U-shape. This allows students to face each other during the discussion while maintaining the authority of the teacher. Such an arrangement also allows room for both the teacher and the students to move about the room.

- Students should wear name tags if they do not know each other.
- The room should be equipped with two projection screens so works of art can be compared and contrasted (see discussion of this method later in this chapter). Screens can be placed at open end of the U-shape where all participants can see them.
- There are no perfect reproductions. Images in books being passed from student to student cannot be discussed. Only two students can look at the images at a time, no one has enough time to view them, and, as discussion takes place, no one can refer back to them. Images have to be large enough for everyone to see them at one time and be able to refer back to them as the discussion progresses. Three-dimensional objects can be placed on a table in the center of the U-shape. Slides are best for discussion, although good, large reproductions have the added advantage of being able to hang on bulletin boards for future viewing after the discussion is over.

The Psychological Environment

The teacher has the professional responsibility to try to meet the educational needs of *all* students. Discussing issues and arguing and defending points of view are essential for *affective* learning to take place. Discussion activities can also be valuable experiences for developing self-esteem and confidence in students by producing intrinsic rewards. However, students are going to be very reluctant to participate in discussion activities, for they recognize, and rightly so, that expressing opinions publicly can make one feel vulnerable. The teacher is responsible for seeing that this does not happen. Here are some things to consider:

- If discussion is to be an important part of the classroom activities, start discussion activities on the very first day of class so students will come to expect it. If discussions take place only on random occasions, they will probably not be effective sessions. Discussions take practice, on the part of the teacher and students.
- Establish some rules. Students should address each other by name and make eye contact if at all possible; comments should not be personalized but focused on topic and questions; and although the teacher may begin the discussion by asking questions, responses should be addressed to fellow students, not the teacher.
- The teacher should attempt to prevent individuals from dominating the discussion, for such students often intimidate less aggressive students. If possible, encourage the more reserved students to participate.

Once students begin to willingly participate, the experience will be a liberating one for them. They will acquire a sense of self-confidence and empowerment, and a valuing of the subject matter being discussed will likely follow.

The Political Environment

Schools are political environments. While they are presumed to instill the values of the larger society and to prepare youngsters to be productive citizens within that society, there is much that contradicts such notions. While American society on the whole is democratic, the political structure within a classroom is autocratic (Efland, 1976). The teacher is the authoritarian figure and the students have few democratic rights or privileges.

The ultimate purpose for using discussion methods in class is to shift the bulk of responsibility for learning from the teacher to the students (Rorschach and Whitney, 1986; Shor & Freire, 1987; Welty, 1989). This naturally implies that the teacher relinquish some authority in the classroom and create an atmosphere in which some democratic notions apply. The teacher must establish the structure for discussions, the questions that challenge the students to think, and assert his authority when students do not adhere to the rules (rules meant to ensure free and open discussion). To create an environment where responsibility is shared, consider doing the following:

- Initial discussions might center on the act of discussing itself; guide students in establishing the rules they will follow in the future.
- Once discussion is underway, refuse to make eye contact with students who are talking. If necessary, point out to students why you are not making eye contact and that you want them to address their fellow students.
- Most authors agree that calling on students by name to answer specific questions will probably not establish a productive atmosphere for discussion. It will, in all likelihood, inhibit open discussion. However, the teacher does have a responsibility to all students and should be sensitive to those who are initially inhibited about participating. If asked with care, open-ended and descriptive questions might draw them into the discussion.
- When the teacher initiates discussion with a question, he must have the patience to wait for a response, even though it may seem to take an eternity. The question might be rephrased if necessary, but expect responses.
- Give the discussion method time to work. Students are used to being told what they should know; they are not used to deducing it for themselves. It will take more than the first few days of the semester for them

to adjust to the new responsibilities expected of them. Use the time to experiment with different kinds of questions, visuals, and problems. Find out what works best for you.

RAISING QUESTIONS FOR DISCUSSION

In order to initiate productive discussion, it is necessary to raise thought-provoking questions. In fact, one of the primary components of critical thinking is the ability to raise basic questions. Questioning initiates inquiry, and discussions should nurture students to think about issues, ideas, and works of art for themselves. That is the "end" for which discussion is the "means." The teacher and the questioning strategies employed should serve as a model for the students' own personal inquiry into art.

Hamblen (1984) provides a useful questioning strategy (Figure 2–1) based on Bloom's (1956) *Taxonomy* (see p. 11), and Feldman's (1981) *Critical Performance* (see p. 11).

THE COMPARE-AND-CONTRAST METHOD

Gestalt psychologists argue that we never perceive things in isolation; instead, we always perceive an object in relation to the things around it. When an art critic discusses a work of art, reference is always made to other works so that a perspective on the judgment of value or rank is established. The same framework for discussion needs to be established in the classroom.

The comparing and contrasting of works of art merits continued emphasis for its potency as a teaching tool. Students do not need a strong background or vocabulary in the arts to participate in the activity. If the works are carefully chosen, an infinite range of concepts and expressions can be examined. For example, if the discussion focuses on how two artists treated the same subject matter, the talk will inevitably raise questions about formal properties, style, differing time periods or cultures, speculation on the artist's intent, and context. For older students who are becoming complacent and narrow in their views of what art is or should be, such a method can be used to jolt them out of their limited perceptions. By showing images that contain the same subject matter but different styles, moods, and meanings, students can be helped to see that there is more to the interpretation of a work of art than merely recognizing the objects in the picture.

Consider some of the questions and ideas that could be dealt with when comparing and contrasting the following three images: Pistoletto's *Sacra Conversazione*, Segal's *Cinema*, and Longo's *Untitled: "Portrait of Kevin."*

KAREN A. HAMBLEN

BLOOM	QUESTIONS	ELABORATIONS AND CLARIFICATIONS	FELDMAN
Knowledge	Who created this object? When was this object created? Where is this object found? What is the title? What is the size? What is the medium used? What technique was used? Identify the subject matter. Identify the elements of design Where do you see order? Where do you see variety? What reasons did the artist/designer give for creating this?	Do you notice how it relates to its environment? Explain. Have you noticed how the subject is conveyed? Explain. Have you seen similar objects elsewhere? Explain. What would you like to know about the artist/designer?	Description
Comprehension	Describe the subject matter. Describe the use of color. Describe the elements of design. Compare this to another work. Explain how this object is used. What is the major theme? Contrast, in subject, style, medium etc., to another work. Give examples of types of textures, types of colors, etc., used. Translate the subject matter into a statement.	What is most pleasing about this object? What other similar objects do you find pleasing? What is least pleasing about this object? Is this an object you would like to own? Explain. What interests you most about this object?	Description
Application	What types of materials would you need to make this object? Clarify the textures, colors, etc. used. In what types of environments would this object be used?	What would you like to know about the technique used? What mood is created? Why? What colors, shapes, etc., influence your mood?	Description Analysis

FIGURE 2–1. Sample art criticism questions within Bloom's taxonomic categories.

KAREN A. HAMBLEN CONT.

BLOOM	QUESTIONS	ELABORATIONS AND CLARIFICATIONS	FELDMAN
	What types of lines, colors, etc., would you use to reproduce this object? From a given group, choose the people that might enjoy this object? Report on other objects that resemble this object. What skills would you need to make this object? Who are the users and appreciators of this object?	What would you like to know about this object? Decide how this object should be treated- now, in 5 years, in 10 years. Would you like to know what critics, historians, etc., have written about this object? Explain. What is your opinion of the object's social significance? In what way would you use or display this in your home?	
Analysis	Decide why this style was used. Why was this medium used? Why was this technique used? Analyze the functions of this object. How does function relate to meaning? Survey the uses of this object and re- late those to its design. Support your reasons for how its form relates to function. Identify the center of interest and give reasons for your choice. Describe the steps used to make this object. How does its meaning relate to the artist's career?	How does this object relate to others in its classification (e.g., painting, draw- ing, etc.)? What characteristics make this object valuable? How do you define valuable? How does this object fit your ideas of beauty, good design, etc.? How would you rank this object with others you value?	Analysis Interpretation

FIGURE 2–1. Continued

BLOOM	QUESTIONS	ELABORATIONS AND CLARIFICATIONS	FELDMAN
Synthesis	Predict the use and meaning of this object in the year 2050. Devise a plan to make this object more valued. Devise a plan to market this object. How many titles can you think of for this object? What would be the meaning if it were made out of…material? Imagine and describe its color, texture, etc., opposites. Create a conversation between this and another object. Suppose the size were changed.	Would you have valued this object 2, 5, 10 years ago? Explain. Do you think you will value this object 5, 10, etc, years from now? Explain. To whom would you give this as a gift? Why? To whom would you not give this as a gift? Why? If you were a different person (describe), would you like this object? Explain.	Interpretation
Evaluation	Decide whether the form fits its use. Assures its personal and social significance. Discuss this object's unique qualities. Rate this object in relation to others. Judge its aesthetic value. Give your opinion as to its treatment for the next 100 years.	Do you value this object? Why? How would you incorporate this object into your life? What personal meaning does it have for you? What other objects that you value relate to this one?	Evaluation

FIGURE 2–1. Continued

FIGURE UA 2–1. *Sacra Conversazione*, 1963, by Michelangelo Pistoletto. 67 x 39 1/2", painted tissue paper on stainless steel. Albright-Knox Art Gallery, Buffalo, New York. Gift of Seymour H. Knox, 1964.

FIGURE UA 2–2. *Cinema*, 1963, by George Segal. 118 x 96 x 39", metal sign, plaster statue, illuminated plexiglass. Albright-Knox Art Gallery. Buffalo, New York, Gift of Seymour H. Knox, 1964.

FIGURE UA 2–3. *Untitled (Portrait of Kevin)*, 1980, by Robert Longo. 28" x 40", crayon on paper. Albright-Knox Art Gallery, Buffalo, New York, James S. Ely Fund, 12/3/80.

1. What do these images have in common?
   - People as subject matter, all fairly realistically represented.
   - Monochromatic, with the exception of the red letters in *Cinema.*
   - Minimal amount of detail, apart from figures.
2. How do the images differ?
   - Singular figures vs. group.
   - Reposed figures vs. suggested movement vs. agitated, uncontrolled movement.
   - Two-dimensional vs. three-dimensional media.
3. What do the poses of the figures suggest?
4. As a viewer, how does your involvement in the images differ?
   - Detached observer vs. being a part of the image (Pistoletto's image is painted on a mirrored surface).
5. Do the images leave you with a sense of comfort? Warmth? Detachment? Isolation? Loneliness? Anxiety?
6. Are the images strictly a personal statement by the artist, or do they speak to society at large?
7. What ideas do these art objects communicate?
8. Is there a thematic relationship between these images?

When guiding a discussion of such works, teachers should be prepared to keep the conversation on a relevant course and to be flexible enough in their preparation to deal with ideas and directions in the discussion that they may not have anticipated.

Additional examples of themes and concepts in works of art that could be focal points for discussion are as follows:

1. What happens when culturally accepted symbols are seen out of context? Subject matter alone is not enough to indicate content and meaning. For example,

Eiffel Tower	Statue of Liberty	Eiffel Tower with Statue of Liberty–Paris

2. Which is the better painting? All three paintings were done by Picasso, the one on the left at the age of fifteen. Why would an artist who could paint like that at fifteen paint images like the one on the right-hand side almost seventy years later?

First Communion	*Girl Before a Mirror*	*Reclining Nude*
Picasso at fifteen	Picasso (1932)	Picasso (1968)

3. Isolation—How alone does one have to be to be alone? What is the role of the viewer?

N.Y. Movie	*Platform with Stairs*	*That Gentleman*
E. Hopper (1939)	R. Shaffer (1980–81)	A. Wyeth (1960)

4. How are people interacting in the images you see? Discuss the relativity of realism.

Sunday Afternoon on the Ile de la Grande Jatte	*The Luncheon of the Boating Party*	*Dempsey and Firpo*
Seurat (1884–86)	Renoir (1881)	G. Bellows (1924)

5. How does the artist interact with those around him? How does he choose to portray himself? Discuss the notion of painterly style vs. slick imagery.

Las Meninas	*Allegory of the Art of Painting*	*The Painter's Studio*
Velasquez (1656)	Jan Vermeer (1670–75)	Courbet (1855)

Self-Portrait	*Myself Painting a Self-Portrait*	*Self-Portrait with Head and Body*
Van Gogh	G. Gillespie (1980–81)	G. Segal (1968)

6. The self-portrait as a record of one's life.

Albrecht Dürer(1483)	*Albrecht Dürer*(1498)	*Man of Sorrows*
		Albrecht Dürer (1522)

7. How does the artist portray others? What does it reflect about the individual, the artist, the age? What remains constant, and what changes over time and culture?

Egyptian Portrait of a Man Mummy Case	*Ann of Cleves*	*Frank*
(160–170 A.D.)	Hans Holbein (1539)	C. Close 1968–69

8. How are couples portrayed? How is intimacy established? How do they interact? How is dramatic impact established?

Mayan Man & Woman	*Arnolfini Wedding*	*Paris Street: A Rainy Day*
700 A.D.	Jan Van Eyck (1434)	Caillabotte (1877)

Interior	*Bout Round II*	*Mr. & Mrs. Clark Percy*
Degas	Kienholzs (1982)	Hockney (1970–71)

9. How does the portrayal of the Madonna and Child differ from artist to artist and age to age?

Enthroned Madonna & Child	*The Alba Madonna*	*The Bath*
13th century	Raphael (1510)	Mary Cassatt (1891)

10. How does the portrayal of the crucifixion reflect the attitude of the artist and his age?

Crucifixion–Tryptych	*The Holy Trinity*	*Christ of St. John of the Cross*
1255–1318	Massaccio (1425)	Dali 1951
Pieta	*Resurrection*	
Michelangelo (1497–99)	El Greco (1597–1604)	

11. Contrast three different modes of expression of a similar theme. Discuss Style.

Guernica	*Elegy to the Spanish Republic #34*	*3rd of May*
Picasso (1937)	Motherwell (1953–54)	Goya (1814)

12. The artist as social protester/commentator.

Nuclear Warhead	*The Execution*	*Mercenaries V*
R. Arneson (1983)	G. Segal (1967)	L. Golub (1984)

13. Art in the service of socialism.

Detroit Industry Series– Ford Motor Assembly Plant	*We Shall Repay the Coal Debt to Our Country*	*Model for the Monument to the 3rd Communist International*
D. Rivera (1933)	G. Klutsis (1930)	V. Tatlin (1920)

14. Why is this considered art? How does Christo's use of the Pont Neuf compare and contrast with that of Renoir's?

Running Fence	*The Pont Neuf Wrapped: Project for Paris*	*The Pont Neuf*
Christo (1972–76)	Christo (1986)	Renoir (1872)

15. How are human beings' relationship to nature conveyed in these works? What does it say about time, place, and attitude?

| *Mont Saint Victoire* | *T.V. Garden Installation* | *Landscape with Figures* |
| Cezanne (1886–87) | Nam June Paik (1982) | G. Tooker (1965–66) |

EVALUATION AND ASSESSMENT IN ART ────────────────

For decades, art teachers were taught that evaluation in art stifled a child's creativity and self-expression:

> There should be one place in the school system where marks do not count. The art room should be a sanctuary against school regulations, where each youngster is free to be himself and to put down his feelings and emotions without censorship, where he can evaluate his own progress toward his own goals without the imposition of an arbitrary grading system. (Lowenfeld and Brittain, 1982, p. 163)

Such notions about evaluation, self-expression, and creativity seem a bit too romantic and unrealistic in an age of tight budgets and educational accountability. Parents, administrators, and taxpayers have a right to expect that quality learning and teaching are taking place in schools. Nurturing creative thinking, self-esteem, self-expression, and a love and appreciation for the subject matter being taught is not the unique domain of art teachers; such noble goals are common to all good teachers and no doubt reflect the primary motivation for good people to enter the teaching profession.

Essential to evaluation in art is the development of curriculum goals for the art program. The teacher has to know what he wants his program to provide for students if he is to evaluate their progress toward achievement of those goals. As the field of art education has shifted away from a child-centered, therapeutic approach to a subject-centered emphasis, students are now expected to acquire a body of knowledge about art as well as develop as observers of art.

There are two distinct aspects to evaluation. *Formative evaluation* takes place while the lesson is being taught. The teacher assesses whether or not the students understand the ideas being taught as reflected in the production of their art products or in their response to questions in discussions. As the lesson progresses, the teacher can adjust his teaching style or reexamine key concepts from different perspectives and examples to enable students to grasp the concepts.

Summative evaluation summarizes the success of individuals and the class as a whole in achieving the goals of the lesson. Traditionally, when art teachers were required to assign grades to student art work, the decisions of success or failure were left to the subjective judgment of the teacher. However, many writers on instruction insist that every lesson should have clearly spelled-out objectives and criteria for determining if the objectives have been achieved (Mager, 1984; Hunter and Gee, 1988). Students should be made aware of the objectives and criteria at the outset of the lesson, so they can organize their own thinking and adapt their personal learning styles to maximize their potential for successfully achieving the objectives. Students have a right to know what is expected of them (See Chapter 2, section on Writing Instructional Objectives, Unit Plans, and Lesson Plans.)

Pope (1990) provides an example of a criterion-based scoring sheet for evaluating a high school freshman, studio-art lesson:

"FRESHMAN FETISH"

NAME: _____ DATE: _____ PERIOD: _____

CRITERIA: SCORE:

1. Student selects a personal event which may require
   a fetish.(A)   - 0 1 2 3 4 5 +
2. Student chooses an appropriate animal to clearly
   represent extra power. (A)   - 0 1 2 3 4 5 +
3. Student decides the purpose of the "packages." (A)   - 0 1 2 3 4 5 +
4. Student explains fetish purpose, animal choice,
   and package function in a written paragraph. (A)   - 0 1 2 3 4 5 +
5. Student develops at least six thumbnail sketches
   of an animal in different positions. (C,P)   - 0 1 2 3 4 5 +
6. Student designs sculpture without long extensions. (C)   - 0 1 2 3 4 5 +
7. Student selects best position of animal for sculpture. (C) - 0 1 2 3 4 5 +
8. Sculpture is simplified. (C,P)   - 0 1 2 3 4 5 +
9. Student draws best thumbnail sketch in 6 points of view:
   four sides, top, bottom. (P)   - 0 1 2 3 4 5 +
10. Student determines size and shape of packages. (C)   - 0 1 2 3 4 5 +
11. Student selects colors of packages and fetishes. (C,A) - 0 1 2 3 4 5 +
12. Student mixes plaster and sand in proper ratio. (P,C)   - 0 1 2 3 4 5 +
13. Student mixes and adds colors to plaster to obtain
    "sedimentary rocks." (C,P)   - 0 1 2 3 4 5 +
14. Student transfers 2-D image onto the 3-D plaster
    form. (C,P)   - 0 1 2 3 4 5 +
15. Student carves plaster "in the round." (P)   - 0 1 2 3 4 5 +
16. Student ties packages to the back of fetish. (P)   - 0 1 2 3 4 5 +

17. Student carving is free of bumps, chisel
    marks. (P)   - 0 1 2 3 4 5 +
18. Student develops proportion in animal's anatomy. (C,P)   - 0 1 2 3 4 5 +
19. Sculpture is no larger than four inches square. (P)   - 0 1 2 3 4 5 +
20. In a paragraph, student compares his or her problems
    of design and process with possible Zuni problems. (C,A)   - 0 1 2 3 4 5 +

KEY: C = Cognitive; A = Affective; P = Psychomotor

Day (1985) suggests that art teachers teaching from a subject-centered approach have a variety of tools that can be used to evaluate learning in the art classroom.

1. *Observation* (formative). The teacher observes student behavior during demonstrations, presentations, and work to identify students that need additional motivation or personalized instruction.
2. *Interview* (formative, summative). This can take place on both an individual and small-group basis, and can be used to determine if students grasp stages of critical process or can interpret metaphoric content in works. It can be used in individual critiques of students' work to guide them in improving their art products, which can reveal the need for additional instruction. It can also be used as one approach for determining if individual has grasped and achieved lesson objectives.
3. *Discussion* (formative). Discussions of works of art or ideas about art can help reveal what student attitudes are toward certain kinds of art work. Future lessons and discussions can be developed to expand and enrich their attitudes and perceptions of art.
4. *Performance* (formative, summative). Specific tasks are assigned to students to reveal their knowledge, skills, and understanding of concepts being taught. For example, the student is asked to demonstrate her knowledge and/or skill of a contour line drawing by producing such a drawing.
5. *Checklist* (formative, summative). This is used to record class participation to determine who is and is not participating. If particular procedures are to be followed, a checklist can also be used to record successful completion of each step.
6. *Questionnaire* (formative, summative). This can be used to record when students have achieved a prescribed level of knowledge or skill before moving on to the next level of performance. For example, before a student can begin work in the photolab, where mistakes can be extremely

costly in terms of time, materials, and equipment, the student must demonstrate an acceptable level of knowledge and/or competence.

7. *Test* (summative). An objective test can be administered following a lesson or unit of study to determine the amount of information and knowledge acquired by the students. Such a test can include both multiple-choice and short-answer questions.

8. *Essay* (summative). The students are asked to write an essay about a topic or a work of art, demonstrating critical, creative, and analytical skills that have been practiced in class discussions.

9. *Visual Identification* (summative). Students view slides and reproductions and are expected to identify the artist, work of art, style and/or historical period, originating culture, and so forth.

10. *Attitude Measurement* (formative, summative). The teacher may be interested in how successfully she is instilling appreciation for art in her students or concerned about their opinions of a new curriculum approach being used in class. Such measurements can be done using carefully constructed questionnaires or by having students rank-order their preferences of art works while viewing slides or reproductions.

11. *Aesthetic Judgment* (summative). The teacher judges the quality of the final products produced by the students. Because specific goals and objectives were established at the outset of the assignment, criteria exists for determining how successfully the student satisfied the assignment. The aesthetic quality of the final product can be judged by the teacher based on the context in which it was created.

Portfolios and Authentic Assessment

Educators have become disillusioned with standardized tests and their inability to measure higher-order thinking skills and affective learning. In recent years, teachers have come to realize that traditional paper-and-pencil objective examinations evaluate only a very narrow aspect of knowledge and thinking, and, too often, schooling is geared to teaching students to pass the test. Today, there is growing interest in all academic disciplines for an assessment concept that originated in the visual arts: the portfolio.

A traditional artist's portfolio contains a sampling of the best work he has produced. However, when portfolios are used for assessment purposes, the content and purpose is much more broadly defined. Portfolios become integral to the curricular process and are referred to as *process portfolios*. A process portfolio is a working portfolio, serving formative as well as summative purposes, and contains a number of materials not found in a traditional portfolio. It can contain preliminary sketches and drafts as well as finished work, reflective logs or journals, written work, video art or videotapes of previous art work, and so on.

Throughout the school year, the students work in their portfolios, adding and revising work. The log or journal requires the students to reflect daily on what they are learning and why it is important to them. Typically, the students take their portfolios home at the end of the fall and spring semesters with a questionnaire to guide a parental review of the portfolio and the evidence of learning that it contains. At the end of the school year, the students spend the last two weeks reviewing their log entries for the year, writing summary statements, and selecting work that best summarizes their learning for the year. This work will include not only their best work, but work that reflects "turning points," or growth, in their understanding of art. The teacher can then put away their final portfolios for the fall semester, when they will again be pulled and reviewed as a starting point for the new year's learning. (See Figures 2–2, 2–3, 2–4, & 2–5.)

The use of portfolios makes assessment an ongoing, integral part of the curriculum and actively engages the student and parents in the process. The benefits of such an approach dovetail with the discussion method of teaching: this method engages the student in critical and reflective thinking, shifts the primary responsibility for learning from the teacher to the student, and nurtures affective behavior—values and attitudes (Silver and Strong, 1992; Wiggins, 1989; Wolf, 1987 and 1991).

While art educators have come to recognize the importance of evaluation in art, the reality of teaching art in an elementary school setting often prohibits adequate assessment of art learning. If the elementary school art teacher sees six to seven hundred students per week for only 35 minutes (and sometimes less) per week, learning that truly carries over and can be reinforced week to week is marginal, and the amount of time and paperwork necessary for adequate evaluation of art learning makes assessment difficult, at best.

To initiate authentic assessment in your classroom, start slowly, experiment with one grade level, and find what works for you. Identify a classroom teacher with similar interests who is willing to allow students extra time for writing in their logs and organizing their portfolios. Keep in mind that students will be working in their portfolios almost every time you meet with them, and that when you are using portfolios for assessment, it is not just an end-of-the-semester "ordeal."

While authentic assessment does require more of the teacher's time, particularly when first initiating the process, the results are rewarding. Students shift from passive to active engagement in their own learning, their time "on task" accelerates, and they value their own efforts because they can see their work and learning evolve. (For more information, see the Authentic Assessment Bibliography.)

ART ROOM NEWS

Sept. 1992
Mrs. Parks

WELCOME BACK!!!!

We have an exciting year ahead of us! I am looking forward to meeting all of my new students at Riverview School. I have recently moved to the Buffalo area from the Hudson Valley. I taught art to elementary students there for six years.

OUR ART PROGRAM

This year in art we will be looking at a variety of artists' works representing various cultures and a range of media. Students will view, discuss, and produce a variety of art works. Some of the art units will reflect areas of study related to what the children are studying in their classrooms.

Journals will be kept and used during the art period. We will be making and working in these journals during the art period. Some research and writing may be required to enhance specific art units. This will be at each child's level.

Each class has an art period one day per week for 55 minutes. Please send a smock (an old shirt is great!). Although we try to use art materials that do not stain, sometimes it cannot be avoided. SO PLEASE DO NOT LET YOUR CHILD WEAR THEIR BEST CLOTHING TO ART CLASS.

PORTFOLIO ASSESSMENT

Each student will keep a working portfolio of his/her work in the art room. This portfolio will be a way to assess and evaluate learning in the arts. A portfolio is an organized collection of a child's work over a period of time. It is used by the teacher, student, and parent to monitor the growth of the student's learning. The portfolio can provide the means for the development of those skills needed to become independent, self-directed learners.

Portfolios are also a way for students to value their own work and to value themselves as learners. The portfolio will include finished art projects, projects in progress, sketches of work, work receipts for each completed project, and journals.

Twice a year, art work, as well as other chosen items will be put into a summary portfolio and will be sent home for parents to view and give feedback. This assessment process will be very a valuable tool for the teacher, parents as well as the students.

TREASURES

Much of what you consider garbage at home could be treasure in the art room. Artists frequently use found objects in their art work. We welcome found objects in our art room! These materials can be sent to the art room with your child on their art day. PLEASE be sure these materials are safe and clean. At the present time we are specifically interested in wood pieces, plaster, screws, nuts, bolts, wire, plaster, buttons, ribbon, thread, and fabric.

HOURS

I will be teaching at Riverview School on Monday, Tuesday, Wednesday, and Friday mornings. If for any reason you would like to meet with me, please feel free to set up an appointment.

FIGURE 2–2.

ART PROJECT
WORK RECEIPT

NAME:_____   CLASS:_____

PROJECT:_____   DATE:_____

DESCRIBE YOUR WORK:_____
_____
_____

LIST THE STEPS:_____
_____
_____

WHAT DID YOU DO TO MEET THE CRITERIA?_____
_____
_____

WHAT DID YOU LEARN?_____
_____
_____

EXPLAIN._____
_____
_____

GRADE YOURSELF: 1 (BEST) 3 (O.K.) 5 (WORST)

ADDITIONAL COMMENTS / SKETCHES_____
_____
_____

FIGURE 2–3.

FINAL ART PORTFOLIO ASSESSMENT REVIEW

THIS IS THE FINAL PORTFOLIO REVIEW FOR THIS SCHOOL YEAR. LOOK THROUGH YOUR PORTFO-LIO AT YOUR WORK YOU SAVED FROM THE FIRST HALF OF THE YEAR, ALL OF YOUR WORK FROM THIS HALF OF THE YEAR, INCLUDING SKETCHES, WORK RECEIPTS, JOURNAL ENTRIES, EVERYTHING!!! ANSWER THE FOLLOWING QUESTIONS AS HONESTLY AND COMPLETELY AS POSSIBLE.

WHICH OF YOUR ARTWORK WAS YOUR FAVORITE? WHAT MADE IT YOUR FAVORITE?

_____
_____

WHICH ART PROJECT WAS THE MOST CHALLENGING FOR YOU? EXPLAIN.

_____
_____

WHICH ARTIST/MOVEMENT DID YOU FIND THE MOST INTERESTING? WHY.

_____
_____

WHAT AREAS IN ART DID YOU IMPROVE THE MOST IN THIS YEAR? EXPLAIN.

_____
_____

RATE YOURSELF IN THE FOLLOWING AREAS. I WILL RATE YOU IN THE SAME AREAS.

MEETS CRITERIA			
PROPER USE OF MATERIALS			
FOLLOWS DIRECTIONS			
ORIGINALITY			
COMPLETES WORK			
ATTITUDE/EFFORT/BEHAVIOR			
	GREAT VERY GOOD SATISFACTORY NEEDS IMPROVEMENT		

THE STUDENT WILL COMPLETE THE PERFORMANCE CHART BY COLORING THE FIRST BAR IN EACH CATEGORY.

THE ART TEACHER WILL COMPLETE THE CHART BY COLORING IN THE SECOND BAR IN THE GRAPH.

TEACHER COMMENTS:_____
_____
_____

PLEASE RETURN THIS REVIEW WITH THE BACK COMPLETED AND SIGNED. THANK-YOU!

FIGURE 2–4

ART PORTFOLIO FEEDBACK SHEET

PLEASE REVIEW THE ITEMS IN THE ART PORTFOLIO AND DISCUSS THE *ART PORTFOLIO REVIEW* WITH OUR ART STUDENT. PLEASE SIGN THIS FEEDBACK SHEET AND RETURN IT TO ME AT RIVERVIEW SCHOOL. IF YOU HAVE ANY QUESTIONS OR CONCERNS PLEASE FEEL FREE TO CONTACT ME AT SCHOOL.

1. I (WE) FEEL THE WORK IN THIS PORTFOLIO SHOWS:

_____
_____
_____

2. I (WE) ARE PLEASED WITH:

_____
_____
_____

3. AREAS THAT NEED FURTHER ATTENTION:

_____
_____
_____

4. OTHER IDEAS, THOUGHTS, COMMENTS, OR CONCERNS:

_____
_____
_____

SIGNATURES: _____

THANKS FOR YOUR COOPERATION! MRS. LISA PARKS

FIGURE 2–5.

SUMMARY ———————————————————————————

For years, art instruction was strictly studio based and art teachers engaged the interests of students through hands-on experiences in the making of art. Today, such activities are encouraged in general education as "active learning." As the field of art education has shifted to a DBAE approach and broadened its view of what art instruction should be, the need for art teachers to expand their methods of delivering art instruction has broadened as well. Teaching art from a discussion methods and portfolio assessment approach requires an artistry of teaching that is as challenging for the instructor as it is for the student.

3 | WHAT CAN YOU TEACH?

In order for one to have a perspective on the teaching of art, it is helpful to have some understanding of the evolution of art education. There is a context for today's "subject-centered" art education and it is the result of a combination of forces within the society as a whole, the educational community, art education itself, and changes that have taken place in the world of art.

HISTORY OF ART EDUCATION

Art in the Service of Industry

1770	Benjamin Franklin; art not required; taught if teacher thought it was important.
1840s	William Minifie; Philadelphia & Baltimore Boys HS; art for industry; based on geometric principles.
	William Bently Fowle; Boston; taught drawing as art; monitorial techniques.

Early 1800s	Art also taught as social refinement to upper-class young ladies.
1850s–1860s	With industralization, vocational value of drawing emphasized even further.
1864	Drawing became required subject in Boston Public Schools.
1871	Walter Smith brought from England to become Director of Art for state of Massachusetts and to be supervisor of art for Boston and Principal of Art Normal School.

Art for Developing the Child

1880s	Child Study Movement (psychologist G. Stanley Hall, leader), based on ideas of Pestalozzi, Herbart, and Froebel and furthered by John Dewey. Concerned not only with what could be impressed upon child, but what child had to express. Encouraged students to draw from nature, study color, learn principles of art, and appreciate beauty in art and nature.
1900–1940s	Picture Study; lay person's tastes in art, contemporary artists absent; ethical and moral values taught.
Early 1900s	Arthur Wesley Dow; elements and principles of design; systematic approach to teaching art.
1910	Walter Sargent; interested in psychology of children's art; drawing as tool for thinking.
1930s	Progressive Education Association; brought Dewey's ideas to fruition; significance of experience in learning and self-expression and noninterference by teacher important. Drawing nurtures creativity.
1920s and 1930s	Freud; art as a type of therapy and as a "preventive medicine" that contributes to psychological health of child.
Early 1950s	Art educators began to recognize the modern aesthetic.
1940s–1970s	Viktor Lowenfeld; creative and mental growth of child; based on ideas of progressive era.

Art As a Subject Worthy of Study

1962	Manual Barkan suggested there might be better way to teach art, based on the behavior of artists, historians, and critics.
1966	Penn State Conference; ideas similar to Barkan's discussed.
1968	The National Art Education Association (NAEA) officially adopted production, history, and appreciation as central to the art curriculum; art became subject worthy of study.

1982   Getty Center for Education in the Arts founded.

1985   Getty published *Beyond Creating: The Place for Art in America's Schools.*

1988   NEA's *Toward Civilization* published.

GOALS FOR QUALITY ART EDUCATION

The National Art Education Association (NAEA) is the largest professional art education organization in the world. In 1968, the NAEA published a statement entitled *The Essentials of a Quality School Art Program,* which signaled an official shift from a child-centered focus to a subject-centered focus for art education. The statement identified three primary goals for art education: (1) teaching art production, (2) teaching art history, and (3) teaching art appreciation. In 1986, the Board of Directors of the NAEA authorized the production of an updated statement prepared by Charles A. Qualley on its behalf entitled *Quality Art Education: Goals for Schools.* In defining quality art education, "…students learn…"

- to develop, express, and evaluate ideas;
- to produce, read, and interpret visual images in an increasingly visually oriented world;
- to recognize and understand the artistic achievements and expectations of civilized societies. (p. 3)

The NAEA identified the following goals for quality art education:

1. All elementary and secondary schools shall require students to complete a sequential program of art instruction that integrates the study of art production, aesthetics, art criticism, and art history.
(1.1) Art instruction shall be conducted by teachers certified in art;
(1.2) Visual arts courses shall be required in elementary, middle, and junior and senior high schools, and should not be scheduled to conflict with other required courses.
2. For graduation from high school, every student shall be required to complete at least one year of credit in one of the fine arts.
(2.1) An acceptable course in visual arts shall include in-depth study in the techniques of at least one art medium, practice in several media, and studies in art history, aesthetics, and criticism.
3. For admission to college or university, every student shall be required to have at least one year of credit in visual art (see 2.1 above).
A complete (and detailed) copy of the "Goals" statement can be

obtained by writing to the NAEA, 1916 Association Drive, Reston, Virginia 22091 (inquire about fee). Some other publications by the NAEA that may be useful for program planning and advocacy include:

- *Purposes, Principles, and Standards for School Art Programs*
- *Microcomputers in Art Education*
- *Standards for Art Teacher Preparation Programs*
- *Who Speaks for Art Education?*
- *Questions You Should Ask About the Art Programs in Your Schools: A Checklist Developed for Members of State Legislatures*
- *A Checklist Developed for Elementary Principals*
- *A Checklist Developed for Secondary Principals*
- *High School Guidance Counselors: Four Things You Should Know About Quality Art Education*
- *Parents: A Quality Education Includes Art Education*
- *The Role of the Art Supervisor*
- *Staffing for Excellence in Elementary and Secondary Schools*
- *Assessing Curriculum Guides for Art Education*
- *College Deans and Departmental Chairpersons*
- *Strengthening Arts Education in Schools.*

THE BODY OF KNOWLEDGE IN ART EDUCATION: WHAT TO TEACH

The field of art education as a whole has created a certain paradox. As art education theory has shifted from a child-centered approach to a subject-centered approach, it has provided a framework for curriculum development, such as in Discipline-Based Art Education (DBAE). However, practitioners in the field generally do not have a background in DBAE, and the field itself has still failed to reach agreement about what all children should know and be able to do with art by the time they graduate from high school (Wilson, 1988).

At issue is whether or not there is a generally accepted body of knowledge in art that artistically literate people possess; and this issue is paralleled by the question of literacy in any field. Hirsch (1983, 1985, 1987) has argued that people considered truly literate are so not because they possess a command of vocabulary and syntax alone, but because they are knowledgeable about people, ideas, and events grounded in the culture itself, which enables them to comprehend and place in context the things they hear, see, experience, and read.

Formalism in art, the chief advocates of which were Bell (1914) and Fry

(1920), was a carryover from modernism and handed down from the teaching practices of Arthur Wesley Dow (Eisner and Ecker, 1966), has been a dominant focus in many art programs. From major emphasis in curriculum materials, to studio activities that approach formal properties as ends in themselves and critiques that focus on composition, art teachers have assumed they were developing art-literate individuals. Unfortunately, research data from the past has not supported this conclusion (Eisner, 1966; National Assessment for Educational Progress, 1981).

If art teachers are expected to develop subject-centered curriculum materials for their districts, there needs to be some consensus as to what constitutes a body of knowledge in art. What should students know about art by the time they graduate from high school? Is there some agreement among "experts" about what that body of knowledge is?

THE SEARCH FOR THE CONTENT OF ARTISTIC LITERACY

If indeed, there is a body of knowledge that literate people possess, what is it, and who decides what it is? Would the contents of such a list be arbitrarily defined? As in the field of censorship, one must ask, who is qualified to make such determinations? What assurances could be made that biased information is not included?

> Although newspaper reporters, writers of books, and the framers of the verbal SAT necessarily make assumptions about the things literate persons know, no one ever announces what that body of information is. So, although we Americans object to pronouncements about what we all should know, there is a body of information that literate people *do* know. And this creates a kind of silent, *de facto* dictating from on high about the things adults should know in order to be truly literate. (Hirsch, 1985, p. 11)

An Analysis of Textbooks

Using the research methodology known as *content analysis,* Parks (1990) analyzed the content of textbooks designed for use in college-level art-appreciation courses (texts designed to provide the non–art major with a broad base of knowledge in art), believing that such an analysis might reveal a base of information about art that could serve as a foundation for curriculum development in the public schools. The following texts were selected for analysis in this study:

Feldman, E. B. (1987). *Varieties of Visual Experience.* Englewood Cliffs, NJ: Prentice-Hall.

Fichner-Rathus, L. (1986). *Understanding Art.* Englewood Cliffs, NJ: Prentice-Hall.

Gilbert, R., and McCarter, W. (1988). *Living With Art.* New York: Knopf.

Knobler, N. (1980). *The Visual Dialogue* (3rd ed.). New York: Holt.

Kurtz, B. D. (1987). *Visual Imagination.* Englewood Cliffs, NJ: Prentice-Hall.

Preble, D., and Preble, S. (1989). *Artforms.* New York: Harper & Row.

Zelenski, P., and Fisher, M. P. (1988). *The Art of Seeing.* Englewood Cliffs, NJ: Prentice-Hall.

The content of each text was sorted into three lists: (1) *artists,* (2) *works of art*, and (3) a broader list labeled *art concepts,* which included such things as intaglio, cubism, African art, and so on. To facilitate the efficient collection of data, the indexes of the texts were used, and for each artist, concept, or work of art recorded, the source/author was also recorded.

Once the lists were compiled, any name or concept used by four or more authors was placed on the appropriate master list. In total, there were 1,219 artists identified, with 146 appearing on the final list. In the seven texts, there were 2,800 specific artworks discussed, but only 63 works identified by four or more authors to warrant their placement on the final list of artworks. In the original list of art concepts, there was a total of 2,024; in the final list, 154.

The lists were as follows:

Artists*

Abakanowicz, Magdelina
Adams, Ansel*
Agesander, Athenodorus
Albers, Josef
and Polydorus of Rhodes
Anuszkiewicz, Richard
Arp, Jean
Balla, Giacomo
Bearden, Romare
Bernini, Gianlorenzo*
Boccioni, Umberto
Bosch, Heironymous
Botticelli, Sandro

Brancusi, Constantine**
Braque, Georges**
Bruegel, Pieter (the Elder)*
Brunelleschi, Filippo
Calder, Alexander**
Callicrates
Caravaggio*
Cassatt, Mary*
Cellini, Benvenuto
Cezanne, Paul**
Chagall, Marc
Christo, Jauacheff*
Close, Chuck

---

*Two asterisks (**) follow the names of artists included in all seven texts; one asterisk (*) follows the names of artists included in six of the seven texts.

Cornell, Joseph
Courbet, Gustave*
Daguerre, Louis
Dali, Salvador**
Daumier, Honoré**
David, Jacques Louis*
Davis, Stuart
Degas, Edgar**
de Kooning, Willem*
Delacroix, Eugene
Derain, André*
Diebenkorn, Richard
Donatello
Dubuffet, Jean
Duchamp, Marcel**
Dürer, Albrecht**
Eakins, Thomas
Eiffel, Gustave
Evans, Walker
Flack, Audrey
Fragonard, Jean Honoré
Frankenthaler, Helen
Fuller, R. Buckminster**
Gabo, Naum
Gauguin, Paul**
Gericault, Theodore
Ghiberti, Lorenzo
Giacometti, Alberto*
Giotto
Goya, Francisco*
Greco, El**
Grooms, Red
Hals, Frans
Hamilton, Richard
Hanson, Duane**
Hokusai, Katsushika
Holbein, Hans
Hopper, Edward
Ictinus
Ingres, Jean Auguste*
Johns, Jasper

Johnson, Philip
Kandinsky, Wassily**
Kelly, Ellsworth
Kirchner, Ludwig
Klee, Paul*
Kokoschka, Oscar
Kollwitz, Kathe*
Lange, Dorothea**
Lawrence, Jacob
LeCorbusier, Charles
Leonardo da Vinci**
Lichtenstein, Roy
Limbourg Brothers
Louis, Morris
Magritte, René
Malevich, Kasimir
Manet, Edouard
Mantegra, Andrea
Masaccio
Matisse, Henri**
Michelangelo Buonarroti**
Mies van der Rohe, Ludwig**
Miro, Joan
Modigliani, Amedo
Mondrian, Piet**
Monet, Claude**
Moore, Henri*
Motherwell, Robert
Mu Ch'i Munari, Bruno*
Munch, Edvard**
Nevelson, Louise
Newman, Barnett
Niepce, Joseph Nicephore
Noguchi, Isamu
Nolde, Emil
Oldenburg, Claes**
Oppenheim, Meret
Orozco, Jose
Paik, Nam June**
Palladio, Andrea
Pei, I. M.

*Two asterisks (**) follow the names of artists included in all seven texts; one asterisk (*) follows the names of artists included in six of the seven texts.

Picasso, Pablo**
Pollock, Jackson**
Raphael Sanzio**
Rauschenberg, Robert**
Ray, Man
Rembrandt, van Rijn**
Renoir, Pierre*
Riley, Bridget*
Roche, Kevin
Rodin, Auguste*
Rosso, Medardo
Rothko, Mark*
Rousseau, Henri
Rubens, Peter Paul*
Saarinen, Eero*
Safdie, Moshe and David Barott
Segal, George
Serra, Richard
Seurat, Georges**

Smith, David*
Smith, Tony
Smithson, Robert*
Steichen, Edward
Stella, Frank
Sullivan, Louis
Tinguely, Jean
Tintoretto
Toulouse-Lautrec, Henri*
van Eyck, Jan**
van Gogh, Vincent**
Vasarely, Victor
Velasquez, Diego**
Vermeer, Jan
Warhol, Andy
Watteau, Jean Antoine
Weston, Edward*
Wood, Grant
Wright, Frank Lloyd**

Art Works**

Agesander, Athenodorus and Polydorus of Rhodes; *The Laocoon Group**

Balla, Giacomo; *Dynamism of a Dog on a Leash**

Bernini, Gianlorenzo; *Cornaro Chapel; Ecstasy of St. Theresa*

Botticelli, Sandro; *Birth of Venus*

Cellini, Benvenuto; *Saltcellar of Francis I*

Cezanne, Paul; *Mont Sainte-Victoire*

Christo; *Running Fence*

Dali, Salvador; *Persistance of Memory*

Daumier, Honoré; *Rue Transnonian*

David, Jacques Louis; *The Oath of Horatii*

de Kooning, Willem; *Woman and Bicycle*

Derain, André; *London Bridge*

Duchamp, Marcel; *Nude Descending a Staircase**; *Mona Lisa (LHOOO)*

Fuller, R. Buckminster; *American Pavilion, Expo '67**

Giotto; *The Lamentation*

*Two asterisks (**) follow the names of artists included in all seven texts; one asterisk follows the names of artists included in six of the seven texts.

**The list of art works is organized alphabetically according to the artist's last name, unless the artist is unknown, in which case the title of the work is used. Works that are included in all seven texts are followed by two asterisks (**), and works included in six texts are followed by one asterisk (*).

Hagia Sophia, Istanbul*

Ictinus and Callicrates; *Parthenon*

Kollwitz, Kathe; *Self Portrait*

Lange, Dorothea; *Migrant Mother, Nipomi, CA*

Le Corbusier; *Notre-Dame-Du Haut, Ronchamp, France*

Leonardo da Vinci; *The Last Supper**; *Mona Lisa*

Limbourg Brothers; *Les Très Riches Heures du Duc de Berry*

Manet, Edouard; *The Luncheon on the Grass*

Mantegna, Andrea; *Dead Christ*

Masaccio; *The Tribute Money*

Michelangelo Buonarroti; *Pieta; St. Peters, Rome; Sistine Chapel frescoes; The Creation of Adam; David*

Mies van der Rohe, Ludwig; *Barcelona Chair; Seagram Building, NYC***

Mondrian, Piet; *Composition with Red, Yellow, and Blue*

Mu Ch'i; *Six Persimmons**

Munch, Edvard; *The Scream*

Nefertiti

Nolde, Emil; *The Prophet*

Notre Dame De Chartres

Oppenheim, Meret; *Object*

Paik, Nam June; *T. V. Bra for Living Sculpture*

Panthenon

Paxton, Joseph; *Crystal Palace, London*

Picasso, Pablo; *Bulls Head; Les Demoiselles d'Avignon; Guernica**

Pont du Gard

Raimondi, Marcantonio; *The Judgment of Paris*

Raphael Sanzio; *The School of Athens*

Rembrandt, van Rijn; *Self Portrait*

Rodin, Auguste; *The Burghers of Calais*

Smith, Tony; *Die*

Smithson, Robert; *Spiral Jetty*

Steiglitz, Alfred; *The Steerage*

Tintoretto; *The Last Supper*

van Eyck, Jan; *Giovanni Arnolfini and His Bride*

**The list of art works is organized alphabetically according to the artist's last name, unless the artist is unknown, in which case the title of the work is used. Works that are included in all seven texts are followed by two asterisks (**), and works included in six texts are followed by one asterisk (*).

van Gogh, Vincent; *The Starry Night*
Velasquez, Diego; *Les Meninas*
Venus of Willendorf
Wright, Frank Lloyd; *Falling Water, Bear Run, PA***; *Guggenheim Museum, NYC.*

Art Concepts*

Abstract expressionism*
Acrylic paint
Action painting
African art
Airbrush
Analytic cubism
Aquatint*
Architecture*
Assemblage sculpture
Balance in composition**
Bauhaus
Byzantine art
Calligraphy
Camera
Camera obscura
Cartoon art
Carving, in sculpture*
Casting*
Cave paintings, Stone Age
Ceramics
Chalk
Charcoal drawing
Chiaroscuro
Children's art
Clay crafts
Collage*
Color field painting
Color*
  Value
Complementary color
Computer-aided design
Conceptual art

Constructivism
Crafts
Crayon drawing
Cubism*
Dada*
Daguerreotype photography
Dome
Drawing
Dry media
Drypoint engraving*
Egg tempera
Egyptian art
Encaustic painting**
Engraving, dry point and line*
Environments
Etch (acid), etching*
Expressionism**
Fauvism*
Fiber arts
Figure-ground relationships
Film
Fine art
Folk art
Form
Fresco**
Furniture (as embodiments of
  ideas and feelings)
Futurism**
Geodesic dome
Gesso
Glaze
Gothic architecture

*Concepts that are covered in all seven texts are followed by two asterisks (**), and concepts covered in six texts are followed by one asterisk (*).

Graphic design
Greek art
Groined vault
Happenings
Hard-edge painting
Hatching
Hue
Humanism
Illustration
Impasto
Impressionism*
Industrial design
Industrial revolution
Intaglio painting*
Intensity
Interior design
International style/architecture
Japanese art: influence on Impressionism
Kinetic (moving sculpture)**
Light*
Line**
Linear perspective
Lithography
Local Color
Lost wax—bronze casting
Mannerism
Manuscript illumination
Mass
Medium, in art
Mesopotamian architecture
Metal crafts*
Mezzotint
Minimalism
Mobiles*
Modeling*
Monotype
Neoclassicism

Nonrepresentational (nonfigurative)
Oil painting**
Op art*
Painting
Pastel drawing
Pencil drawing
Pendentive
Performance art
Perspective*
Photography**
Photorealism
Picture plane
Pigment
Planographic lithography
Pointalism
Pop art
Post and lintel architecture
Post-Impressionism**
Postmodern architecture*
Printmaking
Proportion
Realism*
Reinforced concrete
Renaissance
Representational art
Rhythm
Rococo
Roman art and architecture
Romanesque art and architecture
Romanticism
Saturation (optical property)
Scale*
Sculpture*
Serigraphy*
Shape
Silkscreen printing
Silverpoint drawing

*Concepts that are covered in all seven texts are followed by two asterisks (**), and concepts covered in six texts are followed by one asterisk (*).

Space	Time
Stoneware	Truss construction
Surrealism**	Typography
Symbolism	Unity in composition
Television**	Value (optical property)
Tempera	Vehicle
Terra cotta clay	Video art
Texture*	Watercolor*

Perspectives on the Findings.

To an extent, one can see a Western bias in the above lists. There is a heavy emphasis on European and American art, and when the authors discuss Japanese art, it is often in terms of its influence on French Impressionism. It is also true that there were only four artists with Asian ancestory included in the final list of artists, and three of them—I. M. Pei, Nam June Paik, and Isamu Noguchi—have lived and worked in the West. Only four of the seven authors included Japanese art in their texts, and only four included a discussion of African art. However, there were forty-two Asian artists identified, which suggests that those texts that included them gave them a fair amount of attention.

While the artists, art works, and art concepts included in the lists were not surprising, some exclusions were. For instance, Gustave Eiffel, the designer of the Eiffel tower, was included in the list of artists (for want of a better place to put him), and authors apparently considered him worthy of discussion. And yet, Einstein was only mentioned by one author, and Freud was excluded entirely. Granted, the former was peripherally related to the arts as an engineer and designer, yet the latter two had profound effects on the attitudes and ideas of twentieth-century artists.

In architecture, Mies van der Rohe and the international style were discussed, as was his chief antagonist Frank Lloyd Wright; yet no reference was made to organic architecture, Wright's reaction to the international style. The industrial revolution is covered, yet no mention of the information age is acknowledged, in spite of the inclusion of television as a concept in all seven texts.

Other surprising omissions were Donald Judd, even though minimalism was included, as was the painter, Ellsworth Kelly. John Cage and Allan Kaprow did not receive enough citations to justify inclusion in the final list, even though "happenings" and other 1960s activities they profoundly influ-

---

*Concepts that are covered in all seven texts are followed by two asterisks (**), and concepts covered in six texts are followed by one asterisk (*).

enced did. Only 9 women artists were included in the final list of 146. Of the 9, one was the op artist Bridget Riley, and yet surprisingly, Georgia O'Keefe was missing from the list, perhaps because she did not fit neatly into a stylistic category. Andrew Wyeth, included in all seven texts, was unexpected, considering the ongoing debate by the art establishment over whether he should be considered an artist or an illustrator. Some might view Wyeth's inclusion as evidence that texts do indeed address works that are considered "popular" art, and not just fine art.

Finally, no mention of artistic pluralism appeared in the texts. Postmodern architecture was mentioned in six of the texts, but not postmodernism as it pertains to the other visual arts. This is not a result of the publication dates of the texts; all were published within the past decade, and, with the exception of Knobler (1980), all were updated and/or published within the last five years. With the exception of some photorealists like Chuck Close and Duane Hanson and earthworks artists like Smithson and Christo, virtually all of the significant artists from the past two decades failed to appear in the master list of artists.

While there are a number of discrepancies and seemingly "sins of omission," the master lists compiled provide a good overview of artists, art works, and art concepts to be considered for inclusion in art curriculum materials. Local districts will naturally need to consider regional and cultural concerns when considering how such material should be used. And, individual art teachers should be encouraged to expand on the ideas included here, teaching about the works and artists with which they are most familiar and for which they have a particular passion.

Themes in Art

Thematic approaches to teaching art will be discussed more specifically in the next section. However, thematic approaches can and generally do span all art disciplines, often providing unique and interesting perspectives on the subject of art, and serve as good motivators to pique student interest and motivation in the classroom. While Parks (1990) did not specifically address the issue of themes in art, he suggests that for students to be artistically literate, they need to be aware that themes are a primary source of meaning in art. The following are some examples of themes that can be used for lessons, units of study, or, in some cases, an entire semester's series of activities.

Why is art necessary?
What is art and its purposes and functions?
Universal expressions of art
Aesthetic vs. monetary values

The touch of the human hand or lack thereof

Fine art as its own subject

Everyman as artist

Folk art vs. fine art

Art as communication

The artist's personal perspective: style

Impressionism (or any period or style) and its influence

Art and the "real" world

Other views of reality: art from other cultures

Distorting the look of reality: Why do artists do that?

Defining Reality: the myths and distortions of photography

Photography's influence on painting, and vice versa

Historical roles of the camera

Art and its impact on social change

Art as social protest

Social, political, and artistic revolution

Power and propaganda: politics and ideology

Politics and art: from engagement to censorship

Art, democracy, and totalitarianism: varying functions

Mexican protest art

Integrating the arts: performance art

Conceptual and performance art

Public art

Conserving and restoring art

The changing role of the artist

Light, color, and form as subject

Escaping history, anticipating the future

Inner experiences, parallel realities

The art of seeing

The loss of innocence: industrialization and modernism

Art as beauty and truth

Making the commonplace monumental

Expressing the human condition: anxiety, joy, and despair

Human beings in historical vs. modern vs. contemporary art

The impulse to create

Art in a social and cultural context

Art as a means to transcend mortality

Spiritual and mystical transcendence in art

Order and harmony in nature and art

Art and nature: Zen, the Hudson River, and Frank Lloyd Wright

Making and looking at art: hand, mind, and heart

Art as stimulating objects to be thought through

Recording and honoring historical events

Expressing the supernatural

Art as magic for survival

Art in the service of religion

Myths, legends, fantasy, and illusion

Gods and heroes: the classical world; the Americas

Decorative art

Art as business, art as commodity

Art as communication

The artist's intentions: Are they necessary to know?

Television vs. film: the relativity of time and space

Secular art: the renaissance begins

Ambiguity in life and art

Is good art eternal? The masterpiece vs. transcient art

What are symbols and how do they function?

Symbolism in sculptures and murals

The fabricated environment: Architecture and interior/exterior/urban space

Architectural considerations and plans

Historical Architecture and postmodernism

The Enlightenment: a little eighteenth-century revolution

Comparing styles and subject matter in world art

Art and technology

Artistic inspiration.

ARTISTIC LITERACY AND ART INSTRUCTION

Many art educators believe that developing a national curriculum in art will "academize" art instruction and kill its spirit. However, for a viewer to respond intelligently to a work of art, the individual must possess a base of knowledge about art to frame the proper context for the experience and to be sensitive to the subtle nuances of the work. This requires some understanding of basic art concepts, familiarity with influential artists and their work, and the vocabulary to think and communicate ideas and opinions about art. The challenge for art teachers is to determine the art content they believe their students should master in order to be prepared for a lifetime of learning in art.

TEACHING ART HISTORY

Art History As a Discipline

As a distinct subject of study, art history is approximately 175 years old, having evolved out of the field of classical archeology. "...in fact the field as we know it did not begin to take shape until the second half of the nineteenth century. It was at that time that the standards for connoisseurs, stylistic analysis and iconographical decoding were established" (Rice, 1986, p. 14). Although a relatively young discipline, various methodological approaches to art historical inquiry have evolved. Katter (1986) discusses eight such methodologies:

1. *As the History of Objects*—Drawing on traditions from the field of archaeology, the art historian identifies, describes, classifies, and arranges works of art chronologically based on "some determined principle" and thorough objective research. See Friedlander (1932) and Gilborn (1978).

2. *As the History of Form*—Highly influenced by art criticism and "formalism," formal aspects of works of art become the primary focus for classifying and sequencing works of art. See Wolfflin (1932) and Fry (1927).

3. *As the History of Style*—Style becomes the criteria for dating and establishing the origins of works of art, and for realizing relationships between genres. See Schapiro (1953).

4. *As the History of Ideas*—"This strand of art history has drawn its tradition from the field of comparative literature and the broad field of the humanities....The generalizations drawn...are largely speculative, and are dependent on continuous application of comparative values" (Katter, 1986, p. 209). See Panofsky (1955).

5. *As the History of Culture*—Recognizing that art is a product of social conditions and forces, artifacts become objects for studying a culture. To understand changes in art, the historian looks to change within the society that produced it. Such an approach is intimately related to sociology and anthropology. See Roskill (1976), Gowans (1974), Chalmers (1973, 1974, 1978), and LaChapelle (1984).

6. *As the History of Symbols*—This aspect of art history is the systematic investigation of (iconography) and interpretation of (iconology) subject matter and symbols in works of art. The emphasis is on representational aspects of work rather than style. See Panofsky (1939).

7. *As the History of Artists*—This approach focuses on a biographical investigation of an artist's personal life and its influences on his or her art work. See Barr (1966) and Russell (1965).

8. *As the History of Personality*—This type of inquiry applies psychoanalytic theory to art history, examining and analyzing works of art as extensions of personality, and is closely related to the biographical approach. See Jung (1964), Freud (1964), Erikson (1958).

While Katter (1986) acknowledges the various approaches scholars may take in art historical investigations, when discussing the teaching of art history in the classroom, he states, "...it seems appropriate to conclude that for a young student to be introduced to the study of art through only one of these approaches would leave that student with a distorted view of history and an inadequate experience of art" (p. 210).

A major criticism of the DBAE approach has been that the definition of the various art disciplines has been too narrowly defined, placing too much emphasis on Eurocentric, male-dominated, and elitist art forms. As Katter (1986) demonstrates, art history can be defined, practiced, and taught from a broader perspective than most art teachers experienced in their own professional training.

Erickson (1983) believes the behavior and practices of art historians provide the best model for organizing art history activities in the classroom. She has identified three broad categories of processes employed by art historians in their pursuit of knowledge about art: (1) processes for establishing facts, (2) processes for interpreting meaning, and (3) processes for explaining change. She then goes on to identify five distinct processes, each of which fall under one of the three categories above:

1. *Reconstruction*—This is a process for establishing facts. Here the historian determines if the work appears the same as it did when it was made, or if it has been broken or damaged, altered, faded, darkened, and so on. The scholar's task is to try to reconstruct, usually through imagination, what the work must have originally looked like.

2. *Description*—This is a process for establishing facts. Based on precise observation, the scholar verbally records a description of the work under study. A factual record of the state of preservation, medium, size, subject, form, and so forth, are produced. Description provides the basis for future scholarly studies.

3. *Attribution*—This is a process for establishing facts. Based on cultural and artistic traditions, knowledge about the individual artist and particular events in his or her life, the scholar explains the reason for, or the origin of, a specific work of art.

4. *Interpretation*—This is a process for interpreting meaning. The historian tries to identify meanings for a work of art that would have been understood by individuals when the work was created (an often difficult task). Such an investigation would involve an examination of both the form and content of the work itself and any other relevant information that would lend insight into the meaning of the work.

5. *Explanation*—This is a process for explaining change. Narrative accounts trace the chronology of the relationships between "identified influences, traditions, and innovations" (p. 30). When the historian explains change through identifying an underlying structure that suggests there are "laws and principles" governing the changes, they are referred to as scientific accounts.

Art History in the Classroom

There are a variety of ways art teachers can approach the teaching of art history—from courses designed as pure art history classes, to those that integrate art history with aesthetics, criticism, and production activities, and to those studio courses that use art history as a source for ideas with which to explore and experiment.

There are various alternatives to organizing art history experiences, each with their own strengths and weaknesses. With an understanding of the various approaches, the art teacher can tailor art history lessons to the particular needs of students and to curricular goals.

The Traditional or Positivist Approach.

Most art teachers received their education in art history and art appreciation by taking courses that were delivered by lecture, were chronologically organized, and that stressed "formalist" concerns. In many cases, such classes were not very interesting for the students. Rice (1986) describes her undergraduate art history training: "I studied the history of style as a closed system with an inner life of its own, independent of outside factors" (p. 13). Pazienza (1986) has noted that such an approach, known as positivism, rose out of nineteenth-century scientific empiricism, in which objective observation of the artifact was presumed to produce facts based on the logic of the methodology that produced them.

The strength of a *positivist* approach is that it demonstrates how ideas and styles in art have evolved, structuring the study of art history and providing a sense of time for both the student and the teacher. Such insights are crucial for the student to grasp. Children need to acquire a "feel" for time and to realize that ideas in art do not just appear by accident, but rather are the result of reactions to previous ideas and events in art. The positivist approach employs three of Katter's (1986) eight art historical methodologies: the history of objects, the history of forms, and the history of style.

The weaknesses of a *pure* positivist approach are fourfold: (1) personal and cultural values exist in works of art in spite of attempts to be objective and ignore them; (2) a formalist approach is rather abstract for school-age children and fails to make important connections with the real-life conditions that cause art works to be produced, a necessary connection if children are to empathize with the work; (3) the frequency with which most art classes meet and the attention spans of children do not allow for the dissemination and retention of detailed information that such an approach requires; and, finally, (4) time is relative, and most children (even high school students) lack the age, experience, and maturity to place an art work in a temporal/historical context.

The Idealist Approach.

Rather than focusing on form and style, as the positivist approach does, the *idealist* approach seeks to understand the context and meaning of works of art. To do so, the historian examines the cultural and historical context of the work and dominant ideas within the culture at the time the work came into existence, whether the artist was conscious of their inclusion or not (Pazienza, 1986). Whereas positivism relies strictly on what is objectively observable in the work itself, idealism makes the invisible in art visible. (UA 3-1)

One of the great strengths of the idealist approach is the relationship it establishes between a work of art and the attitudes and values, the quality of life, and the spiritual beliefs held by the culture that produced it. The art object is viewed as a meaning-laden artifact, and any information that aids in peeling back its layers of meaning is useful to the inquiry. Such an approach employs the remaining methodological approaches identified by Katter (1986): the history of ideas, of culture, of symbols, of artists, and of personality. By establishing that a work of art was created by a real, live individual with feelings and needs who was motivated to do so by real-life events, the art teacher can help students to understand that works of art are living objects that continue to communicate centuries after they were created. If students are to respond affectively to works of art, if they are to identify and empathize with the work (and they must if they are going to "appreciate" it), links must be established between the artist, the artistic act, and the social reality that produced it. (UA 3-2)

Another motivating aspect of the idealist approach is the recognition

FIGURE UA 3–1. Saturday Children's Art Classes at Buffalo State College.

that a work of art is a symbolic object. Older children, particularly adolescents, are often intrigued with the idea of symbols. Lessons and units of study that focus on iconography can be exciting, thought-provoking art history lessons. (UA 3-3)

Rather than an extensive look at the chronological development of styles in art, the idealist approach concentrates intensively on a particular theme, work, artist, or period. If there is a weakness to this approach, it is in terms of its disinterest in the chronological ordering of objects and styles. However, children do need to acquire a sense of time, space, and place, and chronology does not have to be mutually exclusive of the idealist approach. In fact, there are variations on the idealist approach that assimilate chronology meaningfully.

The *thematic* approach advocated by Feldman (1970, 1981) can incorporate chronology. For instance, if the theme were *The Influence of Photography on Painting* (see other thematic ideas on page 70), the unit might begin by examining the changes in attitude and quality of life brought on by the industrial revolution, how the new age motivated individuals to invent, how the invention of photography was the marriage of two ideas that had been around for several centuries (knowledge of light-sensitive chemicals and the camera obscura), how photography called into question the nature of reality *and* the function of art, and how photography influenced what artists were

FIGURE UA 3–2. Saturday Children's Art Classes at Buffalo State College.

doing, namely: new ways to think about composing pictures; capturing the immediacy of the moment; and freeing artists from traditional tasks like portraying historical events, beginning the modernist practice of looking into the nature of art itself (a formalist concern). Beginning with the impressionists, the camera's influence on painting could then be traced through the twentieth century, concluding with the works of Cindy Sherman and/or the photorealists.

FIGURE UA 3–3. Saturday Children's Art Classes at Buffalo State College.

Several writers have suggested that art history needs to place greater emphasis on a sociology of art. Katter (1986) includes such a point of view in the methodological approach *As the History of Culture* outlined on page 73. Through the modern "formalist" period in the development of art history, historians applied empirical objectivity to the study of art, ignoring the human and social values embodied in the work. Chalmers (1973, 1974, and 1978) among others (McFee and Degge, 1977; Chapman, 1982) has advocated the need for art historians to focus on *why* art is made. He states:

> Our literature is full of terms suggesting that judgment is crucial to appreciation, but rarely is appreciation related to understanding the nature and meaning of art in multicultural societies. Typically appreciations and judgments are based on the assumption that "good" art has universal and timeless formal properties and stylistic qualities across all cultures and that it is more important to know what art is, particularly what is good Western art, than to know why art is made....The popular, folk, and environmental arts of many cultures and subcultures deserve a place in an art history curriculum that encourages students to view art as intimately related to other aspects of culture. (p. 18)

LaChapelle (1984) also emphasizes the need for sociological approaches to examining periods in art history, particularly the modern period. He raises arguments that creative human beings are not only stimulus-reducing organisms, but stimulus-seekers as well; not only problem-solvers, but also problem-finders.

> ...given our modernist fine art sensibility with its aggressive acceptance of a stimulus seeking–problem finding role, art has become so complicated that it is necessary to search out the conventions and values of the producing group in order to find meaning in that art. (p. 38)

A sociological and anthropological approach to art history can be organized *thematically,* can be integrated with activities in social studies, economics, music, and other subject areas, and can open up avenues for empathic, intrinsic responses from students. It has particular relevance for looking at and discussing contemporary works of art, where the division between fine art and popular art is breaking down, where notions of personal expression are being supplanted with calls for social expression, where "global village" and multicultural concerns are examined, and where content takes precedent over form.

Another variation on the idealist approach is the *inquiry* model proposed by Erickson (1983) and Erickson and Katter (1981). Erickson (1983) proposes teaching art history as an inquiry process, where students are given actual artifacts such as old sheet music, "Coca-cola ads, record-album covers, photographs of gravestones, or other collections of artifacts available for a period of years..." (p. 29) on which they can practice art historical inquiry processes (as found on p. 74). By approaching art history lessons as an inquiry process, the students are learning not only *what* art historians have concluded, but *how* they arrived at those conclusions.

Wilson (1986) describes another inquiry approach to teaching art history. He raises the very real issue that art teachers have not been well prepared to teach art history, especially the broad survey-type courses usually associated with art history classes. He suggests that what may be more valuable for youngsters to experience is an in-depth look at a few artists or works of art, rather than a breadth of exposure to art history. He raises several pertinent questions:

> Is it not possible that the important benefits that come from the study of the history of art can be received through the study of a few works of art? And is it not possible for each art teacher to become a specialist in a few works of art just as some art historians devote much of their professional careers to the study of the work of one artist and sometimes to one or a few works of art? (p. 145)

Working with nine elementary and secondary art teachers four hours a day for three weeks, Wilson studied Picasso's *Guernica*. They applied Arnheim's (1962) approach, examining, discussing, and writing about Picasso's preliminary sketches for the painting, and examined photograph's of Picasso while he worked on the mural. There was an ongoing discussion of the "...symbolic, allegorical, mythical, structural, expressive and stylistic aspects..." (p. 145) of the work. They examined various historians' and critics' writings and interpretations of the painting. They concluded their weeks of work by choosing a position about the painting and writing their own persuasive art historical account of Picasso's work.

While Wilson recognized that the art historical inquiry process practiced by him and his students was undertaken in ideal conditions, it does provide an interesting alternative model (when appropriately geared for the age level of student) for the teaching of art history.

The Instrumentalist Approach.

Instrumentalism is the most common approach to art history lessons used by art teachers. *Instrumentalism* implies that art history is used as an instrument or tool within a studio curriculum, rather than as a distinct, autonomous subject. The teacher may precede a figure-painting assignment by showing how various artists through the centuries, or in different cultures, have approached the human figure as a subject in their paintings. Medieval icons and celebrity images by Warhol might be used as a catalyst for students to develop their own contemporary icons. Even formal properties or techniques might be explored using historical works of art as exemplars for the students to emulate.

> Hurwitz (1986) suggests reversing the objective:...by applying studio experience to a particular moment in art history....Pretend you are a fellow student of Ingres at the Academy of Beaux Arts in Paris in 1800, and see if you can apply the rules of Neo-Classical painting to your drawing..." (p. 70)

The rationale for approaching art history in such a manner is that the studio/sensory experience reinforces learning in art history and art history reinforces learning in the studio activity. An instrumentalist approach also insures that studio activities remain focused on the subject of art, as a means to an end, and will not digress into mindless "artsy-craftsy" activities. However, such an approach seldom provides much "depth" in learning art history because art history is generally not the primary focus of the activities.

While an instrumentalist approach is appropriate for most studio activities, by the time children reach adolescence and are capable of expressing opinions and ideas in writing, their exposure to art history ought to be broadened to include writing and discussion activities, if they are to acquire a good knowledge foundation in art history.

SENSIBLE APPROACHES TO ART HISTORY

Works of art are idea-laden objects that reflect the values of the people that created them. To not teach art history in the classroom is to not teach art. Art history is essential to a foundation for lifelong learning in the arts. However, a strict positivist approach that emphasizes only formalist and chronological information will have a deadening influence in a K-12 classroom. Time is relative and students lack the experience or maturity to find interest or value in such an abstract approach.

A more useful way to organize art history activities in the classroom will be a hybrid of the approaches discussed. Thematic approaches can be the "hook" or motivation that grabs the interest of students. Idealist concerns like cultural and historical context will make the lessons meaningful, while accompanying studio activities will reinforce the concepts being taught. Students do need some sense of chronology which can be emphasized as they come to realize that artists across cultures and throughout time have grappled with similar themes and concerns. If handled artistically by the teacher, such approaches to instruction will be rich learning experiences for students.

TEACHING AESTHETICS

Since the ancient Greeks, philosophers have considered the arts to be a subject worthy of thought and contemplation. The Greeks argued over the nature of beauty and art, and Plato questioned whether or not art had a moral or immoral influence on man. Aesthetic issues are no longer examined solely by philosophers; with the advent of scientific methodology in the nineteenth-century and the birth of the fields of psychology and anthropology, researchers began scientifically testing ideas that were testable and that had traditionally been the sole domain of philosophy.

To focus on aesthetic issues from a strictly philosophical perspective is no longer considered adequate:

> An accounting of why and how people attend to, understand, and respond to art in both spontaneous and deliberate ways is a desirable goal for those seeking to incorporate aesthetics into art education....Cognition, mutable behaviors, enculturation, and holistic structures of thought, feeling and sensation all seem to come into play. (Lankford, 1986, p. 51)

Contemporary approaches to aesthetic issues can be divided into two categories: *philosophical aesthetics* and *scientific aesthetics.* In order to deal with such issues, one needs to be able to think critically (see p. 87) and to raise questions. Langer (1957) distinguished between philosophical questions and scientific questions:

> A philosophical question is always a demand for the meaning of what we are saying. This makes it different from a scientific question, which is a question of fact...(p. 2)

Philosophical Aesthetics

> Art more than any other discipline save perhaps philosophy requires one to develop a view of the world and to become aware of the set of relations that one bears to it and which constitutes the perspective from which it is perceived. (Haldane, 1983, p. 9)

Traditional philosophical issues in aesthetics can be divided into three groupings: (1) theory of the aesthetic; (2) philosophy of art; and (3) philosophy of criticism (See Hagaman, 1988). Discussion questions related to each grouping are as follows:

Theory of the Aesthetic.

What are aesthetic experiences and why do we have them? Why does a sunset or a work of art grab and hold our attention, how does it differ from other forms of experience, and why are we so moved by them? Is it possible to have an aesthetic experience if we do not possess an "aesthetic attitude" or a mindset that is willing to have such experiences? Is an aesthetic experience the result of the properties of the aesthetic object? Do works of art have to be aesthetically appealing to be art or to be good works of art?

Philosophy of Art.

What are works of art? Is there something that all works of art, from all cultures and all periods in history have in common? What about cultures that produce artifacts and decorate their bodies, their homes, tools, and furnishings, yet have no word in their vocabulary for art? Does the function of an object play a part in whether or not to define it as art? Does something have to have physical form to be considered a work of art, or is the art concept enough? How much alteration to materials has to take place before objects can be declared works of art? Does an artist declaring something to be a work of art make it a work of art?

Philosophy of Criticism.

How does one go about determining meaning and value in works of art? What criteria does one use to judge the quality of a work of art? Does one judge all art by the same criteria, or does criteria have to be flexible and adaptive to a variety of works of art? How does one maintain an open mind when looking at works of art? Is judgment of meaning and significance in works of art based solely on what is visually present in the work, or are there external factors that can or should be considered? Is context to be considered (context in which work is seen or created)? How much emphasis in criticism should be placed on *FORM* (elements and principles of design) versus *CONTENT* (subject matter, theme, metaphor, style, cultural references, historical references, and so forth)? (See section on Teaching Criticism, p. 88.)

Scientific Aesthetics

Scientific aesthetics can be divided into two categories: (1) experimental/empirical aesthetics, and (2) sociological/anthropological aesthetics. The field of psychology began in the mid-1800s when scientists who were philosophers by training began applying the new scientific methodology to test traditional philosophical ideas about the human psyche. Similarly, sociologists and psychologists today examine aesthetic questions and issues that are testable, using scientific methodology.

Experimental/Empirical Aesthetics.

Empirical aesthetics implies that there are aesthetic concerns that are physically testable. Empirical aesthetics falls within the domain of the field of psychology and questions how works of art come to be what they are.

What is the role of the artist's conscious/unconscious state on the creation of a work of art? How does an artist perceive and organize perceptions and thoughts; and, in turn, do works of art serve as physical models of human thought itself? What is the nature/role of creativity in the aesthetic experience of a work of art? (See Child, 1970; Arnheim, 1969, 1983; Jung, 1964; Gardner, 1983).

Sociological/Anthropological Aesthetics.

Art is always produced in a social and cultural context. Individuals cannot escape the value and perceptual systems of the culture to which they belong. Therefore, a number of aesthetic questions arise concerning such issues. How does a work of art reflect the culture in which it was created? Is it possible for an individual to truly empathize with a work of art produced in a culture other than his own? Can one ever perceive a work of art from the context of the culture or time period in which it was produced? What is the social relevance of a particular work of art in relation to the time in which it was created? Is there a universal aesthetic, or is what is good in one culture awful in another? (See McFee and Degge, 1977; Chalmers, 1973, 1974, 1978, 1987; Mukerjee, 1959).

Classroom Approaches to Aesthetics

Although many art teachers do not realize it, aesthetic issues surface in classroom dialogue all the time. For example: How might your image be strengthened? Should artists be allowed to produce and exhibit anything they want without fear of censorship? Is it constructive for the federal government to financially support the arts, or does government involvement naturally corrupt and/or encourage mediocrity?

There are many aesthetic issues related to art that are relevant to children's knowledge and experience of art. E. Louis Lankford provides an example of a discussion topic and questions that deal with relevant, real-life aesthetic issues.

THE P.M.A.M. DECISION

A Fictional Scenario for Aesthetic Inquiry

Prepared by E. Louis Lankford, Ph.D
Department of Art Education
The Ohio State University

Since 1908 the Petersburg Municipal Art Museum (P.M.A.M.) has housed a painting titled "Jacob's Ladder," attributed to Rembrandt van Rijn. The painting, one of the museum's showpieces, was a gift from the estate of a wealthy collector, and it exhibits the Biblical content, bold brushstrokes, sombre palette and luminous highlights so characteristic of Rembrandt's later years.

On March 4th, a madman entered the museum and, to the horror of museum visitors, produced a carving knife and managed to cut several long slits through the canvas before he could be stopped by museum guards. The damage was extensive. The painting was immediately transferred to the Restoration Department.

On March 8th, chief restorer Dr. Sonya Pierre entered the museum Director's office looking somewhat distraught, and closed the door behind her.

"We've run tests on the pigments and grounds of the slashed painting in order to restore it properly. The tests have been duplicated once by us, and the results confirmed by the University lab. There can be no doubt about it: 'Jacob's Ladder' is not by Rembrandt. Some of the pigments used were not available until 100 years after Rembrandt's death. I cannot say with any certainty yet, but it may be a forgery. Shall I proceed with the restoration?"

QUESTIONS FOR DISCUSSION

1. If you were the Director, what would be your decision: to restore, or not to restore? On what basis would you rest your decision? What additional information would you want to help you form your opinion? What factors, or what people, might influence your decision?
2. Has the value of the painting changed due to Dr. Pierre's discovery? Try to discriminate among different types of values (e.g., aesthetic, historical, religious, economic, social status) and consider how each type may have changed.
3. Can you identify other issues that could relate to this scenario? For example, would Dr. Pierre's discovery change the way an art critic or art historian would deal with the painting?
4. How might this scenario be adapted or utilized to serve as part of a unit of instruction? What other lessons might be built around it? Can you relate this scenario with lessons in history, criticism, studio, multicultural concerns, building vocabulary, or other content areas in a school curriculum?

Based on Lankford's model, one can develop a series of discussion topics that focus on aesthetic issues. For example:

The Art Market
The art world of nineteenth-century France was dominated by the French Academy, L'Ecole des Beaux Arts. Founded by Louis XIV in 1648 as the Academie Royale de

Painture et de Sculpture, its purpose was to be a guiding force for French art, establishing criteria for judging the quality of art and defining what good art is. The most popular French artist of the nineteenth century and a prominent member of the Academy was William-Adolphe Bouguereau, whose painting *Invading Cupid's Realm* is seen on the screen.

Vincent van Gogh, a Dutchman born in 1853, decided at the age of twenty-seven (after failing as a Christian evangelist) to become an artist and spent the next two years teaching himself to draw. A manic depressant, he took his own life at the age of thirty-seven. In the short ten years of his artistic life, he sold only one painting and that was to his brother Theo, who told him he was serving as a middleman for an art collector.

Recently, van Gogh's painting *Irises,* shown on the screen, sold at auction for $53.9 million. The same year, a Bouguereau sold for $75,000.

QUESTIONS FOR DISCUSSION*

1. Does the recent price paid for a van Gogh mean that Vincent was a better painter than Bouguereau? What is the relationship between artistic value and monetary value?
2. Are the technical merits of the Bouguereau and the van Gogh comparable? If so, what is there about van Gogh's work that demands greater recognition today than the work of Bouguereau?
3. Is there a relationship between popular taste and artistic value? Is it possible for an artist to be an accepted, admired member of society and still achieve greatness in the art world and in the history of art?
4. Why would someone pay almost $54 million for a painting? Does the price of the painting prejudice our viewing of it? Should the art establishment be concerned with the trend toward inflated prices for works of art?
5. Can living artists who receive tens of thousands of dollars for a single work of art remain true to themselves and to art, or does the notion of "art as commodity" corrupt them? Is the concept of "art as commodity" an artistic problem or a cultural problem?

Other discussion topics might focus on issues of beauty in art and nature, how they differ, and whether or not beauty is necessary for an object to be a work of art. Is it possible that five different people can see the same work of art and have different interpretations about the work? Why? What is the difference between public and private responses to works of art? What

*(Answers may overlap.)

makes a work of art revolutionary at a particular historical moment when that same work might be judged mediocre, were it to be painted today. Does the person judge the picture, or the picture judge the person?

Aesthetic Dialogue in the Classroom

Throughout history, human beings have pursued truth and reality through science, religion, philosophy, and art. Art objects have long been recognized as having ideas and values imbedded in them. To engage students in aesthetic discussions unlocks issues related to the nature of art and the human experience that cannot be confronted in any other way. Such activities hone students' inquiry and thinking skills, expose them to aesthetic issues they will later be making decisions on as adults, and broaden their vision and understanding of the nature of art.

TEACHING ART CRITICISM

The education community has come to the realization that the ability to think critically is a basic skill of an educated person. While the field of art education has only recently begun stressing the importance of developing critical-thinking skills in students so they can approach works by mature artists with openness, enthusiasm, and intelligence, art teachers have long used the critique as a means of guiding students in the production of their own art work.

For a student to think critically, he or she needs to possess three skills:

1. Students need to know how to raise basic questions about the ideas or objects into which they are inquiring. Once initial questions are raised, additional questions that build on previous discoveries need to follow *(Socratic questioning)*.
2. Students need to be able to assume a point of view other than their own *(reciprocity)*. This requires the ability to empathize with others and with art objects themselves. How did the artist feel or think? Why would someone arrive at such an interpretation?
3. Students need to learn how to carry on a reasonable discussion over issues and ideas with people they disagree with *(dialectical exchange)*. Discussions centered on works of art should naturally arouse diverse opinions, which can become topics for discussion. And, such discussions should provide opportunities for students to defend their points of view, a crucial activity if students are to develop an appreciation for art (see the discussion of the affective domain, p. 11).

Sternberg (1987) has identified several essential aspects to consider in developing critical-thinking skills in students. The teacher needs to be aware of her role as a model for students. In critical thinking, there is always room for growth, and traditional teacher/authority–student/learner relationships can be counterproductive. The teacher needs to be as flexible, open, and receptive to ideas as her students. The teacher also needs to be thinking about the questions and problems posed for students and think out responses for herself. In other words, the teacher must be willing to relinquish some of her traditional authority and be an active participant in the problems presented to the students. (For insights into conducting such activities, see p. 30, Discussions About Art in the Classroom.)

Sternberg suggests that students need some direct instruction in how to think critically, but the component skills that they learn need to be infused meaningfully into the larger whole of instruction. The ability to think both analytically and synthetically are equally important. Critical thinkers are able to synthesize ideas as well as analyze them.

Art Criticism in the Classroom

As a branch of aesthetics (see previous section on Teaching Aesthetics), art criticism began about the third century B.C. in ancient Greece, where philosophers contemplated the relationship between the personality of the artist and judgments about the works of art they produced. Once the Academie Royale de Painture et de Sculpture opened its exhibition to the public in 1648, modern approaches to criticism began (Cromer, 1990). However, even today the criteria a critic uses to judge the quality of a work of art is rooted in his "philosophy" of art.

When the field of art education shifted from a child-centered to a subject-centered focus, questions arose concerning what all children should know and be able to do in relation to the visual arts. Recognizing that most children do not grow up to be artists, educators began to reduce the heavy emphasis on studio activities and to concentrate more on developing a curriculum that would offer a foundation of understanding of art. To be a critic requires an extraordinary amount of experience, knowledge, insight, and maturity; all the things that children often lack. However, children can be provided with a framework for experiencing art that will make their encounters richer and more meaningful.

A framework for art criticism should be flexible enough to apply to a wide range of artworks and adaptable enough to evolve with changes that take place in art and in the child's growing understanding of art. When looking at works by mature artists, judgments of quality should be avoided, although the opinions of art historians and professional critics can make for informed and interesting discussion topics. The framework for criticism that the teacher selects should be consistently used and reinforced, and the rationale for its use should reflect that it is a method of inquiry; an organized, systematic way of gaining knowledge and meaning from works of art.

Two approaches to criticism that can be applied to classroom use are Edmund Burke Feldman's (1981) *critical performance* and E. Louis Lankford's (1984) *phenomenological approach.* Following a description of each, Feinstein's (1989) method of metaphoric interpretation will be discussed.

Feldman's "Critical Performance".

Feldman's approach to criticism is the most commonly used today. He describes criticism as "talk about art." There are four stages in Feldman's approach: (1) description, (2) formal analysis, (3) interpretation, and (4) judgment (See Hamblen's questioning strategy based on Feldman's model and Bloom's *Taxonomy,* page 41.) The purpose of following a four-stage, systematic approach is to slow down the tendency to make hasty judgments about works of art so that an adequate amount of evidence can be collected for making such judgments.

Description: Feldman defines *description* as the process of "taking inventory" of what is in an image. For representational images, description would include the recognizable objects in an image. If the work is too abstract to identify the objects within it or the image is nonobjective, description would focus on the colors, shapes, and so on present in the image. Such a description does not require an extensive knowledge of art; it describes what any attentive individual would perceive in the work of art.

Description will also include a discussion of media and the techniques employed by the artist. Again, it is important for the viewer to postpone making judgments about the work until the first three stages in the process have gathered evidence on which to base a judgment.

Formal Analysis: Once a basic description of the work has been completed, one begins to *analyze* the form of the work. This process is also descriptive, but it requires a greater understanding of art. It describes the relationships between the things we see in the work and the qualities of color, shape, line, and so forth that cause us to see them. How has the artist organized and composed the image? What principles of design have been employed to create a coherent whole?

Interpretation: Once we have completed description and formal analysis, we are ready to begin speculating about the meanings of the image we see. What ideas, values and themes exist in the work? What artistic problems

Elements of Design

Principles of Design	Point	Line	Shape	Light & Value	Texture	Color	Time	Motion	Mass	Space & Volume	Plane
Scale											
Proportion											
Unity Within Variety											
Repetition & Rhythm											
Balance											
Contrast											
Directional Forces											
Emphasis & Subordination											

FIGURE 3–1. Formal analysis grid.

were explored or solved in the image? What relationship do the ideas have with the human condition? Feldman considers *interpretation* to be the most important part of the critical process.

Because works of art are created within a cultural-historical context, and because viewers vary in their experiences with works of art and cultural-historical backgrounds, multiple interpretations of a work of art are quite feasible. Feldman suggests beginning with one or more *hypotheses,* or speculations about the possible meanings of the work. Once an hypothesis is established, one can examine the visual evidence present in the work revealed through description and formal analysis to determine whether to accept or reject the hypothesis.

Interpretation will require knowledge of art. An understanding of metaphor and artistic and cultural traditions all contribute to a work's meaning. Therefore, it is essential that the art teacher be knowledgeable and sensitive in guiding students to an interpretation of a work of art—guiding the interpretation with questioning when possible, and providing an explanation of the syntax of visual language when necessary.

Judgment: With the exception of critiques of student work, judgments of quality about works by mature artists are unnecessary and inappropriate, because judgment implies giving rank to a work of art, and children often do not have the knowledge, expertise, or need to do such a thing. However, it is important for older students to have an understanding of how critics, curators, and collectors arrive at a judgment about works of art, and discussions about why particular works of art have been judged important or great is a very relevant topic for the classroom.

In order to pass judgments on works of art, a critic needs to possess an extensive knowledge of art historical models, which he can use for comparison purposes when ranking a work of art. How does the work characterize a particular time in history or culture? Does it break from tradition or reflect it? Does it fulfill its intended purpose or function? What artistic problem does the work attempt to solve, and does it do so successfully?

Lankford's Phenomenological Approach.

Lankford's (1984) approach to art criticism works toward an interpretation of a work of art, rather than a judgment of the rank or worth of the object under scrutiny. His phenomenological approach emphasizes the role of perception in the experience of a work of art. He suggests that the individual's perception, how one receives information through the senses and processes it, is as "charged with significance" as the art object itself. He states, "What an object means depends as much upon a viewer's perception as upon the properties of the object" (p. 152).

To experience a work of art, one needs to be aware of the things that influence his or her perceptions of the work and that no interpretation of a work of art is absolute. Lankford (1984) states:

> First, any property of a work...as perceived depends for its significance upon its relation to other properties...the context in which it is used. Second,...it is a tenet of phenomenology...that nothing exists absolutely; knowledge acquired through perception is always subject to revision....Third,...there are no guarantees in the contiguity of experience between conscious subjects....Fourth, no funded interpretation of a work of art ever exhausts the possibilities of meaning inherent in the work. A single work...may speak with fresh significance to different people at different times under different circumstances. (p. 154)

One of the great benefits of critical dialogue about works of art is that it clarifies what is public and what is private about our responses to individual works of art. By discussing personal experiences and personal interpretations of a work with others, we can determine if others share the same experiences and insights. By doing so, we broaden and enrich our own perceptions of works of art.

Lankford's critical method has five components that are arranged sequentially but are integrated from one component to the next as the process evolves.

1. Receptiveness: *Receptiveness* refers to the mindset an individual brings to a work of art. Like Feldman, who stresses delaying interpretation and judgment until description and formal analysis have taken place, Lankford also stresses the importance of approaching a work of art without any preconceived notions about the work's meaning or value. Receptiveness also implies approaching the work with curiosity.

2. Orienting: Here, the individual consciously focuses on the conditions that will maximize her experience of the work of art, establishing a "communicative relationship" with the work. What physical conditions affect perception of the work? Location? Context? Lighting? Noise?

When perceiving and contemplating the work, what needs to be considered to properly focus on the work? Is the work strictly a visual work? Are spatial concerns an issue? Is time a factor? Is the work intended to be viewed strictly as a sensual experience, or is their content with symbolic or conceptual meanings that will require more involved decisions?

What should her physical orientation to the work be? Is she too close or too far away from the work? Does the work need to be viewed from varying perspectives in order to fully perceive and experience it?

3. Bracketing: The individual consciously focuses on issues that contribute to an interpretation of the object's meaning. Past experience in life and with works of art is valuable, as is the context in which he currently experiences it and the contemporary art context in which the work resides.

4. Interpretive Analysis: Here the individual describes the work of art she is perceiving. Formal properties, subject matter, symbolic content, thoughts, and sensual and emotional feelings are described in interpretive analysis. This is the central component of Lankford's methodology, for it clarifies the importance and impact of the work under scrutiny. For the individual, critical dialogue takes place between the object and the viewer; in group discussion, varying perceptions of the work by individuals are revealed. Lankford stresses striking a balance between the visual and the ideational, between form and content.

5. Synthesis: Once varying experiences and information about a work of art are revealed, viewers are prepared to synthesize their experiences into a final interpretation of the work. Lankford stresses that reflections on the meaning of a work may extend beyond the work itself, as long as such reflections remain relevant to the context of the work itself. Immediate perceptions of the work should confirm and enrich the viewer's thoughts about the work's meaning.

Feinstein's Art Response Guide.

Feinstein (1989) has developed a critical method, based on a modified version of Feldman's, that stresses reading works of art for meaning. Placing stress on the use of language in the criticism of works of art, she distinguishes between literal and figurative language, which, in turn, parallel two general kinds of meaning: *literal* and *metaphoric*. For example, in a work of art, the literal meaning of a female figure would be woman. Historically, however, the female figure has metaphorically served as a symbol of beauty, love, liberty, sacrifice, fertility, life-force, and so on. Literal language is factual, whereas figurative language is symbolic, or metaphorical.

Feinstein's modification of Feldman's Critical Performance includes five, rather than four, categories of activities: (1) description, (2) analysis of form, (3) metaphoric interpretation, (4) evaluation, and (5) preference. *Description* and *analysis of form* are factual activities and employ literal language. *Metaphoric interpretation* uses figurative language and a method known as clustering. Feinstein emphasizes that *evaluation* (which parallels Feldman's *judgment,* or giving rank) is inappropriate for classroom use because children do not possess the knowledge and experience to evaluate fairly works of art by mature artists. *Preference* is the final activity in this model and involves stating whether one likes or dislikes the work under scrutiny.

"Clustering is an associative search strategy that facilitates metaphoric interpretation" (1989, p. 46). When examining a work of art, the viewer begins by listing quickly his dominant impressions, or *word descriptors,* of the things he sees in the work; the descriptors are figurative words and are circled. Next, descriptors of visual/expressive qualities are identified. And, finally, feeling/thoughts that are aroused in the viewer are identified using descriptors and circled. Around each of these descriptors are clustered other figurative words that describe what is perceived in the work and that supports the *root descriptor.* The root descriptors could be thought of as metaphoric hypotheses or as speculations about the possible meaning of a work of art that are accepted or rejected through the clustering process.

The viewer is building a linguistic metaphor constructed from a visual metaphor. Feinstein argues that figurative language that employs vivid descriptors, similes, and analogies arouses and enriches sensory and emotional responses to works of art.

The Why's and How's of Art Criticism

Students need to understand that there are systematic ways of organizing one's thoughts and judgments about the meanings and qualities found in works of art. Such thinking skills will enable students to make constructive decisions about their own work and the work of their peers, and will also enable them to arrive at understandings of meaning in the works of mature artists.

As in all learning and teaching situations, consistency and practice are crucial. Once a format for art criticism is established in the classroom, it should be used on a consistent basis so that students learn how to structure their thinking when viewing works of art. For older students, the critical format itself can serve as a topic for discussion.

4 SUMMARY AND CHRONOLOGY OF WESTERN ART HISTORY

The information that follows is organized chronologically according to artistic style or cultural period, followed by a brief description of what was happening during that period in other aspects of human accomplishment.

ANCIENT GREECE AND ROME (540 B.C. TO FIRST CENTURY A.D.)

Chronology

Exekias (eh-*zee*-kee-ahs)	Grk: Archaic	c. 540 B.C.
Psiax (*see*-ahx)	Grk: Archaic	c. 540 B.C.
Douris (doh-ris)	Grk: Archaic	c. 490 B.C.
Ictinus (ick-*tee*-nuhs)	Grk: Architect	c. 450 B.C.
Callicrates (kah-*lik*-rah-teez)	Grk: Architect	c. 450 B.C.

Mnesciles (min-neh-skil-leez)	Grk: Architect	c. 437 B.C.
Lysippus (lie-see-puhs)	Grk: Pre-Hellenistic Sculp.	c. 370 B.C.
Scopas (skoh-pahs)	Grk: Pre-Hellenistic Sculp.	c. 355 B.C.
Bryaxis (brie-axis)	Grk: Pre-Hellenistic Sculp.	c. 300 B.C.
Agesander (ah-juh-sahn-der)	Grk: Hellenistic Sculp.	c. First century A.D.
Athenodorus (ah-thee-noh-doh-ruhs)	Grk: Hellenistic Sculp.	c. First century A.D.
Polydorus (pol-ee-doh-ruhs)	Grk: Hellenistic Sculp.	c. First century A.D.
Vitruvius (vee-*troo*-vee-uhs)	Roman: Architect	c. First century A.D.

Parallel Historical Events

Rome is declared a republic; Cleisthenes of Athens initiated a number of democratic reforms in 510 B.C.; Pythagoras introduced the notion of the octave in music; a theater is built in Delphi; both the Romans and the Babylonians develop a lunar calendar; Phoenicians, under orders from the Pharoah of Egypt, circumnavigate the continent of Africa; Greek anatomist Alemaeon of Croton discovers difference between veins and arteries, and that the brain is connected to the senses; banking is established in Babylon and coins are introduced as currency; public libraries are established in Athens; Dionysus theater is opened in Athens in 493 B.C.; Greek theater at its zenith with Sophocles, Pratinas, Aeschylus, Euripides writing and inventing drama; Persian Wars, 490–449 B.C.; age of religious prophets and philoso-phers—Buddha (550–480 B.C.), Confucius (551–479 B.C.), Socrates (470–399 B.C.), Plato (427–347 B.C.), Aristotle (384–322 B.C.), and Jesus Christ (4 B.C.–30 A.D.).

Hellenistic period in Greece, 320–30 B.C.; Alexander the Great (356–323 B.C.) conquers much of the known world; Euclid lays foundation for geome-try in 323 B.C.; patricians and plebeians granted full equality in 287 B.C.; Eratosthenes (276–194 B.C.) believes earth revolves around the sun; the Great Wall of China is built in 215 B.C.; Rome begins world domination in 168 B.C.; trigonometry invented in 160 B.C. by Hipparchus of Nicaea; Roman poets Virgil (70–19 B.C.) and Horace (65–8 B.C.); Ceasar murdered in 44 B.C. by Brutus and Cassius Longinus; a Roman theater is built in Verulamium, England in 140 A.D..

ROMANESQUE AND GOTHIC PERIODS (1100 A.D. TO 1400 A.D.)

Chronology

Renier of Huy (ray-nyeh)	Romanesque: Sculptor	c. 1110 A.D.
Benedetto Antelami (bay-nay-day-toh ahn-tay-lah-mee)	Romanesque: Sculptor	c. 1180 A.D.
Nicholas of Verdun	Romanesque: Painter	c. 1181 A.D.
Villard de Honnecourt (vee-lahr duh awn-nay-koor)	Gothic: Architect	c. 1240 A.D.
Naumburg Master (nowm-burk)	Gothic: Sculptor	c. 1240 A.D.
Giovanni Pisano (pee-sah-noh)	Gothic: Sculptor	c. 1245–1314 A.D.
Cimabue (chee-mah-boo-ee)	Gothic: Painter	c. 1250–1300 A.D.
Duccio of Siena (doo-chee-oh)	Gothic: Painter	c. 1255–1319 A.D.
Giotto (joht-toe)	Gothic: Painter	c. 1267–1336 A.D.
Nicola Pisano (pee-sah-noh)	Gothic: Sculptor	c. 1269 A.D.
Simone Martini (see-moh-nay mahr-tee-nee)	Gothic: Painter	c. 1284–1344 A.D.
Master Honore (awn-ohr-ay)	Gothic: Illustrated Manus.	c. 1295 A.D.
Arnolfo Di Cambio (ahrn-nohl-foh dee kahm-bee-oh)	Gothic: Architect	c. 1296 A.D.
Lorenzo Maitani (loh-rayn-zoh mah-ee-tahn-nee)	Gothic: Architect	c. 1310 A.D.
Ambrogio Lorenzetti (ahm-broh-gee-oh loh-ren-zet-tee)	Gothic: Painter	c. 1330 A.D.
Pietro Lorenzetti (pee-ay-troh loh-ren-zet-tee)	Gothic: Painter	c. 1330 A.D.
Giovanni da Milano (joe-vahn-nee dah mee-lahn-noh)	Gothic: Painter	c. 1346–1369 A.D.
Lorenzo Ghiberti (loh-ren-zoh ghee-bair-tee)	Gothic: Sculptor	c. 1381–1455 A.D.
Claus Sluter (klows zloot-air)	Gothic: Sculptor	c. 1385 A.D.

4

The Limbourg Brothers (leem-boork)	Gothic:Illuminated Manus.	c. 1400 A.D.
The Master Flemalle (flay-mahl)	Late Gothic: Painter	c. 1420 A.D.
Jan and Hubert van Eyck (van ike)	Late Gothic:Painters	c. 1390–1432 A.D.
Rogier van der Weyden	Late Gothic: Painter	c. 1399–1464 A.D.
Jean Fouquet (zhon foo-kay)	Late Gothic: Painter	c. 1420–1481 A.D.
Martin Schongauer (shown-gower)	Late Gothic: Printmaker and Painter	c. 1430–1491 A.D.
Hugo van der Goes	Late Gothic: Painter	c. 1440–1482 A.D.
Hieronymus Bosch (heer-ahn-ni-mus bosh)	Late Gothic: Painter	c. 1500 A.D.

Parallel Historical Events

Period of Gothic architecture begins; The Pueblo culture in North America is in its third period; The Christian Crusades are in their heyday causing the decline of Islamic science and culture; Bologna University founded in 1119; the marriage of priests is discouraged by the First Lateran Council in 1123; St. Bartholomew's Hospital is founded in London in 1123; the earliest-known mariner's compass is invented by Alexander Neckam in 1125; in 1150, Arabs in Spain invent paper; explosives are used by the Chinese in warfare; Notre Dame Cathedral is built in Paris, 1163–1235; Oxford University is founded in 1167; private houses in England start using glass windows; in 1191, the second era of Mayan civilization begins in Central America; engagement rings are introduced in 1200.

Genghis Khan becomes the Chief Prince of the Mongols in 1206, captures Peking China in 1214, and Persia in 1218; the building of Rheims Cathedral begun, 1212–1311; the Magna Carta is sealed by King John in 1215; an Arab geographical encyclopedia is published in 1224; in 1252, torture is being used by the Inquisition; the House of Commons is established in England in 1258; Marco Polo travels to China in 1271, where he serves the Emperor Kublai Khan from 1275–1292, and is jailed when he returns to Italy in 1295; Roger Bacon, the greatest scientist of his age, is imprisoned for heresy from 1277–1292; the glass mirror is invented in 1278; eyeglasses are invented in 1290.

Edward I of England standardizes the yard and the acre in 1305; gunpowder is invented in Germany in 1313; Mexico City is founded by the Aztecs in 1327; first attempt to scientifically forecast weather in England, 1337; the bubonic plague (black death) begins in India in 1332, devastates Europe between 1347 and 1351, killing 75 million people, including one-third of the population of England; Tenochtitlan, capitol of the the Aztecs, is built in 1364; Chaucer writes "Canterbury Tales," 1387–1400; the revival of Greek literature begins in Florence in 1396, when Greek classes are opened by Manuel Chrysoloras.

RENAISSANCE (1400 TO 1580 A.D.)

Chronology

Jacopo della Quercia   Early Renaissance: Sculptor   c. 1374–1438 A.D.
(Jah-koh-poh del-lah kwair-chee-ah)

Fillipo Brunelleschi   Early Renaissance: Architect   c. 1377–1446 A.D.
(fee-lee-poh broo-nel-les-kee)

Donatello   Early Renaissance: Sculptor   c. 1386–1466 A.D.
(doh-nah-tel-loh)

Paolo Uccello   Early Renaissance: Painter   c. 1397–1475 A.D.
(pah-oh-loh oo-chel-loh)

Fra Angelico   Early Renaissance: Painter   c. 1400–1455 A.D.
(frah ahn-jay-lee-coe)

Luca della Robbia   Early Renaissance: Sculptor   c. 1400–1482 A.D.
(loo-hak del-lah roh-bee-ah)

Leone Battista Alberti   Early Renaissance: Architect   c. 1402–1472 A.D.
(lay-ohn-nay bah-tees-tah ahl-bair-tee)

Fra Fillipo Lippi   Early Renaissance: Painter   c. 1406–1469 A.D.
(frah fill-leep-poh leep-pee)

Bernardo Rossellino   Early Renaissance: Sculptor   c. 1409–1464 A.D.
(bair-nahr-dho roh-zay-lee-noh)

Domenico Veneziano   Early Renaissance: Painter   c. 1410–1461 A.D.
(doh-may-nee-koh vey-ney-zee-ah-noh)

Masaccio   Early Renaissance: Painter   c. 1420 A.D.
(mah-sach-chyo)

Piero della Francesca   Early Renaissance: Painter   c. 1420–1492 A.D.
(pee-air-roh day-lah fran-chess-kuh)

Andrea del Castagno   Early Renaissance: Painter   c. 1423–1457 A.D.
(ahn-dray-ah dayl kah-stah-noh)

Antonio Rossellino   Early Renaissance: Sculptor   c. 1427–1479 A.D.
(ahn-toh-nee-oh roh-zay-lee-noh)

4

Andrea Mantegna (ahn-dray-ah mahn-ten-yah)	Early Renaissance: Painter	c. 1431–1506 A.D.
Giovanni Bellini (joe-vahn-nee bel-lee-nee)	Early Renaissance: Painter	c. 1431–1516 A.D.
Andrea del Verrocchio (ahn-dray-ah dayl vay-roh-kee-oh)	Early Renaissance: Sculptor	c. 1435–1488 A.D.
Sandro Botticelli (sahn-drow baw-tee-chel-lee)	Early Renaissance: Painter	c. 1444–1510 A.D.
Domenico Ghirlandaio (doh-may-nee-koh geer-lon-day-oh)	Early Renaissance: Painter	c. 1449–1494 A.D.
Pietro Perugino (pee-ay-troh pay-roo-ghee-noh)	Early Renaissance: Painter	c. 1450–1523 A.D.
Piero Cosimo (pee-ay-roh coh-see-moh)	Early Renaissance: Painter	c. 1462–1521 A.D.
Donato Bramante (dohn-nah-toh brah-mahn-tay)	High Renaissance: Architect	c. 1444–1514 A.D.
Leonardo da Vinci (lay-oh-nahr-doh dah vin-chee)	High Renaissance: Painter, Architect, Poet, Engineer, and Inventor	c. 1452–1519 A.D.
Michelangelo Buonarotti (my-kel-an-jay-loe)	High Renaissance: Sculptor, Painter, Architect	c. 1475–1564 A.D.
Giorgione (jee-orge-o-nay)	High Renaissance: Painter	c. 1478–1510 A.D.
Raphael (rah-fay-el)	High Renaissance: Painter	c. 1483–1520 A.D.
Titian (tish-in)	High Renaissance: Painter	c. 1488–1576 A.D.

NORTHERN RENAISSANCE (1490 A.D. TO 1590 A.D.) _____

Chronology

Matthias Grunewald (maht-thee-ahs groo-in-vahlt)	Northern Renais.: Painter	c. 1471–1528 A.D.
Albrecht Dürer (ahl-brekht duh-ruhr)	Northern Renais.: Painter	c. 1471–1528 A.D.
Lucas Cranach the Elder (loo-kahs krah-nahx)	Northern Renais.: Painter	c. 1472–1553 A.D.

Albrecht Altdorfer (ahl-brekht ahlt-dohr-fehr)	Northern Renais.: Painter	c. 1480–1538 A.D.
Hans Holbein the Younger (hahns hohl-byn)	Northern Renais.: Painter	c. 1497–1543 A.D.
Pieter Aertsen (pee-ter airt-zen)	Northern Renais.: Painter	c. 1508–1575 A.D.
Jean Goujon (zahn goo-zhohn)	Northern Renais.: Sculptor	c. 1510–1565 A.D.
Hector Schier (hehk-tohr sheer)	Northern Renais.: Architect	c. 1515 A.D.
Pierre Lescot (pee-ayr lehs-koh)	Northern Renais.: Architect	c. 1515–1578 A.D.
Pieter Bruegel (The Elder) (pee-ter broy-guhl)	Northern Renais.: Painter	c. 1525–1569 A.D.
Germain Pilon (zher-mehn pee-yohn)	Northern Renais.: Sculptor	c. 1535–1590 A.D.
Nicholas Hilliard	Northern Renais.: Painter	c. 1547–1619 A.D.

4

MANNERISM (1500 TO 1600 A.D.)

Chronology

Girolamo Savoldo (gee-roh-lah-moh sah-vohl-doh)	Mannerism (Realism): Painter	c. 1480–1550 A.D.
Correggio (kohr-ray-jee-oh)	Mannerism (Proto-Baroque): Painter	c. 1489–1534 A.D.
Alonso Berruguete (ah-lohn-soh beh-roo-gweht)	Mannerism: Sculptor	c. 1489–1561 A.D.
Pontormo (pohn-tohr-moh)	Mannerism: Painter	c. 1494–1556 A.D.
Rosso Fiorentino (roh-soh fee-ohr-rehn-tee-noh)	Mannerism: Painter	c. 1495–1540 A.D.
Benvenuto Cellini (behn-vehn-noo-toh cheh-lee-nee)	Mannerism: Sculptor	c. 1500–1571 A.D.
Parmigianino (pahr-mee-jee-ah-nee-noh)	Mannerism: Painter	c. 1503–1540 A.D.
Francesco Primaticcio (frahn-ches-koh pree-mah-tee-chee-oh)	Mannerism: Sculptor	c. 1504–1570 A.D.

Giacomo Vignola (jee-ah-koh-moh vee-nyoh-lah)	Mannerism: Architect	c. 1507–1573 A.D.
Giorgio Vasari (jee-ohr-jee-oh vah-sah-ree)	Mannerism: Architect, Art Historian, and Critic	c. 1511–1574 A.D.
Bartolommeo Ammanati (bahr-toh-loh-may-oh ah-mahn-nah-tee)	Mannerism: Architect	c. 1511–1592 A.D.
Andrea Palladio (ahn-dray-ah pahl-lah-dyo)	Mannerism: Architect	c. 1511–1592 A.D.
Agnolo Bronzino (ah-nyoh-loh brohn-zee-noh)	Mannerism: Painter	c. 1518–1594 A.D.
Tintoretto (teen-toh-reh-toh)	Mannerism: Painter	c. 1518–1594 A.D.
Paolo Veronese (pah-oh-lo vay-roh-nee-zee)	Mannerism (Realism): Painter	c. 1528–1588 A.D.
Giovanni Bologna (joe-vah-nee boh-lohn-yah)	Mannerism: Sculptor	c. 1529–1608 A.D.
Giacomo della Porta (jee-ah-koh-moh day-lah pohr-tah)	Mannerism: Architect	c. 1540–1602 A.D.
Domenico Theotocopoulos ("El Greco") (el greh-co)	Mannerism: Painter	c. 1541–1614 A.D.

Parallel Historical Events

The Medici family rise to power in Florence in 1400; in North America, the Middle and Upper Mississippi phases of the Moundbuilders culture are developing in 1400; a 22,937-volume encyclopedia is compiled in China in 1403; Filippo Brunelleschi establishes "Rules of Perspective" in 1412; the papacy establishes the Medici of Florence as its banker in 1414; The Great Temple of the Dragon is built in Peking, China in 1420; in 1428, Joan of Arc leads the French army into battle against the English and is burned at the stake in Rouen in 1431; the cast-iron gun is invented in 1430; Portuguese encounter their first Africans near Cape Blanc, Western Africa in 1441, and reestablish slave trade; in 1450, Florence becomes the center of humanism and the Renaissance under the leadership of the Medici; Johann Gutenberg, the inventor of the printing press in Europe, prints the Mazarin Bible at Mainz, 1453–1455; the French royal mail service is established in 1464; Lorenzo de Medici begins ruling Florence from 1469–1492; Dante's *Divine Comedy* is published for the first time in 1472; and Newfoundland is "discovered" by the Danish navigator Deitrich Pining in 1472; in 1480, Leonardo da Vinci invents the parachute; the Spanish Inquisition begins in 1481; in 1489, the "+" and "-" come into use in mathematics; in 1492, Ferdinand and Isabella of Spain agree to finance the voyage of Christopher Columbus, and he set sail on August 3 from Palos, Spain and arrived in the Bahamas on October 12; beginning in 1495, the first editions of the Greek Classics were printed by Aldus Manutius.

Juan de la Cosa published a map of the New World in 1500; Christopher Columbus is arrested and returned to Spain in irons for rehabilitation in 1500; by 1501, over one thousand printing shops existed in Europe, and approximately thirty-five thousand books had been published since the invention of the printing press; after his second voyage to South America in 1502, Amerigo Vespucci concludes that it is not India! Martin Waldseemuller proposes in 1507 that the New World be called "America" after Amerigo; Copernicus declares in 1512 that the earth and other planets revolve around the sun; in 1513, Balboa crosses Panama and "finds" the Pacific Ocean, while Juan Ponce de Leon "discovers" Florida.

The Roman Catholic Church in 1515 forbids the printing of books without its permission; in 1517, Martin Luther posts his ninety-five theses on the Palast Church door in Wittenberg and starts the beginning of the German Reformation; Ferdinand Magellan leaves Spain in 1519 to circumnavigate the globe; Cortés arrives in North America in 1519 with horses, introducing them to the continent for the first time; Cortés destroys the Aztec civilization and assumes control of Mexico in 1521; Henry VIII recognized as head of church in England, rejecting papal influence, 1531; Pizarro eliminates the Inca in Peru, 1533.

The diving bell is invented in 1535; the Spanish Inquisition begins burning Protestants at the stake in 1543; in 1541, Coronado explores areas now known as New Mexico, Texas, Oklahoma, and Kansas, while de Soto "discovers" the Mississippi River; Konrad von Gesner publishes a book on modern zoology in 1551; an Aztec dictionary is published in 1555; pencils are manufactured in England, 1565; first newspaper is published in Venice, 1566; decimal fractions were introduced in 1576 by Francois Viete; work is begun in 1578 on the Pont Neuf bridge that crosses the Seine in Paris.

Kabuki theater begins in Japan, 1586; in 1589, forks are introduced in the French court; Shakespeare writes "Henry VI," "Richard III," "Comedy of Errors." and "Taming of the Shrew," 1590–1593; the buried city of Pompeii is discovered in 1592; Galileo invents the thermometer in 1596; the iron-clad warship is invented in Korea in 1598; Ieyasu defeats his rivals and becomes ruler of Japan in 1600, moving the capital from Kyoto to what is now Tokyo; William Gilbert publishes a treatise on magnetism and electricity, and the telescope is invented by Dutch opticians, both in 1600.

BAROQUE AND ROCOCO PERIODS (1590 TO 1780 A.D.) ─────────

Chronology

Annible Carracci (ahn-nee-blay kah-rah-chee)	Baroque: Painter	c. 1560–1609 A.D.
Sanchez Cotan (sahn-chehz koh-tahn)	Baroque: Painter	c. 1561–1627 A.D.
Michelangelo da Caravaggio (my-kel-an-jay-loe da car-ah-vah-jyoh)	Baroque: Painter	c. 1571–1610 A.D.
Ingio Jones (enn-jee-oh joe-nays)	Baroque: Architect	c. 1573–1652 A.D.
Peter Paul Rubens	Baroque: Painter	c. 1577–1640 A.D.
Frans Hals	Baroque: Painter	c. 1580–1666 A.D.
Hendrick Terbrugghen (hehn-dreek tehr-broo-gehn)	Baroque: Painter	c. 1588–1629 A.D.
Artemisia Gentileschi (ahr-tay-mee-see-ah jehn-tee-les-kee) (female)	Baroque: Painter	c. 1593–1653 A.D.
Louis Le Nain (loo-ee luh nahng)	Baroque: Painter	c. 1593–1648 A.D.
Georges de la Tour (zhorzh duh lah toor)	Baroque: Painter	c. 1593–1652 A.D.
Nicolas Poussin (poo-san)	Baroque: Painter	c. 1593–1665 A.D.
Jan van Goyen	Baroque: Painter	c. 1596–1656 A.D.
Pietro da Cortona (pee-ay-troh dah cohr-toh-nah)	Baroque: Painter	c. 1596–1669 A.D.
Francesco de Zurbaran (frahn-see-skoh de soor-bar-rahn)	Baroque: Painter	c. 1598–1664 A.D.
Francois Mansart (frawn-swah mahn-sahr)	Baroque: Architect	c. 1598–1666 A.D.
Gianlorenzo Bernini (jahn-lowhren-tsoh ber-nee-nee)	Baroque: Sculptor, Architect	c. 1598–1680 A.D.
Anthony van Dyck	Baroque: Painter	c. 1599–1641 A.D.
Diego Velazquez (dee-aye-goh vay-las-kes)	Baroque: Painter	c. 1599–1660 A.D.
Francesco Borromini (frahn-ches-koh bohr-roh-mee-nee)	Baroque: Architect	c. 1599–1667 A.D.
Claude Lorraine (klohd luh-ran)	Baroque: Painter	c. 1600–1682 A.D.
Rembrandt van Rijn (rem-brant van ryne)	Baroque: Painter	c. 1606–1669 A.D.

Judith Leyster (female)	Baroque: Painter	c. 1609–1660 A.D.
Andre Le Notre (ahn-dreh luh noh-treh)	Baroque: Architect	c. 1613–1700 A.D.
Lebrun (luh-brewn)	Baroque: Painter	c. 1619–1690 A.D.
Guarino Guarini (gwah-ree-noh gwah-ree-nee)	Baroque: Architect	c. 1624–1683 A.D.
Pieter Saenredam	Baroque: Painter	c. 1625 A.D.
Jan Steen (yahn steen)	Baroque: Painter	c. 1625–1679 A.D.
Jacob van Ruisdael (rise-dale)	Baroque: Painter	c. 1628–1682 A.D.
Sir Christopher Wren	Baroque: Architect	c. 1632–1723 A.D.
Jan Vermeer (yahn ver-mair)	Baroque: Painter	c. 1632–1675 A.D.
Giovanni Battista Gualli (joe-vah-nee bah-tees-tah)	Baroque: Painter	c. 1650 A.D.
Jan Davids de Heem	Baroque: Painter	c. 1650 A.D.
Claude Perrault (klohd peh-roh)	Baroque: Architect	c. 1650 A.D.
Louis Le Vau (loo-ee luh voh)	Baroque: Architect	c. 1650 A.D.
Johann Fischer von Erlach (yoh-hahn fees-shehr vahn air-lahk)	Late Baroque: Architect	c. 1656–1723 A.D.
Jakob Prandtauer	Late Baroque: Architect	c. 1660–1726 A.D.
Pierre Puget (pee-air poo-zhay)	Baroque: Sculptor	c. 1660 A.D.
Jules Hardouin-Mansart (jhewl ahr-dween mahn-sahr)	Baroque: Architect	c. 1670 A.D.
Francois Girardon (frawn-swah zhee-rahr-dohn)	Baroque: Sculptor	c. 1675 A.D.
Antoine Coysevox (an-twahn kohj-say-vohz)	Baroque: Sculptor	c. 1675 A.D.
Antoine Watteau (an-twahn wah-toe)	Baroque: Painter	c. 1684–1721 A.D.
Dominikus Zimmermann	Baroque: Architect	c. 1685–1766 A.D.
Balthasar Neumann	Baroque: Architect	c. 1687–1753 A.D.

4

Giovanni Battista Tiepolo (joe-vah-nee bah-tees-tah)	Baroque: Painter	c. 1696–1770 A.D.
William Hogarth	Baroque: Painter	c. 1697–1764 A.D.
Louis Roubiliac (loo-ee roo-bee-lee-ahk)	Baroque: Sculptor	c. 1702–1762 A.D.
Joshua Reynolds	Baroque: Painter	c. 1723–1792 A.D.
Thomas Gainsborough	Baroque: Painter	c. 1727–1788 A.D.
Jean-Baptiste Simeon Chardin (zhon-bah-teest see-may-on sharr-dan)	Rococo: Painter	c. 1699–1779 A.D.
Germain Boffrand (zher-mayn boh-frahn)	Rococo: Sculptor	c. 1700 A.D.
Francois Boucher (frawn-swah boosh-ay)	Rococo: Painter	c. 1703–1770 A.D.
Jean Honoré Fragonard (zhon oh-no-ray fra-go-nahr)	Rococo: Painter	c. 1732–1806 A.D.
Marie-Louise- Elisabeth Vigée-Lebrun (vee-zhay luh-brewn)	Rococo: Painter	c. 1755–1842 A.D.
Étienne Maurice Falconet (ay-tee-n mah-rees fahl-koh-nay)	Rococo: Sculptor	c. 1760 A.D.
Clodion (kloh-dee-ohn)	Rococo: Sculptor	c. 1770 A.D.

Parallel Historical Events

The plans of 777 fixed stars, produced by Tycho Brahe is published posthumously in 1602; Johann Kepler publishes "Optics" in 1604; the English establish their first colony in North America in 1606, Jamestown, Virginia; the astronomical telescope is invented by Galileo in 1608 and he then observes and names the satellites of Jupiter in 1610, and in 1616 the Catholic Church forbids him to pursue any more scientific work, and finally in 1633 he is forced by the Inquisition to renounce the theories of Copernicus; the Native American Indian Princess Pocahontas marries John Rolfe in 1614; in 1616, William Shakespeare dies; in 1619, the first African slaves arrive in Virginia; Pilgrim Fathers leave Plymouth, England and land at New Plymouth, Massachusetts, 1620; Johann Kepler's writings on Copernican astronomy banned by the Catholic Church in 1621; Peter Minuit buys the island of

Manhattan in 1626 with merchandise estimated to be worth about $24; the English High and Latin School is established in Boston, 1635.

In 1637, European books, religion, and contacts are forbidden in Japan; England abolishes torture in 1638; between 1642 and 1660, all theaters in England were ordered closed by the Puritans; in 1641, Theophraste Renaudot proposes a plan for free medical treatment of the poor in Paris, and, in 1644, he is forbidden to practice medicine; John Milton argues for freedom of the press, while Roger Williams publishes on the topic of separation of church and state, 1644; King Louis XIV performs in 1651 as a dancer in a ballet at the age of thirteen, and the following year he reestablishes lawful government in France and begins the building of Versailles in 1662; England begins turnpike tolls, 1662; Antonio Stradivari produces his first violin, 1666; Isaac Newton measures the orbit of the moon in 1666; in 1667, the French army uses hand-grenades on the battlefield, and, in 1670, uniforms and paper cartridges; ice cream is created in 1677; Niagara Falls is "discovered" by Father Louis Hannepin in 1679; in 1680, the Dodo bird becomes extinct.

In 1685, Chinese ports are opened to foreign trade, and J. S. Bach and G. F. Handel are born; the first alphabetically arranged dictionary is published in England, 1703; Isaac Newton publishes his "Optics," 1704; British conduct their last execution for witchcraft in 1712; in 1717, school attendance is made compulsory in Prussia, and an innoculation against smallpox is introduced in England; Jonathan Swift publishes *Gulliver's Travels* in 1726; Isaac Newton dies in 1727; Ben Franklin and his brother James publish *The Pennsylvania Gazette* in 1729; the same year, the Emperor of China prohibits the smoking of opium; composer F. J. Haydn is born in 1732; in 1736, the first successful appendectomy is performed; E. J. von Kleist invents the electrical capacitator in 1745.

In 1751, the British Parliament declares January first to be the start of the New Year; the first female M.D. is graduated from a German university in 1754; W. A. Mozart is born in 1756 and, at age 6, tours Europe as a prodigy; in 1764, James Watt invents the condensor and foreshadows the dawn of the steam engine and the industrial age, and the numbering of houses begins in London, with the first paved sidewalks appearing two years later; the New York Assembly is disbanded in 1767 for refusing to house and support British troops, and the Massachusetts Assembly is disbanded the following year for refusing to assist in the collection of taxes; L. van Beethoven is born, and the industrial revolution begins in England, 1770; in 1773, the first cast-iron bridge is built in England; J. H. Pestalozzi starts his school in Zurich in 1774 that revolutionizes educational theory and practice, and the Continental Congress meets in Philadelphia and bans the importation of British goods; the American Revolution begins in 1775; the Declaration of Independence is issued in 1776, the Stars and Stripes are adopted as the flag of the Continental Congress in 1777, and the British finally recognize America's independence in 1783; the fountain pen is invented in 1780.

NEOCLASSICISM AND ROMANTICISM (1750 TO 1875 A.D.) ───────

Chronology

Jacques Germain Soufflot (zhahk zher-mayn soo-floh)	Neoclas.: Architect	c. 1713–1780 A.D.
Étienne-Louis Boullée (ayn-tee-n loo-ee boo-lee)	Neoclas.: Architect	c. 1728–1799 A.D.
Horace Walpole	Neoclas.: Architect	c. 1717–1797 A.D.
Jean Antoine Houdon (zhahn an-twahn oo-dohn)	Neoclas.: Sculptor	c. 1741–1828 A.D.
Thomas Jefferson	Neoclas.: Architect	c. 1743–1826 A.D.
Jacques Louis David (zhahk loo-ee dah-veed)	Neoclas.: Painter	c. 1748–1825 A.D.
Antonio Canova (ahn-toh-nee-oh kah-noh-vah)	Neoclas.: Sculptor	c. 1757–1822 A.D.
Benjamin Latrobe	Neoclas.: Architect	c. 1764–1820 A.D.
Jean-Auguste Dominique Ingres (zhahn oh-goos-tay doh-mee-neek een-gray)	Neoclas.: Painter	c. 1780–1867 A.D.
John Nash	Neoclas.: Architect	c. 1815 A.D.
George Stubbs	Romantic: Painter	c. 1724–1806 A.D.
John Singleton Copely	Romantic: Painter	c. 1738–1815 A.D.
Benjamin West	Romantic: Painter	c. 1738–1820 A.D.
John Henry Fuseli	Romantic: Painter	c. 1741–1825 A.D.
Francisco Goya (frahn-sees-coh go-yah)	Romantic: Painter	c. 1746–1828 A.D.
William Blake	Romantic: Painter	c. 1757–1827 A.D.
Joseph Nicephore Niepce	Romantic: Photographer	c. 1765–1833 A.D.
Caspar David Friedrich	Romantic: Painter	c. 1774–1840 A.D.
Joseph M. W. Turner	Romantic: Painter	c. 1775–1851 A.D.
John Constable	Romantic: Painter	c. 1776–1837 A.D.
Francois Rude (frawn-swah roo-day)	Romantic: Sculptor	c. 1784–1855 A.D.

Theodore Gericault (zhay-ree-koh)	Romantic: Painter	c. 1791–1824 A.D.
Camille Corot (kah-meel koh-roh)	Romantic: Painter	c. 1796–1875 A.D.
Eugene Delacroix (oo-zhen duh-lah-kwah)	Romantic: Painter	c. 1798–1863 A.D.
Honoré Daumier (awn-ohr-ay doh-mee-ay)	Romantic: Painter	c. 1808–1879 A.D.
Auguste Preault (oh-goost preh-ohl)	Romantic: Sculptor	c. 1809–1879 A.D.
George Caleb Bingham	Romantic: Painter	c. 1811–1879 A.D.
Francois Millet (frawn-swah mee-lay)	Romantic: Painter	c. 1814–1875 A.D.
Alexander Gardner	Romantic: Photographer	c. 1821–1882 A.D.
Rosa Bonheur (roh-sah-bohn-yuh)	Romantic: Painter	c. 1822–1899 A.D.
Matthew Brady	Romantic: Photographer	c. 1823–1896 A.D.
Jean-Baptise Carpeaux (zhahn bahp-tees kar-poh)	Romantic: Sculptor	c. 1827–1875 A.D.
Timothy O'Sullivan	Romantic: Photographer	c. 1841–1882 A.D.

4

Parallel Historical Events

In 1781, the planet Uranus is discovered by Herschel; the rotary steam engine is invented by James Watt, and a hot-air balloon is constructed, 1782; a paddle-wheel steamboat is sailed in 1783; George Washington is inaugurated the first President of the United States, the Bastille is stormed in France as the French Revolution begins, and the first steam-powered factories are opened in Britain, 1789; in 1790, Washington, D.C. is founded; in 1791, a motion passes the British Parliament abolishing the slave trade, while in the United States, laws are passed in 1793 forcing escaped slaves to be returned to their owners; also in 1793, Louis XVI is executed in France by the newly invented guillotine; the first telegraph is developed in Paris, 1794; in 1796, Peking bans the importation of opium into China; lithography is invented in Germany, 1798; the Rosetta Stone is discovered in 1799, allowing for the deciphering of Egyptian hieroglyphics, while in Switzerland in the same year, Pestalozzi opens his school.

The first electric battery is invented by Alessandro Volta in 1800; in 1801, Robert Fulton invents the first submarine, while in England, the first iron trolley tracks are laid; Napoleon is crowned Emperor in 1804 and rockets are introduced as weapons in the British army; in 1808, the Africans are prohibited from being brought to the U.S. as slaves, and in the same year, excavations that will continue for seven years begin at Pompeii; in 1812, the U.S. declares war on Britain and the Brothers Grimm publish their fairy tales; Buffalo, New York is burned to the ground by the British in 1813, while Francis Scott Key writes the poem that later becomes the U.S. national anthem; in the same year, the first practical steam locomotive is built in England by George Stephenson and Mexico declares its independence; in 1815, roads are being built in England from crushed stone; Indiana becomes a state in 1816, while the Erie Canal is begun between Buffalo and Albany in 1817; in 1819, the U.S. purchased Florida from Spain, and the British government established a 12-hour work day for children; the first iron railroad bridge is built in England, 1822; in Rochester, New York, a baseball club is organized in 1825.

Joseph Niepce produces a photograph on a metal plate in 1827; the first railroad for hauling passengers and freight, the Baltimore and Ohio, begins construction in 1828; Mexico abolishes slavery, and the first American-invented typewriter is patented, 1829; the first prototype of the sewing machine is invented in 1830; slaves in Virginia revolt in 1831, killing fifty-five whites; the Spanish Inquisition, in operation since the thirteenth century, is eliminated, while the forerunner of the modern computer (analytical engine) is invented by Charles Babbage, 1834; in 1835, Texas declares its independence from Mexico and becomes a republic the following year; the phrase, "Art for art's sake" comes into general use in 1835; in 1837, Friedrich Frobel opens his first kindergarten in Germany, and the U.S. Congress passes a gag law to discourage debate on the issue of slavery, while the editor of an abolitionist newspaper is murdered by a mob in Alton, Illinois; Charles Dickens publishes *Oliver Twist* in 1838; the first baseball game is played in Cooperstown, New York in 1839.

In 1841, the first women to graduate from American universities receive their degrees; the New York Philharmonic is founded in 1842; Samuel Morse is commissioned by the U.S. Congress to build the first telegraph line between Baltimore and Washington, 1843; paper made from wood pulp is invented in 1844; the first underwater cable is laid across the English Channel in 1845; in 1847, the gold rush begins in California, and the U.S. military capture Mexico City; revolutions are taking place in 1848 across Europe in Vienna, Venice, Milan, Berlin, and in Paris, where Louis Napoleon is elected President of the Republic (he has himself declared Emperor, four years later), and Marx and Engels publish their "Communist Manifesto."

In 1850, 14 percent of the U.S. population were black slaves, and California becomes a state; *The New York Times* begins publication, 1851; Harriet Beecher Stowe publishes *Uncle Tom's Cabin*, and Herbert Spencer proposes the notion of "evolution," 1852; U.S.N. Commodore Perry negotiates a treaty with Japan, and Heinrich Goebel invents the light bulb, 1854; in 1855,

Principles of Psychology is published by Herbert Spencer; the first transatlantic cable begins to be laid in 1857; in 1859, Dickens' *A Tale of Two Cities*, Darwin's *On the Origin of Species by Natural Selection*, and Marx's *Critique of Political Economy* are all published, and the first oil well in the U.S. is drilled at Titusville, Pennsylvania.

The first practical internal combustion engine is built in 1860; in 1861, Lincoln is inaugurated President and the American Civil War begins; the first machine-driven refrigerator system is built, 1861; the Gatling gun is developed in 1862, and President Lincoln issues the " Emancipation Proclamation," declaring slaves free in Confederate States as of January 1, 1863; Roller skating becomes a form of recreation in America in 1863; in 1864, Cheyenne and Arapahoe Indians are massacred in Colorado; in that year, Tolstoy publishes *War and Peace*, Louis Pasteur invents pasteurization, and "In God We Trust" first appears on U.S. coins; in 1865, President Lincoln is assassinated, the Civil War ends, Lewis Carroll publishes *Alice in Wonderland*, the Ku Klux Klan is founded in Tennessee, Yale University opens the first Department of Fine Arts in the U.S., and Vassar College appoints the first female professor in the U.S.; Alfred Nobel invents dynamite, 1866; the Cincinnati Red Stockings introduce uniforms to baseball in 1868 and become the first salaried team in 1869.

In 1870, Jules Verne publishes *Twenty Thousand Leagues under the Sea*, the Catholic church promotes the notion of papal infallibility, and the Standard Oil Company is founded by J. D. Rockefeller; in 1871, labor unions are legalized in Britain, Darwin publishes *The Descent of Man*, and the city of Chicago burns to the ground; the first color photographs are produced, 1873; the first impressionist exhibit is held in Paris, 1874; Mark Twain publishes *The Adventures of Tom Sawyer* in 1875.

4

REALISM, IMPRESSIONISM, AND POSTIMPRESSIONISM (1840 TO 1900 A.D.)

Chronology

Gustave Courbet (goos-tahv koor-bay)	Realism: Painter	c. 1819–1877 A.D.
Edouard Manet (ay-dwahr mah-nay)	Realism: Painter	c. 1832–1883 A.D.
William Morris	Realism: Painter	c. 1834–1896 A.D.
James McNeill Whistler	Realism/Impression.: Painter	c. 1834–1903 A.D.

Edgar Degas (ed-gahr duh-gah)	Impressionism: Painter	c. 1834–1917 A.D.
Winslow Homer	Impressionism: Painter	c. 1836–1910 A.D.
Auguste Rodin (oh-goost roh-dan)	Impressionism: Sculptor	c. 1840–1917 A.D.
Claude Monet (klohd muh-nay)	Impressionism: Painter	c. 1840–1926 A.D.
Berthe Morisot (bairt moh-ree-zoh)	Impressionism: Painter	c. 1841–1895 A.D.
Auguste Renoir (oh-goost ren-wahr)	Impressionism: Painter	c. 1841–1919 A.D.
Thomas Eakins (ay-kins)	Impressionism: Painter	c. 1844–1916 A.D.
Mary Cassatt (cah-sat)	Impressionism: Painter	c. 1845–1926 A.D.
Henry O. Tanner	Impressionism: Painter	c. 1859–1937 A.D.
Julia Margaret Cameron	Postimpressionism: Photographer (Pictorialist)	c. 1815–1879 A.D.
Oscar Rejlander (ray-lahn-der)	Postimpressionism: Photographer (Pictorialist)	c. 1818–1875 A.D.
Gustave Moreau (goo-stahv moh-roh)	Postimpressionism: Painter (Symbolist)	c. 1826–1898 A.D.
Henry Peach Robinson	Postimpressionism: Photographer (Pictorialist)	c. 1830–1901 A.D.
Eadweard Muybridge (ed-wurd my-brij)	Postimpressionism: (Motion Photography)	c. 1830–1904 A.D.
Étienne-Jules Marey (ay-tee-n zhewl mah-ray)	Postimpressionism: (Motion Photography)	c. 1830–1904 A.D.
Paul Cézanne (say-zahn)	Postimpressionism: Painter	c. 1839–1906 A.D.
Odilon Redon (oh-dee-lahn reh-dahn)	Postimpressionism: Printmaker	c. 1840–1916 A.D.
Henri Rousseau (on-ree roo-soh)	Postimpressionism: Painter	c. 1844–1910 A.D.
Paul Gauguin (go-gan)	Postimpressionism: Painter (Symbolist)	c. 1848–1903 A.D.
Jacob Riis	Postimpressionism: Photographer (Documentarian)	c. 1849–1914 A.D.

Vincent van Gogh (van goe)	Postimpressionism: Painter	c. 1853–1890 A.D.
Peter Henry Emerson	Postimpressionism: Photographer (Naturalist)	c. 1856–1936 A.D.
Georges Seurat (zhorzh sir-ah)	Postimpressionism: Painter	c. 1859–1891 A.D.
James Ensor	Postimpressionism: Painter	c. 1860–1949 A.D.
Aristide Maillol (ah-ree-steed mah-johl)	Postimpressionism: Sculptor	c. 1861–1944 A.D.
Henri de Toulouse-Lautrec Postimpressionism: Painter (on-ree duh too-looz low-trek)		c. 1864–1901 A.D.
George Minne	Postimpressionism: Sculptor	c. 1866–1941 A.D.
Edouard Vuillard (eh-doo-ahr vee-lahr)	Postimpressionism: Painter (Symbolist)	c. 1868–1940 A.D.
Ernst Barlach (airnst bahr-lahk)	Postimpressionism: Sculptor	c. 1870–1938 A.D.
Aubrey Beardsley	Postimpressionism: Draftsman (Symbolist)	c. 1872–1898 A.D.
Gertrude Kasebier	Postimpressionism: Photographer (Secessionist)	c. 1879–1973 A.D.
Edward Steichen	Postimpressionism: Photographer (Secessionist)	c. 1879–1973 A.D.
Wilhelm Lehmbruck	Postimpressionism: Sculptor	c. 1881–1919 A.D.
Pablo Picasso (pah-bloh pee-kah-soh)	Postimpressionism: Painter (Blue Period)	c. 1881–1974 A.D.

4

Parallel Historical Events

Alexander Graham Bell invents the telephone and the National Baseball League is founded, 1876; Thomas Edison invents the phonograph in 1877; the repeater rifle is invented by Mannlicher in 1878; the streets of London are lit by electricity in 1878, followed by New York City in 1880; hypnosis is used to treat hysteria, marking the beginnings of psychoanalysis, and the first hydro-electric plant is designed by Edison, 1882; Chicago's first skyscraper is built in 1883, the same year William Thomson speculates on the size of atoms; Twain's *Huckleberry Finn* and London's first subway "tube" are completed in 1884; the individuality of fingerprints is established, and George Eastman produces coated photographic paper, 1885.

   In 1886, structures for producing electricity at Niagara Falls are begun, the Statue of Liberty is dedicated, and Marx's *Das Kapital* is published in English; in 1888, the electric motor, the Kodak box camera, and the pneumatic tire are developed, the first beauty contests are held, and women are being murdered in London by "Jack the Ripper;" A. Gustave Eiffel designs the Eiffel Tower, 1889.

In 1890, the first motion pictures are shown in New York City, and the first all-steel frame skyscraper is built in Chicago; the "zipper" is invented in 1891; the first Ford is built in 1893, the year the Columbian World Exhibition is held in Chicago; in 1894, the flat phonograph disc is developed and a committee is formed to organize the first modern "olympics;" Armenians are massacred in Turkey in 1895, while Cubans fight for their independence from Spain; also in 1895, H. G. Wells publishes *The Time Machine*, and Freud publishes his theories on hysteria; radioactivity is discovered in 1896 by Becquerel, the electron in 1897 by Thomson, radium and polonium by Pierre and Marie Curie in 1898, alpha and beta waves by Rutherford in 1899, and radon by Dorn in 1900; H. G. Wells publishes *The War of the Worlds* in 1898; quantum theory is published by Planck in 1900, while Freud publishes *The Interpretation of Dreams.*

TWENTIETH-CENTURY WESTERN ARTISTS (1900 TO PRESENT)

During the twentieth century, Euro-American art became progressively diverse, styles and ideas overlapped more and more, and artists were less and less inclined to be categorized in a particular movement. To facilitate the listing of artists and styles, this section begins with a timeline of Western art that lists approximate dates when a particular movement was in its prime and shows the interrelationships between artistic styles (Figure 4–1).

Chronology

Fauvism (1905 to 1910)

Henri Matisse (on-ree mah-tees)	Fauves: Painter	c. 1869–1954 A.D.
Georges Rouault (zhorzh roo-oh)	Fauves/Expressionist: Painter	c. 1871–1959 A.D.
Maurice de Vlaminck (moh-rees duh vlah-meenk)	Fauves: Painter	c. 1876–1958 A.D.
Raoul Dufy (rah-ool dew-fee)	Fauves: Painter	c. 1877–1953 A.D.

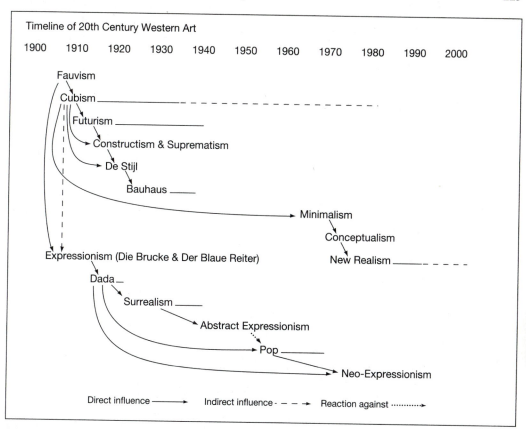

FIGURE 4–1. Timeline of Twentieth-Century Western Art.

André Derain   Fauves: Painter   c. 1880–1954 A.D.
  (on-dray duh-ran)

Expressionism (1903 to 1915)

Wassily Kandinsky   Expressionist/Bauhaus:
                      Nonobjective Painter   c. 1866–1944 A.D.
    (vass-see-lee can-din-skee)

Emile Nolde   Expressionist: Painter
                      German, Die Brucke   c. 1867–1956 A.D.
    (ay-muhl nohl-duh)

Lyonel Feininger   Expressionist/Cubist/
                      Bauhaus: Blaue Reiter   c. 1871–1956 A.D.
    (lew-yoh-nehl fine-neen-kehr)

Georges Rouault	Fauves/Expressionist: Painter	c. 1871–1959 A.D.
(zhorzh roo-oh)		
Otto Mueller	Expressionist: Painter German, Die Brucke	c. 1874–1930 A.D.
(ah-toh mew-lair)		
Franz Marc	Expressionist: Painter German, Blaue Reiter	c. 1880–1916 A.D.
(frahnz mahrk)		
Ernst Ludwig Kirchner	Expressionist: Painter German, Die Brucke	c. 1880–1938 A.D.
(airnst loot-vik keerkh-ner)		
Arthur Dove	Expressionist: Painter (Stieglitz Group)	c. 1880–1946 A.D.
Hans Hoffman	Expressionist/Abstract Expressionist: Painter	c. 1880–1966 A.D.
(hahns hohf-mahn)		
Max Pechstein	Expressionist: Painter German, Die Brucke	c. 1881–1955 A.D.
(mahks pehk-shtine)		
José Clemente Orozco	Expressionist: Painter	c. 1883–1949 A.D.
(hoh-zeh klay-mehn-tay oh-rohz-koh)		
Erich Heckel	Expressionist: Painter German, Die Brucke	c. 1883–1970 A.D.
(eh-rik heh-keel)		
Max Beckman	Expressionist: Painter	c. 1884–1950 A.D.
(mahks behk-mahn)		
Karl Schmidt-Rottluff	Expressionist: Painter German, Die Brucke	c. 1884–1976 A.D.
(kahrl shooh-mit raht-loof)		
Oskar Kokoschka	Expressionist: Painter Blaue Reiter	c. 1886–1980 A.D.
(os-kar koh-kosh-kah)		
Georgia O'Keefe	Expressionist: Painter (Stieglitz Group)	c. 1887–1986 A.D.
George Grosz	Expressionist: Painter German	c. 1893–1959 A.D.
(gross)		
Chaim Soutine	Expressionist: Painter	c. 1894–1943 A.D.
(shehm soo-teen)		

Parallel Historical Events, 1905–1915

Freud publishes *The Psychopathology of Everyday Life* in 1904, and *Three Contributions to the Theory of Sex* in 1905; Pavlov tests his theories of conditioned reflexes in 1907; in 1912, Alfred Adler publishes *The Nervous Character,* and C. G. Jung *The Theory of Psychoanalysis;* in 1914, J. B. Watson publishes *Behavior: An Introduction to Comparative Psychology,* while Magnus Hirschfeld publishes *Homosexuality of Man and Wife.*

Cubism (1907 to 1940s)

Lyonel Feininger (lew-yoh-nehl fine-neen-kehr)	Expressionist/Cubist/Bauhaus: Blaue Reiter	c. 1871–1956 A.D.
Jacques Villon (zhak vee-joh)	Cubist: Painter (Section d'Or)	c. 1875–1963 A.D.
Albert Gleizes (ahl-bair glayz)	Cubist: Painter	c. 1881–1953 A.D.
Fernand Leger (fair-non lay-zhay)	Cubist: Painter	c. 1881–1955 A.D.
Pablo Picasso (pah-bloh pee-kah-soh)	Cubist: Painter, Sculptor	c. 1881–1974 A.D.
Georges Braque (zhorzh brahk)	Cubist: Painter	c. 1882–1963 A.D.
Jean Metzinger (zhahn meht-zeen-zhay)	Cubist: Painter	c. 1883–1956 A.D.
Henri Laurens (on-ree lah-rehn)	Cubist: Sculptor	c. 1885–1954 A.D.
Juan Gris (whahn grees)	Cubist: Painter	c. 1887–1928 A.D.
Alexander Archipenko	Cubist: Sculptor	c. 1887–1964 A.D.
Marcel Duchamp (mahr-sell doo-shahm)	Cubist/Dada/Futurist: Painter, Sculptor (Section d'Or)	c. 1887–1968 A.D.
Raymond Duchamp-Villon (reh-mohn doo-shahm vee-joh)	Cubist: Sculptor (Section d'Or)	c. 1896–1938 A.D.

Futurism (1909 to 1940)

Giacomo Balla (jah-koh-moh bahl-la)	Futurist: Painter	c. 1871–1958 A.D.

Joseph Stella	Futurist: Painter	c. 1877–1946 A.D.
Kazimir Malevich	Cubo-Futurist/Suprematist:	
	Painter	c. 1878–1935 A.D.
Carlo Carra	Futurist: Painter	c. 1881–1966 A.D.
(kahr-loh kar-rah)		
Umberto Boccioni	Futurist: Painter, Sculptor	c. 1882–1916 A.D.
(oom-bair-toh boh-choh-nee)		
Gino Severini	Futurist: Painter	c. 1883–1966 A.D.
(jee-noh seh-veh-ree-nee)		
Luigi Russolo	Futurist: Painter, Composer	c. 1885–1947 A.D.
(loo-ee-jee roo-soh-loh)		
Liubov Popova	Cubo-Futurist: Painter	c. 1889–1924 A.D.

Constructivism and Suprematism (1913 to 1928)

Kazimir Malevich	Suprematist: Painter	c. 1878–1935 A.D.
(kah-sim-eer mahl-yay-vitch)		
Vladimir Tatlin	Constructivist: Painter,	
	Architect, Stage Designer	c. 1885–1953 A.D.
(vlad-ih-mir tat-lin)		
Liubov Popova	Constructivist/Suprematist:	
	Painter, Textile Designer	c. 1889–1924 A.D.
Eleazer Lissitzky	Constructivist/Suprematist/	
	De Stijl/Bauhaus: Painter,	
	Typographer, Designer	c. 1890–1941 A.D.
Naum Gabo	Constructivist: Sculptor	c. 1890–1977 A.D.
(nawm gah-boh)		
Alexander Rodchenko	Constructivist/Suprematist:	
	Painter, Photographer,	
	Designer	c. 1891–1956 A.D.

Parallel Historical Events, 1907–1940s

Rutherford establishes his theory of atomic structure in 1911; Wilson detects protons and electrons in 1912; Hess discovers cosmic radiation; in 1913, Geiger invents the Geiger counter to measure alpha rays, and the term isotope is used; Jeans publishes *Radiation and the Quantum Theory* in 1914; Einstein proposes his *General Theory of Relativity* in 1915; the dimensions of the Milky Way are discovered by Shapley in 1918; in 1919, Einstein's theory of relativity is demonstrated through observations of solar eclipses, and studies confirm that the atom is not the smallest particle in the universe; using photography, Wolf reveals in 1920 the structure of the Milky Way; Chadwick and Rutherford run preliminary experiments for splitting the atom, 1921; in 1925, Heisenberg, Bohr, and Jordan establish quantum mechanics for atoms, while Franck and Hertz are acknowledged for the discovery of the laws governing the impact of the electron on the atom; Goddard launches the first successful liquid fuel rocket in 1926; in 1930, Eddington works to unify quantum theory with relativity; Lawrence develops the cyclotron in 1931; Einstein and Infeld publish *The Evolution of Physics* in 1938; intensive research begins in 1941 on the Manhattan Project to develop an atomic bomb.

Dada (1916 to 1922)

Francis Picabia	Dadaist/Surrealist: Painter	c. 1879–1953 A.D.
(frahn-chees pee-kah-bee-ah)		
Kurt Schwitters	Dadaist: Painter, Sculptor, Architect	c. 1887–1948 A.D.
(koort shvit-uhrs)		
Jean Arp	Dadaist: Collage, Sculptor	c. 1887–1966 A.D.
(zhahn ahrp)		
Marcel Duchamp	Cubist/Dadaist/Futurist: Painter, Sculptor	c. 1887–1968 A.D.
(mahr-sell doo-shahm)		
Man Ray	Dadaist/Surrealist: Painter Photographer, Film maker	c. 1890–1977 A.D.
Max Ernst	Dadaist/Surrealist: Painter	c. 1891–1976 A.D.
(mahks ehrnsht)		

De Stijl (1917 to 1923)

Piet Mondrian	De Stijl: Painter	c. 1872–1944 A.D.
(peet mohn-dree-ahn)		
Constantin Brancusi	De Stijl/Expressionist: Sculptor	c. 1876–1957 A.D.
(kahn-stuhn-teen brahn-koo-see)		
Theo van Doesburg	De Stijl/Dadaist/Bauhaus: Painter, Writer, Poet	c. 1883–1931 A.D.
(tay-oh van dohz-buhrg)		
Gerrit Rietveld	De Stijl: Architect, Designer	c. 1888–1964 A.D.
(gair-it ryt-velt)		
Eleazer Lissitzky	Constructivist/Suprematist/ De Stijl/Bauhaus: Painter, Typographer, Designer	c. 1890–1941 A.D.
Alexander Calder	De Stijl/Dada: Sculptor	c. 1898–1976 A.D.

Bauhaus (School) (1919 to 1933, 1938–1946)

Wassily Kandinsky	Expressionist/Bauhaus: Non Objective Painter	c. 1866–1944 A.D.
(vass-see-lee can-din-skee)		

4

Lyonel Feininger	Expressionist/Cubist/Bauhaus: Blaue Reiter	c. 1871–1956 A.D.
(lew-yoh-nehl fine-need-kehr)		
Paul Klee	Fantasy, Pri-Mordial/Bauhaus: Painter; Pre-Cursor to Surrealism	c. 1879–1940 A.D.
(clay)		
Walter Gropius	Bauhaus: Architect	c. 1883–1969 A.D.
(val-tuhr grow-pee-us)		
Ludwig Mies van der Rohe	Bauhaus/International Style: Architect	c. 1887–1969 A.D.
(leet-vik mees vahn dair roh-eh)		
Oskar Schlemmer	Bauhaus: Sculptor, Painter	c. 1888–1943 A.D.
(shlem-uhr)		
Laszlo Moholy-Nagy	Bauhaus: Sculptor, Painter, Photographer, Designer	c. 1895–1946 A.D.
(lahs-loh moh-hoh-lee-nahd-yuh)		

Surrealism and Its Precursors (1924 to 1940)

Paul Klee	Fantasy, Primordial/Bauhaus: Painter; Precursor to Surrealism	c. 1879–1940 A.D.
(clay)		
Francis Picabia	Dada/Surrealist: Painter	c. 1879–1953 A.D.
(frahn-chees pee-kah-bee-ah)		
Marc Chagall	Fantasy/Nostalgia: Painter	c. 1887–1985 A.D.
(shah-gahl)		
Giorgio de Chirico	Fantasy/Metaphysical: Painter; Precursor to Surrealism	c. 1888–1978 A.D.
(johr-jyo de key-ree-co)		
Max Ernst	Dada/Surrealist: Painter	c. 1891–1976 A.D.
(mahks ehrnsht)		
Joan Miró	Surrealist: Painter	c. 1893–1983 A.D.
(zhoh-ahn mee-roh)		
Paul Delvaux	Surrealist: Painter	c. 1897–
(pohl dehl-voh)		
Alberto Giacometti	Surrealist: Sculptor, Painter	c. 1901–1966 A.D.
(ahl-bair-toh jah-ko-met-tee)		
Arshile Gorky	Surrealist/Abstract Express: Painter	c. 1904–1948 A.D.
Salvador Dali	Surrealist: Painter	c. 1904–
(sahl-vah-dore dah-lee)		

Yves Tanguy (ee-veh tahn-gee)	Surrealist: Painter	c. 1900–1955 A.D.
René Magritte (ruh-nay muh-greet)	Surrealist: Painter	c. 1898–1967 A.D.

Abstract Expressionism and Its Precursors (1942 to Early 1960s)

Hans Hoffman (hahns hohf-mahn)	Expressionist/Abstract Express: Painter	c. 1880–1966 A.D.
Mark Rothko (rawth-koh)	Abstract Expressionist: Color Field Painter	c. 1903–1973 A.D.
Adolf Gottlieb (gawt-leeb)	Abstract Expressionist: Color Field Painter, Pictographs	c. 1903–1974 A.D.
Arshile Gorky	Surrealist/Abstract Express: Painter	c. 1904–1948 A.D.
Clyfford Still	Abstract Expressionist: Color Field Painter	c. 1904–1980 A.D.
Willem de Kooning (vill-em duh koe-ning)	Abstract Expressionist: Action Painter	c. 1904– A.D.
Barnett Newman	Abstract Expressionist: Color Field Painter	c. 1905–1970 A.D.
David Smith	Abstract Expressionist: Sculptor	c. 1906–1965 A.D.
Lee Krasner	Abstract Expressionist: Action Painter	c. 1908–1984 A.D.
Franz Kline (frahnz klyn)	Abstract Expressionist: Gesture Painter	c. 1910–1962 A.D.
Jackson Pollock (pah-lock)	Abstract Expressionist: Action Painter	c. 1912–1956 A.D.
Morris Louis	Abstract Expressionist: Color Field Painter	c. 1912–1962 A.D.
Ad Reinhardt (add ryn-hahrt)	Abstract Expressionist: Color Field Painter	c. 1913–1967 A.D.
Robert Motherwell	Abstract Expressionist: Color Field Painter	c. 1915–

4

Grace Hartigan	Abstract Expressionist:	
	Action Painter	c. 1922–
Sam Francis	Abstract Expressionist:	
	Color Field Painter	c. 1923–
Ellsworth Kelly	Abstract Expressionist/	
	Minimalist: Painter, Sculptor	c. 1923–
Kenneth Noland	Abstract Expressionist:	
	Color Field Painter	c. 1924–
Helen Frankenthaler	Abstract Expressionist:	
	Color Field Painter	c. 1928–
Frank Stella	Post-Painterly Abstraction:	
	Painter	c. 1936–

Parallel Historical Events, 1917–1950s

In 1917, C. G. Jung publishes *Psychology of the Unconscious* and Freud publishes *Introduction to Psychoanalysis.* and controversy over their ideas follow in 1918; J. B. Watson's *Psychology from the Standpoint of a Behaviorist* appears in 1919; published in 1920 are A. Adler's *The Practice and Theory of Individual Psychology* and C. G. Jung's *Psychological Types,* and Rorschach develops his inkblot test, publishing his *Psychodiagnostic* in 1921, the same year that the National Institute for Industrial Psychology is established in London; Freud publishes *The Ego and the Id* in 1923; H. de Man publishes *The Psychology of Socialism,* 1925; in 1927, Freud publishes *The Future of an Illusion,* Pavlov *Conditioned Reflexes;* Jung's *Relationships between the Ego and the Unconscious* appears in 1928.

Civilization and Its Discontents by Freud appears in 1930; in 1933, C. J. Jung's *Psychology and Religion,* C. G. Jung's *Modern Man in Search of a Soul,* and Reich's *Character Analysis* are published; Horney's *The Neurotic Personality of Our Time,* 1937; C. G. Jung's *The Interpretation of Personality,* 1940; Malraux publishes the *Psychology of the Arts* in 1948; Berdyaev's *Dreams and Reality* appears in 1950; B. F. Skinner publishes *Science and Human Behavior* in 1953.

Pop and Op Art (1956 to 1970)

Victor Vasarely	Op Art: Painter	c. 1908–
Richard Hamilton	Pop Art: Painter, Printmaker	c. 1922–
Roy Lichtenstein (lick-ten-styn)	Pop Art: Painter, Sculptor	c. 1923–
Larry Rivers	Pop Art: Painter	c. 1923–
George Segal	Pop Art: Environmental Sculptor	c. 1924–

Robert Rauschenberg (rou-shen-burg)	Pop Art: Painter, Sculptor	c. 1925–
Allan Kaprow	Pop Art: Happenings, Sculptor	c. 1927–
Robert Indiana	Pop Art: Painter	c. 1928–
Andy Warhol	Pop Art: Painter, Printmaker, Filmmaker	c. 1928–1987
Claes Oldenburg	Pop Art: Sculptor, Happenings, Performance	c. 1929–
Jasper Johns	Pop Art: Painter	c. 1930–
Tom Wesselmann	Pop Art: Painter, Sculptor	c. 1931–
Bridget Riley	Op Art: Painter	c. 1931–
James Rosenquist	Pop Art: Painter	c. 1933–

Parallel Historical Events, The Television Age

John L. Baird transmits an image of people by television in 1925, and demonstrates color television in 1928; the phenomena of technocracy and its domination enters the vocabulary in 1930; by 1938, there are twenty thousand television sets in use in New York City; the prototype of the modern computer is built at Pennsylvania University in 1946; color television makes its U.S. debut in 1951; by 1954, 29 million homes in the U.S. have a television set; "Rock and Roll" is popular in 1956; in 1957, the Soviet Union launches Sputnik I and II, the first satellites to orbit the earth, and they send two monkeys into space in 1959; by 1960, there are 85 million television sets in the U.S.

4

Minimal Art (1964 to 1975)

Louise Nevelson	Abstract Expressionist/ Minimalist: Sculptor	c.1899–1988
Ellsworth Kelly	Abstract Expressionist/ Minimalist: Painter, Sculptor	c.1923–
Donald Judd	Minimalist: Sculptor	c. 1928–
Robert Morris	Minimalist: Sculptor, Performance	c.1931–
Dan Flavin	Minimalist: Light Sculptor	c. 1933–
Carl Andre	Minimalist: Sculptor	c. 1935–
Robert Smithson	Minimalist: Earthworks, Sculptor	c. 1938–73
Richard Serra	Minimalist: Sculptor	c. 1939–
Douglas Huebler	Minimalist/Conceptualist: Sculptor	c. 1942–

Conceptual Art (1968 to 1975)

Joseph Beuys	Conceptualist: Sculptor, Performance, Installation	c. 1921–
Miriam Schapiro	Feminist: Collections, Painter, Printmaker	c. 1923–
Edward Kienholz	Conceptualist: Sculptor, Installation	c. 1927–
Sol LeWitt	Minimalist/Conceptualist: Sculptor, Draftsman, Author	c. 1928–
John Baldessari	Conceptualist: Painter, Printmaker	c. 1931–
Nam June Paik	Conceptualist: Performance, Installation	c. 1932–
Faith Ringgold	Feminist: Quilter, Painter Printmaker	c. 1934–
"Christo" Javacheff	Conceptualist/Arte Povera: Environmental Sculptor	c. 1935–
Walter De Maria	Conceptualist: Environmental Sculptor	c. 1935–
Hans Haacke	Conceptualist: Painter, Installation	c. 1936–
(hahnz hah-keh)		
Eva Hesse	Conceptualist: Painter, Assemblage	c. 1937–1970
Nancy Holt	Conceptualist: Environmental Sculptor	c. 1938–
Judy Chicago	Feminist: Painter, Installation	c. 1939–
Vito Acconci	Conceptualist: Sculptor, Poet, Performance	c. 1940–
Jennifer Bartlett	Conceptualist: Painter, Sculptor, Installation	c. 1941–
Bruce Nauman	Conceptualist: Sculptor	c. 1941–
Richard Tuttle	Conceptual/Process Art:	c. 1941–
Douglas Huebler	Minimalist/Conceptualist: Painter, Photographer, Sculptor	c. 1942–
Jonathan Borofsky	Conceptual/Installation: Sculptor	c. 1942–
Gilbert and George	Conceptual: Performance, Living Sculptors	c. Gilbert 1942– George 1943

(Gil. Proesch, Geo. Passmore)

Michael Heizer	Conceptual/Earthworks: Sculptor, Painter	c. 1944–
Mary Miss	Conceptual/Site Works: Sculptor	c. 1944–
George Trakas	Conceptual/Site Works: Sculptor	c. 1944–
Joseph Kosuth	Conceptualist: Installations, Author	c. 1945–
Alice Aycock	Conceptualist: Site Sculpture	c. 1946–
Alan Sonfist	Conceptual/Earthworks: Sculptor	c. 1946–
Michael Singer	Conceptual/Site Works: Sculptor	c. 1946–

New Realism (1968 to 1980s)

Philip Pearlstein	Realist: Figurative Painter	c. 1924–
Duane Hanson	Super Realist: Sculptor	c. 1925–
Audrey Flack	Photo Realist: Painter, Photographer	c. 1931–
Robert Bechtle	Photo Realist: Painter	c. 1932–
Malcolm Morley	Photo Realist: Painter	c. 1933–
Richard Estes	Photo Realist: Painter	c. 1936–
John De Andrea	Super Realist: Sculptor	c. 1940–
Chuck Close	Photo Realist: Painter	c. 1940–

Neoexpressionism "Bad Art" (1975 to 1980s)

Joseph Beuys (yoh-sehf boys)	Conceptualist: Sculptor, Performance, Installation	c. 1921–1986
Leon Golub	Neoexpressionist: Painter	c. 1922–
Georg Baselitz (gay-ohrk bahz-leetz)	Neoexpressionist: Painter	c. 1938–
Pat Stier	Neoexpressionist: Painter	c. 1940–
Laurie Anderson	Neoexpressionist: Performance	c. 1942–
Anselm Kiefer (ahn-selm kee-fair)	Neoexpressionist: Painter	c. 1945–
Sandro Chia (sahn-droh kee-ah)	Neoexpressionist: Painter	c. 1946–
Eric Fischl	Neoexpressionist: Painter	c. 1948–
Jenny Holzer	Neoexpressionist: Electronic Installation	c. 1950–
Charles Clough	Neoexpressionist: Painter	c. 1951–

Julian Schnabel	Neoexpressionist: Painter	c. 1951–
Francesco Clemente	Neoexpressionist: Painter	c. 1952–
(frahn-chehs-koh clay-mehn-teh)		
David Salle	Neoexpressionist: Painter	c. 1952–
Robert Longo	Neoexpressionist: Painter, Performance, Installation	c. 1953–

5 │ NON-WESTERN ART AND ARTISTS

When outlining historical styles, periods, and artists in the European tradition, specific dates and names can generally be identified. There are a number of reasons why this may not be the case when examining the art from non-European cultures. Many cultures do not view the making of art as a separate, autonomous activity. Aesthetic products may be intimately tied to ritual objects, dress, and body ornamentation. An artifact may be intended for daily utilitarian use and its maker anonymous, because the product is something that everyone makes and its existence is not considered to be anything out of the ordinary, or the culture maintains a verbal, rather than a written history. Therefore, the information provided here will differ from culture to culture, depending on what is known and available about their art and artists.

Because of the tremendous amount of information and the diversity of the world's various cultures, this list should not be considered to be all inclusive.

AFRICA

Africa is the second largest continent on earth with a diverse range of cultures including those often associated with Western culture, such as Egypt. The performing and literary (in most cases oral) arts play an equally important role with the visual arts in many African cultures. The mask, which westerners generally associate with Africa, will be most prominent in cultures where secret societies and ritualistic practices are important.

The history of African art is at best sketchy for several reasons: the history of most African cultures was verbally passed down from generation to generation, not written; artists were generally anonymous; and materials used were often susceptible to deterioration. Therefore, the information that follows should be considered a sampling, rather than an all-inclusive listing, of some of the more prominent African cultures and their art: rock paintings and engravings ca. 3000 B.C.

Sahara Desert

Nok Culture of Nigeria   ca. 500 B.C.–200 A.D.
  produced pottery head and figure sculptures as well as ironworking

Igbo of Nigeria   ca. 9th century A.D.
  use of copper, alloys, and caste bronze; earliest known textiles found in village of Igbo-Ukwu

Bandiagara region of Mali   ca. 11th century
  cotton and woolen cloths

Ife Culture of Nigeria   ca. 11th–15th century
  One of the most influential and important of African cultures
  brass, bronze portrait castings from city of Yoruba which were so realistic that when seen by Europeans were assumed to be a result of exposure to the Italian Renaissance—casting techniques were superior to European products, terra cotta sculpture

Benin Culture of Nigeria   ca. 15th–19th century
  One of the most influential and important of African cultures and building on knowledge of the Ife
  realistic brass and bronze castings of heads, terra cotta sculpture, carvings in ivory

Sherbro of Sierra Leone   ca. 16th century
  carvings in ivory

Kuba of Zaire   ca. 17th century
  earliest known wood carvings

Ashanti Tribe of Ghana

kingdom at zenith	c. 1700 A.D.

gold and brass casting, gold portrait masks, symbolic stools (gold for the king, black for the souls of ancestors), textiles

Karumba Tribe of Upper Volta and Mali

believed to be the earliest inhabitants of region, known for their graceful antelope inspired carvings used to disperse ancestral spirits following a period of mourning

Bambara Tribe of Mali

great warriors who ruled the city of Timbuctu from the 17th through the 19th centuries, known primarily for carved wood "antelope" headresses known as "Chi Wara" and animal face masks of geometric abstraction

Dogon Tribe of Upper Volta and Mali

cliffdwelling people whose folklore is secretive, known for ancestor figures and masks which are geometric and "cubist" in appearance and carved by the smithy of the clan who is of the sacred class

THE AMERICAS

Archaic period	ca. 40,000–2000 B.C.

stone points	ca. 10,000 B.C.

evidence of humans through-
out the Americas	ca. 8,000 B.C.

Early Pre-Classic	ca. 2,000 B.C.

agricultural development, settlements, formal burial of dead with artifacts suggesting belief in life after death, development of pottery, stone-grinding

Preclassic or Formative period	ca. 1500 B.C.–300 A.D.

similar to Neolithic period in Europe, agricultural system based on maize (corn) production, further refinement of pottery, loom weaving, small painted terra cotta figurines found throughout the Americas that are believed to be used in fertility cults, many artifacts found in central Mexico: Tlatilco, Chupicuaro, Puebla-Guerrero

Olmec Civilization	ca. 1200–400 B.C.

the earliest known culture in the Americas, best known for their skills as stone carvers, particularly monumental heads and sculptures, figurines in jade and serpentine, concentrated in Southern Mexico but influential throughout Middle America: Honduras, Campeche, Veracruz, Tabasco

5

Teotihuacan (Home of the Gods)   ca. 200–600 A.D.

well planned city-state in central Mexico of stuccoed pyramids and palaces, peaceful and highly organized society noted for its architecture, stone carving and sophisticated pottery, built the Pyramid of the Sun near Mexico City which is one of the largest man-made structures in the world

Toltec (Early Post-Classic)   ca. 900–1200 A.D.

a unifying force in Middle America that spread to the Yucatan Peninsula, mingled with the Itza and the Mayan to build the great ceremonial site at Cichen Itza

Aztec (Late Post-Classic)   ca. 1300–1530 A.D.

barbarians who invaded from the north, appropriated the skills, ideas, and craftsmanship of those they conquered, culture and religious practice based on human sacrifice, developed their own distinct style of sculpture, built city of Tenochtitlan ca. 1367 and brought Mixtec craftsmen to city to produce pottery and jewelry, dominated until the Spanish Conquest

Maya   ca. 300–1200 A.D.
Classic Maya   ca. 300–900 A.D.
Toltec-Maya   ca. 900–1200 A.D.

knowledge of mathematics and astronomy far surpassed European counterparts; masters of architecture, sculpture, painting and pottery; found in Mexico, Honduras, Guatemala

Inca   ca. 1200–1532 A.D.

consolidated the west coast of South America, superior engineers, pottery, masters of work with gold and silver decorated in repousse, bronze casting, most famous Inca city Machu Picchu (the lost city of the Incas) built at 8,000 foot elevation in the Andes mountains

Algonquians

made up of the Micmac, Abenaki, Narragansett, and Delaware tribes; lived in what is now the Northeast United States and Canada; carved in shell and stone

Iroquois

Iroquois confederation made up of the five "nations" of New York State—Mohawk, Oneida, Onondaga, Cayuga, and Seneca; closely related in language were the Huron, Neutral, and Erie; agriculturally based; noted for their masks, pottery

Great Lakes Area Indians

Shawnee, Kickapoo, Miami, Winnebago, Fox, and Ottawa spoke in

Algonquian and Sioux dialects; spanned the Great Lakes region and south into Ohio, Kentucky, and West Virginia

Plains Indians

Mandan, Hidatsa, Arikara, Pawnee, Ponca, Omaha, Oto, Iowa, Missouri, Kansa, Osage, Wichita, Sioux occupied what are now the plains states in the central United States; produced pottery, beadwork, carvings

Far West United States

Hotchkiss, Pomo, Wintun, Miwok, and Yokuts; noted for their basketry, stone carvings, and decoys

Northwest United States

Chinook, Athapaskan, Wakashan, Penutian, Salish, Tlingit, Haida, Bella Coola, Kwakiutl, Nootka, Eyak, Tsimshian; noted for stonecarvings, carvings in bone, masks, totems, weavings

Southwest United States

Mogollon, Hohokam, Anasazi, Pueblo, Sinagua, Salado, Mimbres Valley people, Yavapai, Havasupai, Walapai, Mohave, Chametla-Aztatlan, Chalchihuite, Apache, Athapaskan, Navajo, Pima, Tewa, Hopi, Towa, Zuni; noted for their pottery, basketry, cliffdwelling architecture, weaving, carvings

CHINA

5

Neolithic period   ca. 2200–1500 B.C.

"painted pottery culture" red pottery from Yangshao black pottery from Lungshan

Shang Dynasty   1523–1028 B.C.

also known as Yin Dynasty bronze casting

Chou Kings   1027–256 B.C.

    Western Chou   1027–771 B.C.

    Eastern Chou   770–256 B.C.

Ch'in Dynasty   221–207 B.C.

China united, Great Wall built

Han Dynasty   206 B.C.–220 A.D.

introduction of Confucianism, export trade, terracotta funerary statuettes including 6,000 life-size warriors and horses found near Hsien in 1974 A.D.

Period of the Six Dynasties   220–581 A.D.

growth of Buddhism and the building of the cave-temples

Ku K'ai-chih	painter	born 345 A.D.
Chang Seng-yu	painter	early 6th century

Sui Dynasty   581–618 A.D.

T'ang Dynasty   618–906 A.D.

period of prosperity and growth, exposure to foreign cultures and
ideas and led to metalwork in gold and jewels, cities were planned
on grid pattern

Wang Wei	painter	699–759 A.D.
Chang Hsuan	painter	8th century

Period of the Five Dynasties   907–960 A.D.

characterized by anarchy and the division of China into independent
kingdoms, great artistic output, introduction of the printing press and
widespread distribution of literary 'classics'

Sung Dynasty   960–1279 A.D.

Northern Sung emperors   960–1126 A.D.

Fan K'uan	painter	early 11th century
Kuo Hsi	painter	11th century
Kao K'o-ming	painter	11th century
Li T'ang	painter	early 12th century
Li Kung-lin	painter	1040–1106 A.D.
Mi Yu-jen	painter	1086–1165 A.D.

Southern Sung emperors 1127–1279 A.D.

Ma Lin	painter	mid 13th century
Wang T'ing-yun	painter	1151–1202 A.D.
Ma Yuan	painter	c. 1190–1230 A.D.
Hsia Kuei	painter	c. 1190–1230 A.D.

Yuan Rulers   1260–1368 A.D.

of Mongolian extraction, first Emperor Kublai Khan
introduced underglazing in pottery, inlaying with mother-of-pearl
and lacquering, painters excelled at landscapes and horses

Ch'ien Hsuan	painter	c. 1235–1301 A.D.
Kao K'o-kung	painter	1248–1310 A.D.
Chao Meng-fu	painter	1254–1322 A.D.
Huang Kung-wang	painter	1269–1354 A.D.
Wu Chen	painter	1280–1354 A.D.
Ni Tsan	painter	1301–1374 A.D.

Wang Meng	painter	c. 1309–1385 A.D.
Sheng Mou	painter	c. 1310–1361 A.D.

Ming Dynasty   1368–1644 A.D.

artistic taste influenced by Persia, craftsmen skilled at cloisonné enamelling

Shen Chou	painter	1427–1509 A.D.
Wu Wei	painter	1459–1508 A.D.
T' ang Yin	painter	1470–1523 A.D.
Wen Cheng-ming	painter	1470–1559 A.D.
Ch'en Shun	painter	1483–1544 A.D.
Lu Chih	painter	1496–1576 A.D.
Chou Ch'en	painter	c. 1500–1535 A.D.
Wen Chia	painter	1501–1583 A.D.
Ch'iu Ying	painter	1510–1551 A.D.
Hsu Wei	painter	1521–1593 A.D.
Sun K'o-hung	painter	1532–1610 A.D.
Tung Ch'i-ch'ang	painter	1555–1636 A.D.
Wang Shih-min	painter	1592–1680 A.D.
Ch'en Hung-shou	painter	1599–1652 A.D.

Manchu Dynasty   1644–1911 A.D.

China opened to European trade, production of ceramic products accelerated to meet trade demands

Hung-jen	painter	c. 1603–1663 A.D.
K'un-ts'an	painter	c. 1610–1693 A.D.
Kung Hsien	painter	c. 1620–1689 A.D.
Chu Ta	painter	1625–c. 1705 A.D.
Wu Li	painter	1632–1718 A.D.
Tao-chi	painter	1641–c. 1717 A.D.
Wang Yuan-ch'i	painter	1642–1715 A.D.
Chang Feng	painter	c. 1645–1673 A.D.
Kao Ch'i-p'ei	painter	c. 1672–1734 A.D.
Huan Yen	painter	1682–1765 A.D.
Kao Feng-han	painter	1683–c. 1747 A.D.
Chin Nung	painter	1687–c. 1764 A.D.
Lo P'ing	painter	1733–1799 A.D.

Sun Yat-sen, ruler   1911–1945 A.D.

Mao Tse-tung, ruler   1945–1976 A.D.

5

INDIA

Protohistorical Period   c. 2500–300 B.C.

most consistent activity took place in the Indus Valley where artifacts reflect the influences of Mesopotamia with distinct Indian characteristics; artifacts include: pottery, terracotta figurines, animal and human figures carved in soapstone which may be forerunners of the god Siva, bronze figures using the lost-wax process, jewelry, and as yet undeciphered hieroglyphics—see the following works:

      Male Torso (limestone) Indus Valley   c. 2400–2000 B.C.

Early Historical Period   c. 200 B.C.–100 A.D.

Mauryan Style   c. 300–100 B.C.

Sunga-Kanva Style   c. 100 B.C.–100 A.D.

period of the stupas (evolved from burial mounds), temples and monasteries cut into the side of mountains, and large free-standing sculptures all of Buddhist influence—see the following works:

      The Great Stupa Sanchi, India   c. 10 B.C.–15 A.D.

The Transitional Period   c. 50 A.D.–400 A.D.

cave architecture, stupas and sculpture continued to develop as the iconography and the aesthetic of Buddhism (an ideal of serenity and calm); architecture reflected a Hellenistic and Persian influence; Buddha is no longer represented by mere symbols but is now portrayed in narrative reliefs and free-standing sculpture; mural paintings are being executed in caves—see the following works:

      Standing Buddha   c. 5th century A.D.
        Carved Red Sandstone

      Pandulena Cave   2nd century A.D.
        Buddhist   Nasik, India

      Vihara Monastery   2nd century A.D.
        Bhaja, India

The Classical Period   c. 400–900 A.D.

the influential Gupta Style evolved during the Gupta Dynasty of the 4th and 5th centuries, Hindu art began to develop, cave architect reached its zenith around the late 8th century as did Buddhist sculpture in the 5th and 6th centuries, the Buddha's hand gestures and signs of saintliness became standardized at this time while Hindu sculpture contrasts with aggravated rhythms and dominate dynamic figures, Islam is introduced in India—see the following works:

"Beautiful Bodhisativa"   c. 600–650 A.D.
       Padmapani   Cave Fresco   Ajanta, India
Siva as King of Dancers   c. 640–675 A.D.
       Hindu   Elura, India
Papanatha Temple   8th century A.D.
       Hindu   Pattadakal, India
Pallava Cave   8th century A.D.
       Delavanur, Tamil Nadu

The Medieval Period   c. 900–1200 A.D.

Islam spread throughout India as Buddhism disappeared from most areas, relief sculpture now covered most of the facade of buildings, free-standing sculptures of stone and bronze were set up inside temples and used in worship, mithunas ('loving couples') and erotic sculptures were produced, bronze casting reached an ideal state—see the following works:

Kandarya Mahadeva Temple   c. 10th–11th centuries
       Hindu   Khajuraho, India
Shiva Nataraja   c. 11th century
       Hindu   bronze statue
Sivaite Temple (Cola Period)   c. 12th century A.D.
       Gangaikondacolapuram, Tamil Nadu

The Muslim and Medieval Period   c. 1200–1800 A.D.

By around 1200 A.D., Islam conquered most of India and the Moghuls (Turks) ruled for the remainder of the period building mosques, citadels, palaces, and bridges with distinctive Islamic influences though they differed from region to region as the style synthesized with regional aesthetic tastes, metal-working achieved new heights as iron, bronze, gold, silver, copper, brass were cast and alloys, enamelling, and inlaying techniques were developed—see the following works:

"Hindu Deities Krishna   c. 1780 A.D.
       and Radha in a Grove"   painting
Kesava Temple   15th century A.D.
       Somnathpur, India
The Taj Mahal   1632–1654 A.D.
       Moslem   Agra, India

5

JAPAN

Prehistoric or Jomon Periods   c. 10,000 B.C.–200 B.C.

Japan at this time is connected to the Chinese mainland. Artifacts include: cord-marked earthenware called jomon doki, statuettes in latter Jomon periods, skillfully crafted stone tools

Yayoi Period   c. 200 B.C.–200 A.D.

agriculture developed, bronze and iron casting learned from Koreans, potter's wheel imported from Korea, large ornate bells called dotaku produced, the restraint feature found in Japanese art began during this period

Tumulus or
Civilization of the Grave Mounds   c. 200 A.D.–500 A.D.

noted for large burial mounds, ceramic figurines used to decorate burial sites, and decorative jewelry

Asuka or Suiko Period   538–645 A.D.

clan that consolidated power became the Imperial family that continues to rule Japan today, Buddhism first became tolerated and then practiced along side the native religion Shintoism, statues of Buddha break with previous artistic traditions

Nara Period   645–793 A.D.

period marked by increasing influence of Chinese culture including the structuring of court life and government, used glaze on pottery for the first time, oldest anthology of poems collected and history books written, largest statue in the world ever produced using the lost wax technique is made

Heian Period (classical period)   794–1185 A.D.

the emperor established Kyoto as the capital of Japan but also of art and literature, Chinese influence on Japanese culture begins to wane

Kamakura Period   1185–1333 A.D.

period began with clan wars leading to the establishment of a military government or shogunate, Kublai Khan twice failed to conquer Japan, power and wealth of the aristocracy decreased as the warrior samurai and merchants gained influence, Zen Buddhism with its sense of the aesthetic began to influence art and life, period ended when war again broke out between feudal lords

Unkei	sculptor	died—1208 A.D.
Tankei	sculptor	c. 1173–1256 A.D.
Fujiwara		
Takanobu	painter	1142–1205 A.D.

Muromachi Period   1333–1573 A.D.

peace eventually returned, relations with China improved after the Ming court overthrew the Mongols, the Golden Pavilion and Silver Pavilion were built at Kyoto, a Portuguese ship wrecked off the Japanese coast in 1543 followed by the arrival of the Spanish who introduced firearms and Catholicism

Goshin	painter	active 1334–1349 A.D.
Mokuan Reien	painter	died-1345 A.D.
Gyokuen Bompo	painter	c. 1347–1420 A.D.
Gukei	painter	active 1361–1375 A.D.
Sesshu Toyo	painter	1420–1506 A.D.
Shubun	painter	active 1423–1460 A.D.
Shokei Tenyu	painter	active 1436–1465 A.D.
Sesson Shukei	painter	c. 1504–1589 A.D.
Kano Eitoku	painter	1543–1590 A.D.

Momoyama Period   1573–1614 A.D.

Portuguese and Spanish were thrown out of Japan while less politically threatening Europeans continued to be welcomed, raku ware is invented by Chojiro, landscape and scroll painting dominate Japanese art

Tanaka Chojiro	painter	1516–1592 A.D.
Kaiho Yusho	painter	1533–1615 A.D.
Hasegawa Tohaku	painter	1539–1610 A.D.
Furuta Oribe	potter	1543–1615 A.D.
Hon'ami Koetsu	metalsmith/ potter	1558–1637 A.D.
Kano Sanraku	painter	1559–1635 A.D.

Edo Period   1614–1868 A.D.

shoguns established a stable and relatively modern style of government, Christians were persecuted, no one was allowed to enter or leave the country until American Commodore Perry arrived with his battle ships, interest in Kabuki theater increased

Kano Naganobu	painter	1577–1654 A.D.
Kano Tanyu	painter	1602–1674 A.D.
Enku	sculptor	1628–1695 A.D.
Ogata Korin	painter	1658–1716 A.D.
Ogata Kenzan	potter	1663–1743 A.D.
Hakuin Ekaku	painter	1685–1768 A.D.

5

Yosa Buson	painter	1716–1783 A.D.
Ito Jakuchu	painter	1716–1800 A.D.
Ikeno Taiga	painter	1723–1776 A.D.
Suzuki Harunobu	printmaker	1724–1770 A.D.
Maruyama Okyo	painter	1733–1795 A.D.
Uragami Gyokudo	painter	1745–1820 A.D.
Gibon Sengai	painter	1750–1837 A.D.
Nagasawa Rosetsu	painter	1754–1799 A.D.
Kitagawa Utamaro	printmaker	1754–1806 A.D.
Katsushika Hokusai	printmaker	1760–1849 A.D.
Aoki Mokubei	painter	1767–1833 A.D.
Sharaku	printmaker	active 1794–1795 A.D.
Ando Hiroshige	printmaker	1797–1858 A.D.

Meiji Era   1868–1912 A.D.

capital of Japan was moved from Kyoto to Edo by the emperor and renamed Tokyo, a centralized and modern government was established, and schools of Western science and literature were started

Kuroda Seiki	painter	1866–1924 A.D.
Hishida Shunso	painter	1874–1910 A.D.
Kobayashi Kokei	painter	1883–1957 A.D.
Maeda Seison	painter	1885–1977 A.D.
Fukuda Heihachiro	painter	1892–1972 A.D.
Tokuoko Shinsen	painter	1896–1972 A.D.
Munakata Shiko	printmaker	1908–1975 A.D.
Yagi Kazuo	potter	1919–1979 A.D.
Nagare Masayuki	sculptor	1923– A.D.
Kan Makiko	painter	1933– A.D.

6 ART EDUCATION DICTIONARY

A

Abstract, Abstraction To think of something apart from the object itself. The underlying relational structure or form of an idea or object. In art, abstraction generally means identifying and representing the form of objects through rearranging or simplifying the subject. The artist may begin with a preconceived notion about artistic or expressive organization, or about the ways we perceive experience, and impose such order on the objects of perception.

Abstract/Implied Texture The artist creates the illusion of natural texture in an image, or observes texture in nature and alters it to suit his expressive needs.

Academic Artistic production that is rule-governed, functioning within accepted standards of organization and taste.

Acceleration The policy of placing gifted or talented students, whose academic performance excels in comparison to the performance of their chronological peers, in more advanced and challenging learning situations.

Accent An aspect of an image or composition that grabs the attention of the observer—for example, value ranges, scale, psychological impact of subject, and so forth.

Achromatic The differences between darkness and lightness in the absence of color.

Actual Texture The real surface qualities of a material or object, either natural or created by the artist. Examples are wood grain, the surface of a painting created by an impasto technique, carved surfaces, and so forth.

Additive Processes A sculptural process that involves the modeling, casting, or assembling of materials; the artist builds up form by adding materials.

Administration Supervisory personnel in charge of overseeing the operation of a museum or school. Responsibilities may include managing custodial, secretarial, counseling, as well as teaching staff; overseeing scheduling, budgeting, and public relations.

Aesthetics Traditionally, the philosophical contemplation and study of beauty in art and nature. The term was first used by the German philosopher Alexander Gottlieb Baumgarten in the mid-eighteenth century. Today a distinction is made between philosophical versus scientific aesthetics. Philosophical aesthetics defines art, the aesthetic experience, what it means to have an aesthetic attitude, and the validity of criteria used to judge quality in works of art. Scientific aesthetics approaches art from psychological, sociological, and anthropological points of view; in other words, the relationship of art to culture (religion, politics, economics, concepts of morality, science).

Allegorical Images that tell a story in which people, things, and events have symbolic meaning; often didactic, or morally instructive. During the Renaissance, allegorical art often focused on Scripture or classical mythology.

Amorphous Having vague, indistinct, or indefinite form.

Analogous Colors Colors that share common hues and are in close proximity to each other on the color wheel; for example, red-orange, orange, and yellow-orange.

Appropriation To steal or adopt subject matter, style, historical references, cultural references, or a "look" in a work of art. Images that are about images, or ideas, or culture itself. By appropriating from other sources, issues of context and creativity may be raised.

Approximate Symmetry Image has a central axis and appears to almost be symmetrical, with each half of the image being very similar yet varied enough to be more interesting to look at than a symmetrically arranged composition.

Art Specialist A person certified to teach or supervise the visual arts.

Art Supervisor Specialists in art curriculum and instruction, whose responsibilities include leadership and supervision of a district's art program.

Artificial Texture Surface texture created by the artist, not by nature; for example, a carved surface rather than the natural grain of wood or stone.

Assessment A systematic, formative process for determining whether or not learning is taking place. The process is used to inform both student and teacher and to aid in setting individual learning goals and objectives for the student.

Asymmetrical Balance Visual elements and objects in an image are not organized and repeated around a central axis to achieve balance. Instead, the objects and elements are placed in varying positions within the pictorial field to create a sense of compositional balance.

Atectonic A quality in three-dimensional work that frequently extends form into space to create a sense of openness; the opposite of tectonic.

Atmospheric (Aerial) Perspective A technique in pictorial imagery that creates the illusion of deep space by softening contours, diminishing the intensity of colors and details, and lightening values and the contrasts between them as objects appear to recede into space.

Authentic Assessment The use of process folios, self-reflective logs, and portfolios to assess learning. Both formative and summative, authentic assessment implies that the way student learning has been assessed in the past is too narrow in what it measures and is therefore false and misleading.

Autism A little-understood condition defined as absorption in fantasy to the exclusion of interest in reality; extreme withdrawal.

B

Balance A sense of equilibrium among the visual elements in the composition of a work of art. Balance in visual weight gives an image a feeling of organic unity and order.

Bauhaus A influential design school in Germany that thrived and prospered between World Wars I and II. Founded by Walter Gropius and based on the premise that the quality of life would be enhanced by infusing concern for the aesthetic into all aspects of design, architecture, and art, the school believed that learning would be enhanced if students worked side by side with artists, craftsmen, architects, and designers.

Behavioral Disorders Psychotic, neurotic, and personality dysfunctions.

Behavioral Objectives With roots in behavioral psychology, proponents argue that teachers cannot see what is going on inside a student's head; therefore, learning objectives should be stated in behavioral terms, or outward "behaviors," that will serve as indicators that the student understands the material at hand and is able to perform related tasks. Most behavioral objectives begin with the statement, "The student will...."

Biomorphic Shape The opposite of geometric/man-made shapes; irregular shapes with free-flowing curves that resemble those found in natural, living organisms.

Body Image Awareness of one's own physical self.

6

C

Calligraphy Writing as an art form. Writing exemplified by flowing, rhythmical lines, reflecting a particular style and the personality of the writer. Characters created with a brush in Oriental cultures. *Shu* is the Chinese word for writing, which translates as "the brush that speaks."

Casting A sculptural technique in which molten material is poured into pre-shaped molds and allowed to harden. When the mold is removed, the formerly liquid material has taken on the shape created by the mold.

Cast Shadow The darkened shape on a surface created by an object, located between that surface and the light source, which prevents the light from directly hitting the surface behind the object.

Chiaroscuro A technique used to create the illusion of three-dimensionality of objects and their placement in space or atmosphere in a two-dimensional image, by blending and bleeding light and shade on objects.

Chromatic Of color or having colors.

Classical Rooted in ideas from the "Golden Age" of Greece (fifth to the fourth centuries B.C.), works of music, literature, and art that are characterized as intellectual, rational, idealistic, and controlled. A model or prototype of first rank. Throughout the history of Western civilization, there have been movements that reflected on and adhered to the principles of Greek culture—for example, Roman classicism, Renaissance classicism, and neoclassicism in the nineteenth century. U.S. government buildings, monuments, libraries, and museums reflect classical style.

Closure The tendency to stabilize, close, or complete a behavior or mental situation. A Gestalt concept that correlates with wholeness and unity in artistic composition.

Clustering An associative search strategy that facilitates metaphoric interpretation in literature and art. The process requires the viewer to quickly identify intuitive impressions from the work, group or cluster them, and then build evidence to accept or reject them as legitimate interpretations of meaning.

Cognitive Style An individual's approach to problem solving and other mental tasks.

Collage A medium in which found materials are used in, or to create, an image.

Color The property of light reflected off a surface in the form of a particular visible wave length and perceived as a hue in the spectrum; that is, red, orange, yellow, green, blue, indigo, and violet.

Color Tonality Refers to color schemes or color combinations involving hue, value, and intensity relationships.

Color Triad A grouping of three colors placed at equal distances from each other on the color wheel; for example, primary colors, secondary colors, and tertiary colors.

Complementary Colors Two colors that contrast most sharply with each other; colors located directly opposite each other on the color wheel. For example, a primary color's complementary is a secondary color made up of the remaining two primary colors.

Composition Order and unity within the arrangement of objects and visual elements in an image. While subjects or elements may have characteristics that attract interest, they are subordinate to the organization of the whole image; the whole is greater than the sum of its parts.

Concept An idea or general notion.

Conceptual Art While all art is conceptually based, conceptual art of the late 1960s and 1970s placed primary emphasis on ideas over form, rejecting the modernist emphasis on form and formalism. In its extreme, works or events were conceived of in the mind of the artist and presented as a concept without ever achieving visual form.

Content Opposite of a work of art's objective, visual-physical form; content refers to the significance, meanings, and values of a work of art; what is known or felt in a piece; what is interpreted; the psychological, sensory, emotional, and metaphorical properties of the work.

Context A concept related to content and meaning in works of art. The meaning of a work of art cannot be entirely understood or revealed if the work is experienced in isolation; the work must be seen and interpreted in relation (or context) to the culture in which it was produced, the prominent ideas in the history of art when the work was made, and in its mode of expression, style, medium, and so on.

Contour The outer edge or "outline" of a perceived shape. Often distinguished by line, contour can also be defined through variations or extremes of value, texture, color, or mass.

Craftsmanship The aptitude and skillful ability to use materials and tools. Characterized by an attitude of, and concern for, quality.

Criterion-Based Evaluation Standards on which the judgment of success in a learning situation will be based. Criteria are used when exact answers and solutions to problems are not possible, such as studio art activities. The teacher establishes expectations and measures of success and students are informed of the criteria at the outset of the lesson so they may organize their work based on their personal learning styles.

Cross-Contour Lines that create the illusion of surface undulations within shapes or objects in an image; for example, in the paintings of Bridget Riley.

Cubism An artistic style in which three-dimensional objects are rendered on a flat, two-dimensional surface by collapsing the middle-ground in the image; foreground and background meld. Founded by Picasso and Braque in 1908, the style is characterized by geometric and cubelike shapes, often showing several views of the subject in one image. An abstract style of art; emphasis on the structure of form and the concept of how we perceive and reconstruct it on a flat surface. Cool and analytical, non-expressionistic.

Curvilinear Imagery and form composed of curved lines rather than straight, rectilinear lines. Associated more with organic forms and expressionistic styles of art.

6

D

Dada Literally meaning "Hobbyhorse;" an attitude in art, rather than a style, Dada began in 1916 and expressed through absurd and outrageous images and actions the social, political, and psychological trauma brought on by World War I. Declaring art to be dead, Dadaists contradictorally created nihilistic, antiart, antirational, anti-everything works and performances. Although a short-lived, self-destructive movement, it was a forerunner and generating force for surrealism.

Deconstructionism Works of art that appear to emphasize content and meaning, yet levels and shades of meaning are intervalidated or are intercut by distinctive oppositions. The resulting experience of the work is one of ambiguousness and disruptive paradoxicality.

Decorative The embellishment of functional objects with aesthetic qualities. Generally associated with the applied arts—that is, ceramics, furniture, glass, and so forth.

Description A stage in some approaches to the process of criticism in which the viewer takes a "visual inventory" of what is seen in the work of art and formulates an objective statement grounded in that thoughtful observation. Based on what is physically present in the work, other viewers should be able to arrive at the same conclusions. Description can include type of media, dimensions, physical condition, subjects and objects in work, and so on. This stage in the critical process is intended to slow down observation and to delay interpretation and judgments of quality until the viewer has adequately built up enough evidence to draw such conclusions.

Design Often used synonymously with form and composition; the rule-governed, underlying structure or organization of an image. Usually presented in terms of elements of design: line, shape, texture, color, value, and so on; and principles of design: balance, repetition and rhythm, scale, and proportion.

Discipline-Based Art Education An approach to teaching art that emphasizes art as a subject worthy of study, not as a handmaiden to other goals. Referred to as a "subject-centered" approach rather than a "child-centered" or "therapeutic" approach advocated by Lowenfeld, proponents argue that art should be taught from the varying perspectives of the four art disciplines: art history, art criticism, art production, and aesthetics.

Distortion In the translation of visually perceived objects into a rendered image, the artist alters the visual appearance of the objects by changing their general characteristics, size, or position. While certain styles of work rely heavily on distortion for expressive purposes, all works of art naturally employ a degree of distortion, highlighting its relativity.

Domain Projects Defined in Arts PRO-PEL as long-term sustained projects that focus on a particular central concept, theme, or problem. Domain projects always interrelate production, perception, and reflection.

Dominance A principle of art relevant to both objective and nonobjective work, which assumes that certain elements within a composition will be more important and receive more emphasis while all others in the image become subordinate to them.

E

Elements of Art/Design The visual building materials of an image. When assembled into a whole using the rules of composition (see Principles of Art/Design), a coherent idea can be communicated or expressed. The basic elements of line, color, value, shape, texture, mass, and volume are often referred to as the "visual language" of the artist.

Empathy The ability to intellectually or emotionally identify with another's plight or experience. The ability to sense how another must feel; "Walk a mile in my shoes." Works of art require the viewer to respond empathically.

Evaluation The process of forming qualitative judgments about how well a student's art product satisfies a set of pre-established criteria.

Expression A term that reflects the way art "communicates." Rather than communicating objective facts as words do, art expresses emotions, values, sensual feelings, and intellectual ideas through visual form and metaphorical content. To "receive" such a communication requires more than just seeing the message and comprehending its meaning; the viewer must empathical-ly experience (see empathy) the work of art.

Expressionism While it can be used as a general, descriptive term, it usually refers to specific kinds of twentieth-century movements in art—that is, German expressionism, abstract expressionism, and neoexpressionism.

Expressionistic Art Imagery that is created to convey emotion and what is felt, rather than work that is meant to represent what is perceived or reasoned. Usually characterized by distortion and exaggeration, bold colors and gestures, and movement; for example, spirit masks, Michelangelo's Sistine Chapel, works by El Greco, Goya, Delacroix, van Gogh, and styles of expressionism.

F

Fantasy (in works of art) Imagery that depicts parallel realities; not limited to a particular style or period in time and often linked with images from the unconscious and/or processes of free association; for example, Hieronymous Bosch, Michelangelo's visions of God, and the works of Dali and Magritte.

Fauvism An expressionistic style of art that began around 1905 in Paris. Meaning literally "Wild Beasts," fauvist imagery used colors expressively and somewhat decoratively, rather than imitatively.

Figure-Ground Perception The ability to distinguish the important from the unimportant; to be able to focus on an object of perception without distraction.

6

Form Generally used to refer to the overall composition or organization of a work of art; the "whole-ness" of the image as more than a sum of its parts or elements; what visually holds the image together into a coherent whole. *Form* is occasionally used to label the three-dimensional equivalent to the two-dimensional element, *shape.*

Formal Refers to any process that is rule-governed or based on custom and tradition; an orderly, stable composition.

Formal Analysis An objective stage in the critical process in which the composition and organization of a work of art is dissected, examined, and described to determine how it is constituted; breaking down into parts to better understand the whole.

Formalism A philosophical position that established criteria for judging quality in works of art. Founded by Roger Fry and Clive Bell, it emphasized the analysis of form and the elements and principles of design over content or context, arguing that if content or subject matter exists in a work of art, it is because the form of the image serves as a vehicle for conveying such meanings. Popular during the twentieth century and in modernism, it provided consistent criteria that could be applied to works of art, at a time when change and rejection of the past was considered a sign of progress.

Fractional Representation A technique in which several spatial aspects of the same person or object are combined in the picture; for example, ancient Egyptian paintings, Cubism.

Futurism An international twentieth-century movement that began in Italy about 1909 and was founded by the writer F. T. Marinetti. It began as a literary movement whose ideas were quickly adopted by abstract artists. Influenced by the "look" of cubism, it rejected artistic conventions, believing that art should celebrate the energy, power, speed, simultaneity (the representation of successive phases of movement) and dynamism of the industrial age, science, and modern life. Futurists welcomed the approach of World War I.

G

Genre In general terms, work that is classified according to its subject matter—that is, still life, landscape, religious, portraiture, and so forth. More specifically, it refers to paintings that show scenes of daily domestic life, sentimental family scenes, and so on; for example, paintings by Pieter Bruegel (The Elder).

Geometric Shapes (forms) Mathematically based geometric shapes invented by human beings. Contrast with organic or amorphic.

Gestalt A psychological theory that emphasizes how human beings perceive and mentally process information. Proponents believe that people seek wholeness in the things they perceive and experience, and when they do not, their mind imposes closure on the experience. In the arts, formal properties of composition parallel the rules that Gestalt psychologists say govern perception; works of art are therefore models of human thought itself. The whole is greater than the sum of its parts.

Giftedness A term used to describe students who excell academically because of a high level of intelligence and the motivation to learn.

Glyptic A carved object. Also refers to the unique qualities of a particular art material that can be carved or engraved like stone, plaster, or wood. Can be used when alluding to a work of art that has retained the qualities unique to the material from which it is made.

Graphic Arts In general use, any two-dimensional image created from the use of elements of design: painting, drawing, printmaking. More specifically, refers to commercial art applications found in magazines, books, newspapers, and other printed materials.

H

Handicapping Conditions A term used to characterize students with physical, emotional, mental, or learning disabilities.

Happening A form of street theatre and an early form of *performance art*, happenings synthesized improvisation, planned events, found objects, audience participation, and composer John Cage's notions of chance. Influenced by early Dadaist performances, happenings first surfaced in the late 1950s and continued through the pop art movement of the 1960s.

Hard-Edge Painting Any abstract painting using sharply defined edges of shapes and flat color.

Harmony A pleasing combination of elements achieved through repetition of similar characteristics within a composition.

Hellenic A period in history dating from the beginning of the Iron Age in the late eleventh century B.C. to the end of the classical period in the fourth century B.C.

Hieroglyphic An ancient Egyptian form of picture writing in which each individual picture symbolizes a word or syllable.

High Art A term used to define works that aspire to elite aesthetic ideals, as opposed to folk or popular art, which is intended for consumption by the masses. Generally used to refer to Eurocentric art that hangs in galleries and art museums, versus art that serves a practical purpose as in art from "primitive" cultures.

High Renaissance A period in history (circa 1495–1520) during which Renaissance ideas reached their most sophisticated state, as exemplified in the works of Michelangelo, Leonardo da Vinci, and Raphael.

Highlight The area of an object within an image that receives the greatest amount of direct light.

Holography A form of photography that uses a laser beam to produce images that appear to be three-dimensional and can be viewed from varying angles and sides, just as one would view the object in the real world.

6

Hudson River School A group of painters who used the Catskill mountains and the Hudson River as their primary subject matter. Active during 1820 to 1850 and exemplified in the paintings of Frederick Church and Thomas Cole, the work captured the grandeur and power of the North American landscape.

Hue Used to designate the specific, visible electromagnetic wave length of a color found in a ray of natural light and its place in the spectrum or on the color wheel. The common name of a color; for example, red, yellow, green, and so on.

I

Icon Any Greek or Russian Orthodox painting of a religious nature, dating from the sixth century to the present, whose rendering is highly stylized following strict rules of representation. In a more generalized sense, the term can also be used to define images in contemporary culture that take on a life of their own, such as Andy Warhol's repetitive representations of Marilyn Monroe.

Iconography The systematic study of subject matter in works of art versus the study of style.

Iconology The interpretation of symbols and subject matter in works of art, based on the historical and cultural contexts in which they were created.

IEPs (See Individualized Education Program.)

Illumination The decorations and illustrations found primarily in medieval manuscripts, which were usually painted individually with tempera and gold leaf.

Illusionism Found in two-dimensional works that intend to "fool the eye" in the work's imitation of visual reality. Artist uses techniques of perspective, chiaroscuro, and so on. See Trompe-l'oeil.

Illustration Imagery that is generally associated with commercial purposes and is often intended to accompany and complement written text; imagery whose meaning is easily read. When the "look" of illustration is employed in a work of fine art, the meaning of the image is meant to be read in the context of the source material from which it is appropriated.

Image The concrete visual representation of a mentally envisioned idea; a visual impression of something as seen through a lens or reflected in a mirror.

Impasto A technique in painting in which the paint is applied in thick layers, creating actual texture on the surface of the image. From the Italian word for paste, the method is used by painters who are uninterested in creating realistic images; such artists want their actions on the surface of the painting to be evident and considered in the interpretation and experience of the work. Generally considered an expressionistic method of working.

Impression The immediate sensory impact on the mind of what is perceived; an indentation.

Impressionism A major art movement of the nineteenth century, often heralded as the beginning of modern art. Exhibiting for the first time in 1874, the impressionists applied new discoveries in physics about the properties of light, exposure to artworks from the Orient, and images created with the recently invented camera to a new attitude and style of work. Abandoning grandiose themes and subject matter rooted in antiquity, the impressionists chose to work out of doors with natural light to capture their immediate sensory impressions on easel-size canvases. Impressionist paintings are characterized by bold color and light applied with quick brush strokes of paint. The first impressionist exhibit included work by Monet, Renoir, Pissaro, Sisley, Cezanne, Degas, Guillaumin, Boudin, and the female artist Berthe Morisot.

Individualized Educational Program (IEP) Within the field of exceptional education, teachers annually develop an IEP for each special-need student. Because of the range of physical, emotional, and mental handicaps a group of children may have, each individual child must regularly be assessed on what they know and what they are capable of doing so that an individualized plan of instruction can be developed.

Infinite Space Resembling nature, space seems to recede endlessly into the background of the picture plane.

Intensity Refers to the brightness or saturation of a color produced by the quality of light reflecting from it; the absence of gray, black, or white from the color; bright colors have high intensity, and dull colors are of low intensity.

International Style A style of architecture that originated in Europe in the 1920s and was based on the ideas of Mies van der Rohe and Le Corbusier,

who later abandoned the style in favor of a more organic approach to design. Decorative ornamentation was abandoned in favor of modernist ideas about purity of form. The idea dominating the movement was "form follows function," or designing a building from the inside out. The movement culminated in "modern" structures that appeared to be rectangular slabs of glass and steel, with little personality or livability.

Interpretation An aspect of the critical process in which the viewer attempts to arrive at an understanding of the meaning of a work of art. An interpretation may be based in part on any of the following: subject matter, theme, style, metaphor, historical and cultural contexts, artistic and psychological contexts, the context in which the work was meant to originally be seen, formal properties, and artistic intent. Interpretations may be personal or public (shared). However, if they are based on reflective thinking rather than personal preference or "gut reactions," they must be defendable based on collected "evidence" found within the works themselves, or evidence that is external to them but shown to be relevant for framing an understanding of the works.

Intuitive Space The illusion of space in a two-dimensional image based on the artist's instinctual use of space-producing devices such as overlapping, receding planes, diminishing sizes, and colors that become less and less saturated as objects recede into the background.

Invented (Implied) Texture Visual texture invented by the artist that is to be read with the eyes rather than tactilely, or through physical touch. Created by repeating lines, colors, shapes or values, it can be used in an illusionary way to look like an actual texture like wood grain. The opposite of invented texture would be the actual texture of materials, or texture created by the artist; for example, carving, impasto, and so on.

Ironic Characteristic of many postmodern works in which the intended meanings of the subject matter are the opposite of their usual or expected sense.

J

Japonisme A term used to refer to Japanese influences on European art, particularly impressionism and postimpressionism.

Judgment A culminating activity in the critical process, judgment involves determining the value of a work of art, establishing its rank and worth among other works of its kind, and/or assessing whether or not the artist succeeded in achieving her intent.

K

Keystone The central wedge-shaped stone in an arch.

Kinaesthetic Art Art that arouses physical as well as visual sensations in the viewer.

Kinetic Art Any art which incorporates movement or the illusion of move-

ment. The work can be mechanized, as in some of the sculpture of Claes Oldenberg; it can rely on wind, as in the mobiles of Alexander Calder; or, in the case of painting, give the impression of movement through optical techniques, as in the work of Bridget Riley.

Kitsch Mass-produced art and artifacts of popular consumer culture that are naive or that poke fun at or ignore standards of good aesthetic taste. They are often so ugly and of such poor taste that they become collectible metaphors of contemporary society.

Kouros A sculpture of a nude youth representing either a god or victorious athlete. Generally associated with the archaic period in Greek art (circa 620–500 B.C.).

Krater An Ancient Greek vase used to mix water and wine.

L

Lesson Plan A written outline of what will be taught in a given class session. A lesson plan is usually one in a series or units of lessons, arranged in sequential fashion, and will include the goals, objectives, materials, procedures, methods of assessment, and possibilities for extending learning into other areas.

Line A mark left by a moving point. Generally produced by a pencil, pen, or brush, line is most commonly used to define and outline the contours of shapes within an image. The simplest element of design.

Linear Perspective (See Perspective.)

Linocut A relief print made from a wood-mounted piece of linoleum with an image gouged into it.

Lintel A horizontal piece of stone or wood resting on two posts to form a door or window and to support the wall above.

Lithography A method of printmaking based on the principle that oil and water do not mix. The artist draws an image on a ground stone surface or zinc plate with a grease pencil. The stone or plate is then treated so that the nondrawn areas of the surface will be water-loving, and the drawn areas of the image will be oil-loving. During the printing process, the stone or plate is continually moistened with water to resist the oil-based ink; thus, the ink only adheres to the original drawn areas of the image. Paper is then placed on the stone or plate and run through a press, transferring the inked areas onto the paper.

Local (Objective) Color The natural color of objects in daylight as perceived by the eye; for example, the red of a male cardinal, blue sky, white snow, and so on.

Local Value The degree of light or darkness as seen on an actual surface that is determined by its particular pigmentation.

M

Mass The actual physical bulk of a solid, three-dimensional object. In two-dimensional imagery, an object or form that appears to have physical bulk.

Medium, Media The actual material(s) and tool(s) from which images and artifacts are created. The term "media" is also used to specify artistic endeavors created electronically—that is, using video, computer-generated images, film, and so on.

Metaphor The use of one thing as if it were another. Both a product and a process of thought, metaphors are nonliteral symbols that serve as vehicles of meaning in literature and in the visual arts. They make possible the layering of meaning in works of art and enable the artist to condense and vivify the expression of ideas and experience.

Mobile A term first used in 1932 by Marcel Duchamp to describe the work of Alexander Calder, it refers to sculpture that employs movement by harnessing wind currents or mechanization. The form of the work is in constant flux and change, as shapes and patterns continually shift into new relationships.

Modeling The creation of a three-dimensional form; in two-dimensional imagery, the illusion of form is created by building up gradations of lights and darks; in three-dimensional work, a form is produced by shaping or carving pliable materials.

Motif While it can be used to refer to the subject of a painting, *motif* is generally used in reference to a distinct or dominant element in the design of a building, pattern, painting, or sculpture; for example, the art nouveau motif in the terra cotta facade of a Louis Sullivan–designed building.

6

N

Narrative Art Work that tells a story or appears to represent a moment in a series of events. Historically and contemporarily produced for a variety of purposes—for example, to interpret or teach religious stories and events; as propaganda in the case of socialist realism or Nazi art; to recreate ironic experiences or moments in time through the appropriation of images found in particular cultural contexts.

Naturalism Often considered synonymous with realism, it is an attitude or approach to art in which the artist's only intentions are to descriptively represent things visually experienced. This intention actually differs from *realism*, in which the artist may be questioning or expressing universal meanings or truths.

Natural Textures Surface textures that are inherent to a material or object or are created through natural processes.

Negative Shapes In sculpture, the areas that are absent of form or material; in imagery, the negative shapes are the empty space left after the positive shapes have been established. Because the negative space is bound by positive shapes or forms, it, too, functions as a shape in an image. In Gestalt terms of figure-ground relationships, the positive shapes are the figure, and the negative shapes are the ground.

Neoexpressionism A postmodern classification of works that contain much emotion and symbolism, sometimes unconventional media, and often using intense colors and turbulent composition. Many artists working in this mode talk of social expression rather than personal expression.

Neutralized Color A color whose saturation or intensity has been reduced, giving it a dulled or grayed appearance. A color is neutralized by mixing it with a neutral color or the color's complimentary.

Neutrals Surface hues that do not reflect one particular color or wave length of light, only a sense of darkness or light. White, black, and the range of grays in between them are considered neutral colors.

Nonobjective Art work that contains no recognizable subject matter. Image or object is created by manipulating formal properties and materials to express ideas and/or feelings. For examples, see the work of Robert Motherwell and Mark Rothko.

Nonrepresentational Imagery Objects whose appearance does not look like or resemble any actual object or thing; the opposite of representational. See abstraction and nonobjective.

O

Objective Something that exists as an object or fact; an unbiased, nonprejudicial statement devoid of emotion or feelings. In art, the artist precisely renders what is seen without altering or interpreting the image for expressive purposes. In education, an objective is a short term goal of instruction that includes (1) *conditions*, the environmental and educational conditions under which the student will be expected to perform; (2) *performance,* or what specifically the student will do to demonstrate that learning has taken place; and (3) *criteria,* or what the teacher will specifically look for in order to assess whether or not the students have learned and to judge the level of their mastery.

Optical Perception A way of seeing in which the mind and eye perform their natural function, that of providing visual sensation for object recognition. This form of perception is most evident in the work of realists. An alternative form of artistic seeing is *conceptual perception,* in which the artist interjects imagination and creative vision into the act of perceiving.

Organic Unity A work of art in which each isolated part of the image is so integral and interdependent with the whole that the work resembles or is analogous to a living organism. Also referred to as living form.

Organizational Control Predetermined or specific relationships of the art elements in pictorial space.

Orthographic Drawing Used by architects and drafters, a graphic representation of an object which includes a plan, a vertical elevation, and/or a section.

Outcomes-Based Education A shift in philosophical attitude from an emphasis on behavioral objectives and minimal standards of performance to an emphasis on identifying levels of performance excellence within subject-matter disciplines and helping students achieve mastery, or working to their full potential.

P

Painterly A method or style of painting in which the surface texture of the paint is obvious and integral to the expressive meaning of the work. The artist wants the viewer to be aware of his actions on the surface of the painting and to take such activity into consideration when experiencing the work.

Papier Collé A form of collage in which papers of various textures and patterns, such as the printed surface of a newspaper, are pasted to the surface of an image.

Papier Maché Paper pulp mixed with wheat paste or glue and sometimes chalk or sand. The pulp is a flexible material that can be cast or shaped and then baked or left to dry in the open air. During the eighteenth and nineteenth centuries, it was frequently used for decorative objects and small pieces of furniture.

Patina A film, usually green or brown, that appears on the surface of certain metals like bronze or brass as a result of oxidation. Can be used to refer to any pleasing change to surface color or texture as a result of age, use, or exposure to elements.

Pattern The recognizable repetition or combination of elements within the composition of an image.

Perception The active response to sensory experience. More than just seeing or hearing, perception engages the physical and mental faculties in recognizing objects and experiences, judging their qualities, and selecting what is important about them to notice and focus

6

on. The senses are extensions of the brain and serve as its receptors, taking in information for the brain to sort and process. Perception is the initial stage of human thought, and the arts, which are created to arouse and appeal to the senses, therefore become models of human thought itself. Perception also becomes an important issue in the viewing and experiencing of art, because how one perceives is often as important as what one perceives.

Perspective The creation of the illusion of three-dimensional objects and space on a flat, two-dimensional surface. Simple perspective uses the overlapping of objects, the placement of distant objects higher on the page, and diminishing size as basic illusionistic tools. More sophisticated forms of perspective are rule-governed and include (1) *linear perspective,* which uses lines drawn from one or more vanishing points on the horizon line to establish the size and position of objects as they recede into the imaginary distance in the picture; and (2) *aerial or atmospheric perspective,* which uses gradations of color, value, and texture to suggest the distancing of objects (that is, the further into the picture plane an object recedes, the less detailed and the more distorted the color and values become because of moisture, dust, pollutants, and so on, in the "atmosphere").

Photogram A photograph produced not with a camera, but by placing objects on photographic paper and exposing the paper to light, creating ghostly images of the objects on the paper. The process was used by Man Ray and Moholy-Nagy in the 1920s and 1930s.

Photomontage An image created of overlapping photographic images and/or photographic fragments cut and pasted onto a pictorial area. See also *collage.*

Photorealism A painting whose subject matter is a photographic image. At a glance, the viewer can be fooled into thinking she is observing a carefully rendered image of the real world. However, under closer scrutiny, the rendering will appear too precise and mechanical. By painting not what one perceives of the real world but rather a photograph, which is once removed from reality, the photorealist challenges the viewer's interpretation of what is real. Also known as *Superrealism.*

Piazza A large, open space in Italian cities, often at the historic center of the city and surrounded by buildings.

Pictograph A highly simplified symbol of an object or action.

Pictorial Area The area on a surface in which an image exists. Usually bound by a mat, frame, line, or the edge of the material on which the image is created.

Picture Plane The actual surface of a canvas or paper on which the artist works. In images that contain the illusion of depth, the imaginary picture plane serves as a plane of reference, or window, through which the viewer looks to perceive the illusory three-dimensionality of the image.

Pier A free-standing rectangular pillar supporting an arch, the span of a bridge, and so on.

Pieta An image or sculpture in which the dead Christ is portrayed in the arms of the Virgin Mary, his mother. The representation was first used in Germany in the fourteenth century.

Pigments A coloring agent, usually ground into a powder, that is mixed with a liquid vehicle such as oil and turpentine, to produce paint and dyes.

Pilaster Usually ornamental, not structural, a rectangular pier incorporated into a wall and projecting slightly from the surface.

Pillar A free-standing upright used in architecture. Usually functional as well as decorative.

Planar Having to do with planes. See planes.

Plane A surface shape that is two-dimensional, having height and width.

Planography Any method of printmaking where a print is produced by transferring an image from a flat surface, such as a plate or stone, onto paper; for example, see lithography.

Plastic Arts The arts produced by modeling and building three-dimensional form; that is, architecture, sculpture, and ceramics.

Pointillism A style of painting that stimulates the optical mixing of colors. Rather than mixing various colors on a palate before applying the paint to an image, the artist systematically applies raw color to the painting in small dabs, requiring the "eye" of the viewer to blend the colors. Also known as divisionism, the style was used by Neoimpressionist Georges Seurat.

Polyptych A painting made up of a number of smaller panels fastened or hinged together.

Pop Art A movement in art that began in the 1950s in England and America and dominated the art world in the early 1960s, it was a reaction against the highly personal style of abstract expressionism. Using the products and "look" of mass culture and consumerism as its subject matter and theme, with its roots in Dadaist absurdity and performance (happenings), pop art reflected the festive and ironic nature of contemporary life. See the work of Richard Hamilton, Andy Warhol, Robert Rauschenberg, James Rosenquist, Claes Oldenberg, Jasper Johns, and Larry Rivers.

Portfolio In general use, a collection of an artist's best work, demonstrating the range and depth of her capabilities. Evidence of a concern for the quality of the packaging and presentation of one's portfolio is an important consideration. In educational assessment, a final portfolio at the end of the school year is assembled from the student's process folio, reflective log, and sketchbooks and will include not only the child's best work but also works that served as landmarks or turning points in his understanding of the subject matter. When the next school year begins, the portfolio from the previous year is reviewed as a starting point for the new year's learning. See Process Folio and Reflective Logs.

Portico Adopted from classical temples, a roof supported by columns that protrudes from the front or side of a building.

Positive Shapes The shapes in an image that make up the objects and subject matter, and they occupy space. They

6

are the "figure" in figure-ground (fore-ground-background) relationships.

Postimpressionism A term first used by artist and critic Roger Fry in 1914 to refer to European artists whose work was influenced by, but had developed beyond, impressionism. Although the work was very diverse, two general styles evolved that dominated Western art into the mid-twentieth century: expressionism, reflected in the works of Van Gogh and Gauguin; and formalism or abstractionism, exemplified in the works of Cézanne and Seurat.

Postmodernism First used in an architectural context in 1949 by Joseph Hudnut and later by Charles Jencks, the term refers to an attitude or trend in art, architecture, and culture that attempts to modify and expand on modernist ideas; it accepts all that modernism rejected. Whereas modernism made distinctions between high art and popular taste, postmodernism makes no such value judgments. Whereas modernism was dominated by formalist ideals, postmodernism places emphasis on content and the search for meaning, often in ironic ways. In architecture it rejects the cold, boring adaptations of the "international style" in favor of a more eclectic, imaginative approach that appropriates from vernacular, classical, and commercial styles. In the other visual arts, "po-mo" is characterized by an acceptance and appropriation of all periods and styles, including modernism.

Post-Painterly Abstraction The label invented by art critic Clement

Greenberg to describe work exemplified by large fields of color that lacked any evidence of painterly brush strokes. Sometimes used interchangeably with the term *color-field painting*, it most precisely refers to paintings by artists like Ellsworth Kelly, Kenneth Noland, and Morris Louis that Greenberg associated with the movement.

Pouncing A technique used by artists over the centuries (for example, Michelangelo on the Sistine Chapel ceiling) to transfer images from one surface to another. An initial drawing or sketch is done on a sheet of paper. The artist then punches holes in the outlines of the drawing, lays the sketch over the surface on which the image is to be copied, then pats finely powdered chalk or graphite through the holes in the sketch, transferring the outline onto the underlying surface.

Precisionist Painters An American school of painters whose subject matter was architectural motifs and industrial scenes that were devoid of human reference. The representational imagery appeared almost abstract because of the simple, straightforward, and formal qualities in the work. Beginning about 1915, the school included Charles Demuth, Georgia O'Keefe, and Charles Sheeler.

Pre-Columbian Artifacts produced by people in the Americas before the arrival of Columbus in 1492.

Primary Colors The foundation hues from which all other colors are derived; colors that cannot be produced by a mixture of pigments. In painting, the primaries (additive) are red, yellow, and blue; in printing, the primaries (subtractive) are magenta, cyan, and yellow.

Priming A sealer applied to canvas or panel to protect it before the final painting, usually a neutral-colored paint.

Primitive Traditionally used to refer to art work by people from tribal social origins or a Neolithic stage of culture; however, the use of "primitive" in this context is today considered derogatory and not widely utilized. The term can also be used to refer to work whose style appears to be unsophisticated, untrained, or naive, such as the paintings of Henri Rousseau.

Primitivism A Russian art movement (1905–1920) headed by Malevich and Goncharova which integrated concepts from futurism and cubism with themes and subject matter from Russian folk art. The term can also be used generically to refer to any art work that appears primitive.

Print An image produced in multiple copies from a plate, stone, block, screen, or photographic negative.

Process Art A movement in the mid-1960s and 1970s that included Richard Serra and Robert Morris in which the process of creation served as subject matter, and viewers were encouraged to reconstruct what had been done by the artist through the evidence provided for them.

Process Folio Used in authentic or portfolio assessment, the process folio is an integral part of the curriculum. It is a working portfolio that the child uses on a day-to-day basis and includes preliminary sketches, reflective logs, and work in progress. It is added to and deleted from as the school year progresses and requires active participation and reflection from the child, as it shifts responsibility for learning from the teacher to the student. At the end of the school year, the student reviews and reflects on the contents of the process folio and assembles a final portfolio that summarizes her learning for the year. See Reflective Logs and Portfolio.

Proof A trial printing of an image from a plate, block, or photographic negative to determine the quality of the image so that final adjustments, including composition, can be made before multiple copies are produced.

Proportion A formal principle of design, *proportion* refers to the size relationships of objects and elements within an image.

Pugging The process of kneading clay to eliminate air bubbles and to insure that all ingredients are consistently and evenly mixed.

Pyramidal Composition A traditional form of composing an image in which the subject matter fills the volume of an imaginary pyramid. Raphael used this method of organization to create a solid, stable composition.

6

R

Raku A form of pottery of irregular shape and texture that originated in Japan about 1580 and continues in popularity today. The pot is fired at a low temperature and covered with a thick lead glaze that is usually dark in hue. The firing is often done in a pit dug into the ground.

Ready-Made The practice of taking an everyday object, changing the context in which it is experienced, and declaring it a work of art. The term was first used by Marcel Duchamp about 1913 and introduced the notion of "selection" as part of the artistic process, leading the way for the new mediums of collage and assemblage.

Realism Used generally to define art that attempts to reproduce the look of reality as accurately as possible. More specifically, realism was a style led by French artist Courbet in the early to mid-nineteenth century. Influenced by the invention of photography, the realists believed in capturing the dignity and beauty present in the daily routines of life. Courbet declared, "I cannot paint an angel because I have never seen one," choosing instead to portray the social and sensory experience around him. Realism was a forerunner of impressionism.

Reducing Atmosphere A process in the firing of ceramic pieces that causes copper-pigmented glazes to turn red or purple. The effect is achieved by creating a carbon-monoxide-rich environment (an oxidizing atmosphere) inside the kiln, often by using water-soaked wood as a fuel.

Reflected Color A change of hue created by color that is reflecting off one object onto another.

Reflective Logs An aspect of authentic assessment, reflective logs are journals kept by each individual student that require the student to think about what he is learning. Entries may be written at the end of each class session as a way for students to review not only what they have learned but also their thinking about it. Questions like "What was the most important thing I learned today?" and "Why was it the most important?" require the student to think about, and place in context, the things they are learning. Reflective logs may accompany, or be part of, a sketch book. See Portfolio and Process Folio.

Regionalism A group of American artists who rejected European or modern influences in art, choosing as their subject matter and inspiration, scenes, and experiences from the rural Midwest. Active during the 1930s and 1940s, many regionalists were involved in the WPA, federally funded projects that put artists to work painting murals in government buildings around the United States which depicted America's history and character. Prominent among them were Thomas Hart Benton and Grant Wood.

Relief A form of sculpture in which part or all of the composition projects from a flat surface. There are varying degrees of relief:

1. High relief—A relief sculpture in which the figures and objects are carved so deeply into the surface that they appear almost free-standing (*Alto rilievo*).
2. Bas-relief—Also referred to as low relief. The sculptural forms protrude less than half their actual depth from the surface (*Basso rilievo*).

3. Embossing—Sculptural forms rise only nominally from the surface (Anaglyph).

Relief Process Any printmaking method in which the image to be inked and printed is in relief, or raised, from the surface of the block or plate; for example, woodcuts, linoleum block.

Remediation The process of providing personalized assistance to students whose progress in a particular subject matter is lagging behind the performance of their peers.

Renaissance One of the great periods in the history of Western civilization, beginning in Italy in the fourteenth century and ending in approximately 1580, it marked the end of the Middle (or Dark) Ages. The period was inspired by a number of ideas and events: a rediscovery of the humanistic and scientific writings of the ancient Greeks and Romans, which inspired new inquiry; the development of the middle class, which put political power and wealth in the hands of people who before were powerless; the invention of the printing press, allowing for the wide distribution of the knowledge base, and, in turn, allowing for broad contributions to that base; and scientific, mathematic, and artistic discoveries that made navigation of the oceans and seas possible, exposing Europeans to diverse cultures and unknown worlds (the Americas).

The arts flourished during this period as wealthy patrons acquired power, providing sources of financial support apart from the Catholic church, which had previously been the sole patron of the arts and therefore had been able to control the kinds of imagery artists produced. As a result, artists were no longer content focusing only on the afterlife; art work now reflected an interest in the real world through the introduction of secular subject matter, an interest in individuality, and the use of linear perspective based on scientific observation. The greatest achievements occurred during the High Renaissance (1480–1527) and were exemplified in the works of Leonardo da Vinci, Michelangelo, and Raphael.

Repetition A principle of design or composition in which subject matter or elements are repeated within the image creating a sense of stability, planned patterning, or rhythmical movement.

Repoussé The process of raising a relief image in metal by hammering from the back; also termed embossing.

Representational Art Imagery that contains recognizable subject matter, although not necessarily realistic; also known as figurative art.

Resist A process using materials that inherently do not mix; specific image areas on cloth, paper, pottery, or printing plates are covered with wax or varnish to protect them from exposure to dyes, paints, or acids.

Rhythm A principle of design or composition that creates a sense of movement or flow within an image through the systematic repetition of subject matter or elements.

6

Rococo An eighteenth-century French style of art popular during the reign of Louis XV. Most readily associated with the decorative arts, the style is defined by the use of florid S-curves and C-scrolls with motifs inspired by nature. In painting, the images were elegant and pleasant, often reflecting the lifestyles and frivolity of the aristocracy.

Romanesque A term used to define art and architecture that predates the Gothic period (eighth through the twelfth century A.D.). Art work expressed religious emotion through subject matter that was elongated and distorted. Architecture did not possess the light and airy feeling of Gothic structures that employed the flying buttress; Romanesque buildings used round arches to create entrances and openings, while the structures themselves appeared heavy and thick-walled.

Romanticism A movement in art that began in the mid-eighteenth century and ended in the first half of the nineteenth century, when it evolved into realism. With proponents like Turner in England and Delacroix and Gericault in France, romanticism was a revolt against the cool intellectualism of Neoclassicism, emphasizing feeling and the right to personal expression. Typical romantic images were painterly, with tumultuous skies and dramatic gestures; subject matter, symbolic content, and style of painting all merged expressively.

S

Salon In general terms, a French word for an exhibition of art by an independent group of people. More specifically, The Salon was an officially sanctioned exhibition held annually or biennually in the Louvre, beginning in 1667 under royal patronage and continuing under government sponsorship after the French Revolution. In 1881, the French government withdrew its support of the exhibition, leaving administration of The Salon to artist organizations from that point on.

Salon des Refusés An 1863 exhibition of artists' works that were rejected from the official Salon that year. Ordered by Napolean III, it marked the first public recognition of impressionism and modernism.

Salon Painting Academic painting; styles of painting that were acceptable by the officially sanctioned salons.

Sand Painting The practice of making temporary and transitory patterns or designs for religious purposes with colored sand. The artform spans time and cultures and is practiced by the Navajos, Australian aborigines, Tibetan monks, and the Japanese.

Saturation The intensity or brilliance of a color.

Scale A principle of design or composition that refers to the size relationship of an actual work of art to the body-size of the viewer, lending psychological or expressive impact to the experience of the work. Scale can also be used to refer to a proportionally accurate rendering of an object—that is, the automobile is drawn one-tenth scale, or drawn one-tenth the actual size of the original.

Sculpture Unlike painting, which is two-dimensional (height and width), sculpture is work created in three dimensions (height, width, and depth). Three-dimensional form can be created by carving away material (subtractive), or by building up form by adding materials (additive).

Second Language (English as...) Students who grew up speaking a language other than English and who frequently come from home situations in which English is not spoken.

Secondary Color Color created by mixing equal amounts of two primary colors.

Self-Contained Classroom A teaching-learning environment in which students remain in the same room throughout the school day to receive instruction in various disciplines, rather than moving from room to room to different subject-matter teachers.

Sequencing The organizing of the content of a course or program of study in a sensibly progressive manner, working from the simple to the complex, and taking into account the developmental needs of the students.

Serial Art Influenced by the importance of sequencing in mathematics and linguistic theory, paintings and sculpture of the 1960s and 1970s arranged in a sequence with little or no variation. Figurative examples can be found in

the work of Warhol; abstract or minimal examples in the sculpture of Donald Judd.

Serigraphy A method of printmaking known as silk-screening that is based on stenciling techniques. A sheet of silk is stretched taut over a wooden frame, an image is created on the silk with noncolor areas of the design masked off with paper or varnish, the frame is placed on top of paper or canvas, and ink or paint is forced through the screen with a brush or squeegee, transferring the image onto the picture surface.

Shallow Space Pictures that lack the illusion of depth or use of perspective. Image seems to be suspended just behind the picture plane or surface. Term is associated with cubism and abstract expressionism.

Shaman Within primitive societies where specific religious beliefs and practices have not yet evolved, the shaman serves as sorcerer, priest, medicine man, and artist. Responsibilities include producing idols, masks, totems, paintings, and organizing music, rituals, and dances. The powerful shaman serves as an intermediary between the real world and the spirit world, which, in primitive life, confusedly mingle. The artifacts, rituals, and dances serve to appease and control the spirit world, making for successful hunts, harvests, regaining health, and initiation into adulthood.

Shape An element of design that refers

to specific areas in a two-dimensional image that are defined by edges or boarders and/or color, values, or texture. *Organic shapes* are amorphic shapes resembling living organisms, and are often found in expressive works of art. *Geometric shapes* are mathematically defined, humanly invented shapes often found in abstract works of art.

Significant Form A term coined by English art critic Clive Bell to define what he considered to be the true essence of art, the forms and their relationship to each other. He argued that form was the primary content of art, not the narrative or symbolic, thus laying the groundwork for formalism, the dominant modernist philosophy in criticism during the first half of the twentieth century.

Silhouette Any profile, object, or scene shown in black with no interior detail.

Silk Screen (See serigraphy.)

Silver Point A medium using a rod of silver to draw on prepared paper. Used primarily during the Middle Ages, the medium was largely replaced by the introduction of the graphite pencil in the seventeenth century.

Simultaneity A concept found in both cubism and futurism in which the same object is presented from varying viewpoints, in different positions of movement, and/or different moments in time, all in a single image.

Siva (Shiva) The Hindu god of creation and destruction.

Size A thin solution of glue used to stiffen paper and to make canvas or other materials less absorbent.

Slip A thick, creamy solution of diluted clay used to join pieces of clay together and for mold casting. When the slip is of a different color than the vessel itself, it can be used for decorative purposes.

Social Realism Realist works of art that focus on social issues and concerns.

Social Reality One's definition of, or perspective on, reality as determined by the culture or social group to which one belongs.

Socialist Realism The official art of the former Soviet Union. With its roots in academic neoclassicism, socialist realism served as a propaganda and indoctrination tool of the Communist party and government from its official adoption in 1927, to the collapse of the Soviet government. The primary themes running through such works focused on the glory of communism, the achievements of the state, and the dignity of manual labor.

Soft Sculpture Three-dimensional forms produced from soft, pliable materials that conform to gravity and the environment in which they are placed. The concept was pioneered by Claes Oldenberg during the pop art movement of the 1960s.

Special Education (See handicapping conditions.)

Spectrum The band of colors produced when pure, natural light passes through a prism, splitting white light into the various electromagnetic wave lengths that make up the hues visible to the human eye. The resulting "rainbow" of colors ranges from infrared at one end to ultraviolet at the other end.

Stabile An abstract, formalist sculpture with no moving parts.

Stenciling The process of cutting a design or image out of a stiff material and transferring the image onto a surface by forcing paint, dyes, or inks through the cut areas; for example, see serigraphy.

Stepped Pyramid A pyramid constructed of large, rectangular, sloping sections of diminishing size stacked one on top of the other. Less refined in appearance than, and a predecessor to, the pyramids in Giza, Egypt.

Stijl, De A group of Dutch artists committed to the evolution of a purely abstract art that would fulfill a direct expression of the universal. Leading the group were Mondrian and Gerrit Rietveld, and their interests spanned painting, architecture, and furniture design.

Still-Life An image of inanimate objects.

Stippling An image created entirely of dots or dabs.

Stoneware A very hard pottery created by mixing clay and fusible stone and firing at a very high temperature.

Street Art Art taken to the people, rather than waiting for the people to come to the art museums and galleries. Often of a political nature, it is performance art staged in the street. It could also include the works of artists like Jenny Holzer, who uses billboards, electronic message boards, and stickers in phone booths and on parking meters.

Stretcher A wooden frame on which canvas is stretched and attached to produce a surface for painting.

Stupa Derived from the Indian burial mound and found in both Buddhist and Jain religions, the stupa was a monument built to house sacred relics on sites made sacred by visits from Buddha.

Style Reflects the unique combination of concepts, content, formal properties, materials, and techniques that distinguish a particular body of art work from others. The term can be used to label work found in a particular culture or period in history like "Japanese art" or "Renaissance painting." Style can refer to the work of a specific school of artists like the "abstract expressionists," or an individual artist's style within the group like the work of Robert Motherwell. Style can also define general categories of work that have similar qualities, like realism, expressionism, and abstraction. Familiarity with a variety of styles enables the viewer to be able to know what kinds of visual cues to look for and what kind of mind set to establish in order to fully experience a work of art.

Superrealism In sculpture, it refers to work that makes use of direct casting from the human figure, as in the work of George Segal. For painting, see Photorealism.

Suprematism Influenced by Cubism, a Russian movement founded by Kazimir Malevich in 1915 that declared "the supremacy of pure feeling in creative art." Work is characterized by geometric, nonrepresentational forms in limitless space.

Surrealism Founded as a literary movement in 1924 by Andre Breton, surrealism absorbed the artists and methods of the Dada movement, shifting the Dadaist focus on shock and the absurd as a rejection of the art estab-

6

lishment and channeling it to explore the regions of the unconscious mind. Influenced by the writings of Freud, surrealism expressed parallel realities in two major directions: *illusionism* or *veristic surrealism*, whose images were painted in exacting detail and realism, yet whose subject matter reflected the illogic of dream states (Salvador Dali, Max Ernst, and Yves Tanguy); and *automatism*, based on free association and automatic writing, which presumably reflects unconscious states before the control of consciousness and expresses primordial states (Paul Klee, Joan Miro, and Andre Masson). Automatism served as a forerunner to abstract expressionism.

Syllabus A document stating the expected learning outcomes in a given course of study, including goals, objectives, concepts, skills, and areas of understanding.

Symbol The use of an object or sign to represent ideas and convey meanings beyond the literal; for example, the object in a painting may be literally interpreted as a dog, but if it is a Renaissance painting, the "dog" symbolizes faithfulness and fidelity. The study and identification of such symbols is called *iconography.*

Symbolism A European literary and artistic movement that aimed to communicate ideas through powerful symbols. Symbolist works, produced between 1885 and 1910, were highly subjective and its proponents were interested in the mystical, erotic, decadent, and primitive. Among its chief advocates were Gustav Klimt in

Austria and Odilon Redon and Gustave Moreau in France.

Symmetry Visual balance achieved by distributing objects, shapes, colors, textures, and so on equally between two halves of a composition.

Synchronism An American art movement that surfaced just prior to the outbreak of World War I. The work emphasized color, which advocates such as Morgan Russell believed was adequate enough to be considered the content of art.

Synthetism A theory of art adopted by Gauguin and his followers in Pont-Aven that advocated broad areas of bold color and subject matter that was primitive and symbolic. Unlike the impressionists who preceded them and promoted the idea of painting directly from nature, the synthetists believed artists should synthesize their impressions and paint from memory.

T

Talent Generally associated with the arts, an innate ability to master and excel at something, not only in terms of performance, but in terms of motivation, quality, and flexibility of thought, as well as sensitivity to materials. In art education, talented students are accelerated, assigned to advanced placement courses, or placed in special programs for the gifted and talented.

T'ao-t'ieh A stylized dragon mask first seen as decoration on bronze vessels from the Shang Dynasty (1766–1122

B.C.) and later in other forms of Chinese art.

Tapestry A European hand-woven fabric of wool and/or silk, carrying non-repetitive designs or figurative images. Dating from the fourteenth century to the present, tapestries were originally used as wall-hangings in castles and palaces both to decorate and to insulate.

Tectonic Generally associated with architecture and construction, it pertains to simple massiveness and "closed-form."

Tempera A type of paint that is water-soluble until it dries and serves as a binder or medium for pigment; usually made of whole eggs, egg yolks, milk, or glue. The primary medium of Italian painters during the fourteenth and fifteenth centuries for both fresco and panel painting, it was largely replaced as the medium of choice when oil painting was invented.

Template A pattern cut out of durable material and used to insure accuracy of measurement when doing repetitive work.

Tenebrism A style of painting that emphasizes night effects and exagerates the effects of chiaroscuro.

Terra Cotta A hard-baked, reddish clay used in earthenware, sculpture, and architecture. While tiles and pipes are most familiarly used in building, the architect Louis Sullivan used cast slabs of terra cotta to create a highly decorative "skin" on the facade of buildings; for example, the Guaranty Building in Buffalo, New York and the Wainwright Building in St. Louis.

Texture The tactile or visual qualities of the surface of a work of art. *Actual texture* is a surface that has authentic texture inherent in the materials (for example, wood grain). *Invented texture* is created by the artist through carving or modeling; in painting, the artist can build up surface texture by applying thick layers of paint using an impasto technique. *Implied or simulated texture* is the illusion of real texture created by the painter.

Throwing The method of producing pottery on a potter's wheel.

Tiki Mythological figure in Polynesian culture believed to be the creator of the first man, the first man himself, or an ancestor.

Ting Ware Originating during the Sung and Yuan Dynasties (tenth to fourteenth centuries), a delicate creamy white porcelain with a clear and colorless glaze, produced in northern China.

Tint A hue that has white mixed with it. Pink is a reddish tint.

Tone The comparative lightness or darkness of a hue.

Totem A symbolic image, usually representing the protective creature that a tribe believes it is related to, and used as an emblem to represent them. A totem can also be symbolic of blood lineage. Totem poles show figures of totemic protectors and ancestors. See totems produced by the natives of the northwest United States.

Tracery Decorative stonework found in Gothic windows, but also used as ornamental relief on solid walls.

6

Transept Architectural space found most frequently in churches and cathedrals that crosses the main space of a structure at a right angle.

Triptych An image consisting of three separate panels.

Trompe-L'oeil A French term meaning "to fool the eye" which refers to imagery rendered in such precise, illusionistic detail that the viewer confuses the picture with reality.

Tusche A black, greasy liquid used to paint an image on a lithographic stone or plate.

Tympanum The triangular or arched, recessed space above a lintel in a classical facade, often containing sculpture.

Typography The practical art of designing printed texts.

U

Ukiyo-e Japanese art, frequently woodblock prints that spanned the seventeenth through the nineteenth centuries and was characterized by the work of Hokusai, Utamaro, and Hiroshige. The subject matter often centered on historic epics and folk tales; however, the dominant subjects were Kabuki actors and geishas.

Underglaze Decorative painting on ceramic, over which glaze is applied. Once the piece is fired, the decoration is permanently fixed.

Underpainting The initial phase of the indirect method of painting. The artist uses monochromes to layout the general forms of the picture on canvas before applying the final layer of paint that constitutes the finished image.

Units of Study A series of lessons, organized sequentially around a particular theme or concept, that provides greater depth of learning than single-day assignments.

Unity A principle of composition in which a sense of oneness and coherency is established among the various parts of a work of art.

V

Value In formal terms, the range of lights and darks in color or tones. In terms of content and aesthetics, the artistic expression of an individual or social need or concern; a perceived quality or source of appeal in a work of art.

Vanishing Point In linear perspective, the point on the horizon at which lines parallel to each other and to the ground appear to recede into the distance and converge.

Vanitas Popular in seventeenth-century Holland, allegorical still-lifes whose themes were the transience of human life.

Vantage Point The position from which a viewer perceives a work of art.

Vault A roof constructed of a series of arches that can be arranged in varying patterns; for example, barrel vault, groin vault, fan vault, and rib vault.

Vehicle A liquid or emulsion, also known as a medium, that carries pigment and makes it adhere to a surface.

Verism A style of realism that is nonselective, revealing the disturbing truth as well as beauty of a subject.

Vernacular Architecture Grassroots structures built of local materials to suit local needs. Making no reference to specific styles or theories of architecture, such structures function as folk art, often becoming identified as characteristic of particular locations or regions.

Video Art The use of television or the medium of television, electronic video-recording technology, as an art medium.

Vignette A decorative design or illustration that has no definite boundaries and dissolves into surrounding space.

Volume The space filled by a three-dimensional figure or object.

Volute A scroll-shaped form used in architectural ornamentation such as Ionic capitals.

Voussoir Wedge-shaped stones used to construct an arch.

W

Warm Color Colors that have the appearance and feel of warmth, such as yellow, orange, and red.

Warp The fixed threads set up on a loom through which the weft threads are woven.

Wash A thin, fluid transparent layer of paint or ink.

Watercolor Transparent paint that uses water as its vehicle and a water-soluble gum as its binder. Other forms of water-soluble paint, such as gouache, are opaque and, therefore, are not watercolor.

Weft Threads woven at right angles to warp threads to form fabric. Patterns are created in the fabric by the various ways the weft crosses the warp. Also called *woof*.

Window View of Art A term used by some art historians to describe the compositional "look" that dominated art from the Renaissance to the mid-nineteenth century. Objects and figures were arranged within the rectangular framework of the picture, giving the viewer the sensation of looking through, or out of, a window. The use of perspective techniques and heavy picture frames enhanced the effect. Once the industrial age began, artists sense of composition changed. They had greater opportunity to see pictures from China and Japan that had a different sense of nature and reality. The invention of the camera also altered the way artists thought about composition: the camera captured reality in whatever direction one pointed it and from angles other than simply frontal views; because the camera captured the moment, photographs did not always have figures neatly arranged within the framework of the image, instead cropping them off at the edges. Once the modern age began, artists abandoned the "window view" of composition.

Wood Engraving A form of printmaking that uses a hardwood block cut across the grain and engraved with a Burin (a sharp, pointed steel tool). The technique produces a much finer, detailed image than a traditional woodcut.

Woodcut A form of relief printmaking invented by the Chinese in the ninth century, in which the artist carves and gouges an image into a flat block of medium hard wood that is cut along the grain. The areas of the image that are to remain the color of the paper are carved away, leaving the raised sur-

6

face of the block to take the ink. Ink is applied to the raised surface, a piece of paper is then laid on the block, and the back side of the paper is rubbed, transferring the image from the block onto the paper.

WPA/FAP An acronym for Works Progress Administration/Federal Art Project, which was a program established by U.S. President Franklin Roosevelt in his 1935 New Deal legislation to put Americans back to work and break the cycle of the Great Depression. Artists were employed to create works of art in tax-supported government buildings, monuments, and post offices. The end result was the support of artists like Jackson Pollock, Adolf Gottlieb, and Arshile Gorky, who were to become prominent leaders of abstract expressionism and the flowering of American art in the 1940s.

X

Xerography The use of a photocopier as an artistic medium for producing imagery.

Y

Yaksha A male earth deity in Hindu belief and often represented as a sculptured figure on the walls of temples.

Yakshi A female earth deity in Hindu belief whose sculptured image was often used to decorate the entrance of sacred structures.

Yantra Also called a *mandala,* which is a geometric diagram of the cosmos used by Buddhist mystics to focus concentration during meditation.

Z

Zeitgeist A German term meaning the "spirit of the age."

Zen A Japanese sect of Buddhism that emphasizes enlightenment.

Zenga Spontaneous bold ink paintings made by Zen Buddhist artists from the fifteenth through the nineteenth centuries.

Ziggurat A structure consisting of a brick-surfaced, pyramidal-shaped pile of rubble with four or five stages stepped back to form terraces. Built by the ancient Babylonians and Assyrians, open ramplike stairways led to temples and shrines at the top.

ALPHABETIZED BIBLIOGRAPHY

ACKERMAN, J. (1973). Toward a new social theory of art. *New Literary History, 4,* 315–330.

ACKERMAN, J., and CARPENTER, T. (1963). *Art and Archaeology.* Englewood Cliffs, NJ: Prentice-Hall.

ADAMS, D., and FUCHS, M. (1985). The fusion of artistic and scientific thinking. *Art Education, 38*(6), 22–24.

ADAMS, R. L. (1980). A survey of attitudes of Alabama primary teachers toward selected concepts of Viktor Lowenfeld's teachings regarding art education. (Doctoral dissertation, The Florida State University). *Dissertation Abstracts International, 41,* 3843A.

ADAMS, R. L. (1985). Aesthetic dialogue for children: Paradigm and program. *Art Education, 38*(5), 12–15.

ADLER, M. J. (1982). *The Paideia Proposal: An Educational Manifesto.* New York: MacMillan Publishing Co., Inc.

ALEXANDER, C. N., Jr., and CAMPBELL, E. Q. (1964). Peer influences on adolescent educational aspirations and attainments. *American Sociological Review, 29,* 568–575.

ALLOWAY, L. (1975). *Topics in America Since 1945.* NY: Norton.

ALLINGTON, R. L. (1984). Oral reading. In P. D. PEARSON (ed.) *Handbook of Reading Research,* (pp. 829–864). NY: Longman.

ANDERSON, F. E. (1978). *Art for All the Children: A Creative Sourcebook for the Impaired Child.* Springfield, IL.: Charles C. Thomas.

ANDERSON, F. E. and MORREAU, L. (1984). Individualized education programs in art: Benefits or burden? *Art Education, 37*(6), 10–14.

ANDERSON, R. C., SOIRO, R. J., and MONTAGUE, W. (1977). *Schooling and the Acquisition of Knowledge.* Hillsdale, NJ: Erlbaum Associates.

ANDERSON, R. C., and others (1985). *Becoming a Nation of Readers: The Report of the Commission on Reading.* Urbana, IL: University of Illinois, Center for the Study of Reading.

ANDERSON, T. (1985). Toward a socially defined curriculum. *Art Education, 38*(5), 16–18.

ANDERSON, T. (1986). Talking about art with children: From theory to practice. *Art Education, 39*(1), 5–8.

APPLEBEE, A. N. (1978). *The Child's Concept of Story: Ages Two to Seventeen.* Chicago: University of Chicago Press.

APPLEBEE, A. N. (1984). *Contexts for Learning to Write: Studies of Secondary School Instruction.* Norwood, NJ: Ablex.

ARNHEIM, R. (1962). *Picasso's Guernica: The Genesis of a Painting.* Berkeley and Los Angeles: University of California Press.

ARNHEIM, R. (1969). *Visual Thinking.* Berkeley: University of California Press.

ARNHEIM, R. (1983). Perceiving, thinking, forming. *Art Education, 36*(2), 9–11.

ARONSON, E. (1966). The psychology of insufficient justification: An analysis of some conflicting data. In S. FELDMAN (ed.), *Cognitive Consistency.* NY: Academic Press, pp. 115–133.

ARONSON, E., and GOLDEN, B. W. (1962). The effect of relevant and irrelevant aspects of communicator credibility on opinion change. *Journal of Personality, 30,* 135–146.

Art Education, (1983, March), *36*(2). Art and the mind (Special issue).

Art Educators of New Jersey. (1984). *Insights—Art in Special Education: Educating the Handicapped Through Art (3rd ed.).* NJ: Author.

AUPING, M. (1987). *Abstract Expressionism.* NY: Abrams.

AUSUBEL, D., NOVAK, J. D., and HANESIAN, H. (1978). *Educational Psychology: A Cognitive view* (2nd ed.). NY: Holt, Rinehart & Winston.

BACHTEL-NASH, A. (1985). Teaching aesthetic perception in the elementary school. *Art Education, 38*(5), 6–11.

BAIGELL, M. (1974). *The American scene: Paintings of the 1930's.* NY: Praeger.

BAKER, A., and GREENE, E. (1977). *Storytelling: Art and Technique.* NY: R. R. Bowker Co.

BARKAN, M. (1962). The visual arts in secondary-school education. *School Review, 70*(4).

BARKAN, M. (1962). Transition in art education: Changing conceptions of curriculum and theory. *Art Education, 15*(7), 12–18.

BARKAN, M. (1963). Is there a discipline of art education? *Studies in Art Education, 4*(2), 4–9.

BARKAN, M. (1966). Prospects for change in the teaching of art. *Art Education, 19*(8), 4–8.

BARNET, S. (1985). *A short guide to writing about art* (2nd ed.). Boston: Little, Brown.

BARR, A. (1966). *Vincent van Gogh.* NY: Arno Press.

BARTHES, R. (1972). *Mythologies.* NY: Hill and Wang.

BARTHES, R. (1981). *Camera Lucida.* NY: Hill and Wang.

BASUALDO, S. M., and BASUALDO, E. A. (1980). *Models to prevent and deal with disruptive behavior(s) in the classroom: A review of the literature.* ERIC Document No. ED 202812.

BATTCOCK, G. (1968). *Minimal Art.* NY: Dutton.

BATTCOCK, G. (1966). *The new art: A critical anthology.* NY: Dutton.

BATTCOCK, G. (1973). *New ideas in art education,* NY: Dutton.

BAXANDALL, M. (1985). *Patterns of Intention: On the Historical Explanation of Pictures.* New Haven: Yale University Press.

BAYER, H. & GROPIUS, W. (1976). *Bauhaus 1919–1928.* Boston: N.Y. Graphic Society.

BEARDSLEY, M. C. (1966). *Aesthetics from Classical Greece to the Present: A Short History.* NY: MacMillan.

BEARDSLEY, M. C. (1981). *Aesthetics: Problems in the Philosophy of Criticism* (2nd ed.). Indianapolis: Hackett.

BECKER, H. J., and EPSTEIN, J. (1982). Parent involvement: A survey of teacher practices. *The Elementary School Journal, 83*(2), 85–102.

BEITTEL, K. R. (1973). *Alternatives for art education research: Inquiry into the making of art.* Dubuque: Wm. C. Brown.

BELL, C. (1914). *Art.* London: Chatto & Windus.

BERGER, J. (1972). *Ways of seeing.* London: BBC and Penguin Books.

BERLINER, D. (1983). The executive functions of teaching. *The Instructor, 93*(2), 28–40.

BERLINER, D. (1984). The half-full glass: A review of research on teaching. In P. L. HOSFORD (ed.), *Using What We Know About Teaching.* Alexandria, VA: Association for Supervision and Curriculum Development.

BERLINER, D., and ROSENSHINE, B. (1976). *The Acquisition of Knowledge in the Classroom.* San Francisco, CA: Far West Laboratory for Educational Research and Development.

BERSCHEID, E. & WALSTER, E. (1969). Attitude change. In J. MILLS (ed.), *Experimental Social Psychology*, Toronto: The MacMillan Company, 121–232.

BERSSON, R. (1986). Why art education lacks social relevance: A contextual analysis. *Art Education, 39*(4), 41–45.

BETTELHEIM, B. (1975). *The Uses of Enchantment: The Meaning and Importance of Fairy Tales*. NY: Knopf.

BIRD, E. (1979). Aesthetic neutrality and the sociology of art. In M. BARRETT, P. CORRIGAN, A. KUHN, & J. WOLFF (eds.), *Ideology and Cultural Production* (pp. 25–48). NY: St. Martin's Press.

BIRD, T., and LITTLE, J. W. (1985). *Instructional Leadership in Eight Secondary Schools*. Final Report to the U.S. Department of Education, National Institute of Education, Boulder, CO: Center for Action Research.

BLANDY, D. (1985). Review of art and mainstreaming: Art instruction for exceptional children in regular school classes. *Studies in Art Education, 26*(?), 189–190.

BLOOM, A. (1987). *The Closing of the American Mind*. NY: Simon and Schuster.

BLOOM, B. S. (Ed.). (1985). *Developing Talent in Young People*. NY: Ballantine Books.

BLOOM, B. S., ENGLEHART, M. D., FURTS, E. J., HILL, W. H., and KRATHWOHL, D. R. (eds.). (1956). *Taxonomy of Educational Objectives: The Classification of Educational Goals. Handbook I: Cognitive Domain*. NY: David McKay.

BLOOM, B. S., and SOSNIAK, L. A. (November 1981). Talent development vs. schooling. *Educational Leadership, 39,*(2), 86–94.

BOORSTEIN, D. (1973). *The Americans: The Democratic Experience*. NY: Vintage Books.

BOSSERT, S. (1985). Effective elementary schools. In R. KYLE (ed.), *Reaching for Excellence: An Effective Schools Sourcebook*. (pp. 39–53). Washington, D.C.: U.S. Government Printing Office.

BRADDOCK, J. H., II. (1981). Race, athletics, and educational attainment. *Youth and Society, 12*(3), 335–350.

BRANFORD, J. D. (1979). *Human Cognition: Learning, Understanding, and Remembering*. Belmont, CA: Wadsworth.

BRODINSKY, B. (1980). Student discipline: Problems and solutions. *AASA Critical Issues Report*. Arlington, VA: American Association of School Administrators. ERIC Document No. ED 198206.

BROOKOVER, W. B., and others (1979). *School Systems and Student Achievement: Schools Make a Difference*. NY: Praeger.

BROPHY, J. (1979). Teacher behavior and its effects. *Journal of Educational Psychology, 71*(6), 733–750.

BROPHY, J. E. (1981). Teacher praise: A functional analysis. *Review of Education Research, 51*, 5–32.

BROPHY, J., and EVERTSON, C. M. (1976). *Learning from Teaching: A Developmental Perspective*. Boston, MA: Allyn and Bacon.

BROUDE, N. and GARRARD, M. D. (1982). *Feminism and Art History: Questioning the Litany.* NY: Harper and Row.

BROUDY, H. S. (1966). The structure of knowledge in the arts. In R. A. SMITH (ed.), *Aesthetics and Criticism in Art Education: Problems in Defining, Explaining, and Evaluating Art* (pp. 23–45). Chicago: Rand McNally.

BROUDY, H. S. (1972). *Enlightened Cherishing: An Essay on Aesthetic Education.* Urbana: University of Illinois Press. Distributed by Kappa Delta Pi, Lafayette, IN.

BROUDY, H. S. (1985). Curriculum validity in art education. *Studies in art education, 26*(4), 212–215.

BROUDY, H. S. (1987). Theory and practice in aesthetic education. *Studies in art education, 28*(4), 195–197.

BROWN, A. L., and SMILEY, S. S. (1978). The development of strategies for studying texts. *Child Development, 49,* 1076–1088.

BRUNER, J. (1977). *The Process of Education* (with new preface). Cambridge: Harvard University Press. (first published 1960).

BURNSTEIN, E.; STOTLAND, E. & ZANDER, A. (1961). A similarity to a model and self-evaluation. *Journal of Abnormal and Social Psychology, 62,* 257–264.

CANFIELD, J. *Self-esteem in the classroom: A curriculum guide.* Pacific Palisades, CA: Self-Esteem Seminars.

CANFIELD, J., & WELLS, H. *100 Ways to enhance self-concept in the classroom.* Santa Cruz, CA: Educational and Training Services, Inc.

CARNINE, D. R., GERSTEN, R., and GREEN, S. (1982). The principal as instructional leader: A second look. *Educational Leadership, 40*(3), 47–50.

CATTERMOLE, J., and ROBINSON, N. (1985). Effective Home/School/Communications— From the Parents' Perspective. *Phi Delta Kappan, 67*(1), 48–50.

Center for Public Resources. (1982). *Basic Skills in the U.S. Work Force: The Contrasting Perceptions of Business, Labor, and Public Education.* New York.

CHALL, J. S. (1983). *Learning to Read: The Great Debate* (2nd ed.). NY: McGraw-Hill.

CHALL, J., CONARD, S., and HARRIS, S. (1977). *An Analysis of Textbooks in Relation to Declining SAT Scores.* NY: College Entrance Examination Board.

CHALMERS, G. (1973). The study of art in a cultural context. *Journal of Aesthetics and Art Criticism, 32*(2), 249–256.

CHALMERS, G. (1974). A cultural foundation for education in the arts. *Art Education, 27*(1), 21–25.

CHALMERS, G. (1978). Teaching and studying art history: Some anthropological and sociological considerations. *Studies in Art Education, 20*(1), 18–25.

CHALMERS, F. G. (1987). Beyond current conceptions of Discipline-based art education. *Art Education, 40*(5), 58–61.

CHAPMAN, L. H. (1985). Curriculum development as process and product. *Studies in Art Education, 26*(4), 206–211.

CHAPMAN, L. H. (1978). *Approaches to art in education.* New York: Harcourt Brace Jovanovich.

CHAPMAN, L. H. (1982). *Instant Art, Instant Culture: The Unspoken Policy for American Schools.* NY: Teachers College Press.

CHILD, I. L. (1970). The problem of objectivity in esthetic value. In G. PAPPAS (ed.), *Concepts in Art and Education.* NY: MacMillan.

CHOMSKY, C. (1972). Stages in language development and reading exposure. *Harvard Educational Review, 42,* 1–33.

CLARK, B. (1983). *Growing up gifted* (2nd ed). Columbus, OH: Merrill.

CLARK, G. A.; DAY, M. D.; & GREER, W. D. (1987). Discipline-based art education: Becoming students of art. *The Journal of Aesthetic Education, 21*(2), 129–193.

CLARK, G. A. & ZIMMERMAN, E. (1984). *Educating artistically talented students.* Syracuse, NY: Syracuse University Press.

CLEAVER, D. G. (1985). *Art: An Introduction* (4th ed.). NY: Harcourt Brace Jovanovich.

CLEMENTS, C. B. and CLEMENTS, R. D. (1984). *Arts and Mainstreaming: Art Instruction for Exceptional Children in Regular School Classes.* Springfield, IL.: Charles C. Thomas.

COHEN, E. G. & BENTON, J. (1988). Making groupwork work. *American Educator, 12*(3), 10–17.

COHN, S. J., GEORGE, W. C., and STANLEY, J. C. (eds.). (1979). Educational acceleration of intellectually talented youths: Prolonged discussion by a varied group of professionals. In W. C. GEORGE, S. J. COHN, and J. E. STANLEY (Eds.), *Educating the Gifted: Acceleration and Enrichment,* (pp. 183–238). Baltimore: Johns Hopkins University Press.

COKE, V. D. (1975). *100 Years of Photographic History.* Albuquerque: University of New Mexico Press.

COLE, D. (1973). *From Tipi to Sky Scraper: History of Women in Architecture.* Boston: Boston Press.

COLEMAN, J. S., HOFFER, T., and KILGORE, S. (1982). *High School Achievement: Public, Catholic and Private Schools Compared.* NY: Basic Books.

COLLIER, G. (1972). *Art and the Creative Consciousness.* Englewood Cliffs, NJ: Prentice-Hall.

COLLINGWOOD, R. G. (1956). *The Idea of History.* Oxford: Oxford University Press.

COLLINGWOOD, R. G. (1958). *Principles of Art.* Oxford: Oxford University Press.

Committee for Economic Development. (1985). *Investing in Our Children: Businesses and the Public Schools: A Statement.* New York and Washington, D.C.

COOK, E. (1969). *The Ordinary and the Fabulous: An Introduction to Myths, Legends and Fairy Tales for Teachers and Storytellers.* Cambridge and New York: Cambridge University Press.

COOK, J. M. (1977). Measurement of affective art objectives. *School Arts, 77*(2), 14–17.

COPELAND, B. (1984). Mainstreaming art for the handicapped: Resources for teacher preparation. *Art Education, 37*(6), 22–23.

COPPLESTONE, T. (1983). *Art in Society: A Guide to the Visual Arts.* Englewood Cliffs, NJ: Prentice-Hall.

CORCORAN, T. (1985). Effective secondary schools. In R. KYLE (ed.), *Reaching for Excellence: An Effective Schools Sourcebook,* (pp. 71–97). Washington, D.C.: U.S. Government Printing Office.

CORWIN, S. (1990). Art as a tool for learning American history: A preliminary report of a study at National Arts Education Research Center New York University. *THE NYSATA BULLETIN, 40*(1), 23–26.

CRABBE, A. B. (1978). A study of the attitudes toward art of 210 elementary children as they relate to grade, age, and sex. (Doctoral dissertation, The University of Nebraska-Lincoln). *Dissertation Abstracts International, 39,* 3992A.

CRAIK, F. I. M., and WATKINS, M. J. (1973). The role of rehearsal in short-term memory. *Journal of Verbal Learning and Verbal Behavior, 12,* 599–607.

CRAWFORD, D. W. (1987). Aesthetics in discipline-based art education. *The Journal of Aesthetic Education, 21*(2), 227–242.

CROMER, J. (1990). *Criticism: History, Theory and Practice of Art Criticism in Art Education.* Reston, VA: National Art Education Association.

DALLIS, C. (1975). The effects of a black-oriented teaching strategy on attitude change, aesthetic taste, and cognitive learning in art appreciation. (doctoral dissertation, University of Georgia). *Dissertation Abstracts International, 36,* 5648A.

DANTO, A. C. (1981). *The Transfiguration of the Commonplace.* Cambridge, MA: Harvard University.

DAVIS, D. (1977). *ArtCulture.* NY: Harper and Row.

DAVIS, D. J. *Behavioral emphasis in art education.* Reston, VA: National Art Education Association.

DAVIS, D. J. (1966). The effects of two methods of teaching art upon creative thinking, art attitudes, and aesthetic quality of art products in beginning college art students. (doctoral dissertation, University of Minnesota). *Dissertation Abstracts International, 27,* 2272A.

DAY, M. D. (1969). The compatibility of art history and studio art activity in the junior high school art program. *Studies in Art Education, 10*(2), 57–65.

DAY, M. D. (1985). Evaluating student achievement in discipline-based art programs. *Studies in Art Education, 26*(4), 232–240.

DAY, M. D. (1987). Discipline-based art education in secondary classrooms. *Studies in Art Education, 28*(4), 234–242.

DAY, M., and others (1984). *Art history, art criticism, and art production.* Santa Monica, CA: The Rand Corp.

DEINHARD, H. (1975). Reflections on art history and sociology of art. *Art Journal, 35*(1), 20–32.

DELANEY, C. H. (1965). A study of the attitudes of eighth grade students toward specific art activities in relationship to their attitudes toward creative activities in english and science and their drawing abilities. (Doctoral dissertation, Arizona State University). *Dissertation Abstracts International, 26,* 2609A.

DERYLAK, R. (1989). *Enhancing Art Learning Based on Social Studies Curriculum Objectives.* Unpublished Graduate Project, State University College at Buffalo.

DEVIN-SHEEHAN, L., FELDMAN, R. S., and ALLEN, V. L. (1976). Research on children tutoring children: A critical Review. *Review of Educational Research, 46*(3), 355–385.

DEWEY, J. (1934). *Art As Experience.* NY: Capricorn Books, Putnam.

DIBLASIO, M. K. (1985). Continuing the translation: Further delineation of the DBAE format. *Studies in Art Education, 26*(4), 197–205.

DIBLASIO, M. K. (1987). Reflections on the theory of discipline-based art education. *Studies in Art Education, 28*(4), 221–6.

DICKIE, G. (1971). *Aesthetics: An Introduction.* Indianapolis: Bobbs-Merrill.

DICKIE, G., and SCLAFANI, R. (eds.) (1977). *Aesthetics: A Critical Anthology.* NY: St. Martin's Press.

DILEO, J. H. (1970). *Young children and their drawings.* NY: Bruner-Mazel.

DIPRETE, T. A. (1981). *Discipline, Order, and Student Behavior in American High Schools.* Chicago: National Opinion Research Center. ERIC Document No. ED 224137.

DOBBS, S. M. (1974). Research and reason: Recent literature and ideas in American art education. *Curriculum Theory Network, 4* (2–3), 169–191.

DOBBS, S. M. (1979). *Art Education and Back to Basics.* Reston, VA: National Art Education Association.

DOBBS, S. M. [Ed.]. (1988). *Research readings for discipline-based art education: A journey beyond creating.* Reston, VA: National Art Education Association.

DOUGLAS, N. J.; SCHWARTZ, J. B.; and TAYLOR, J. B. (1981). The relationship of cognitive style of young children and their modes of responding to paintings. *Studies in Art Education, 22*(3), 24–31.

DOYLE, W. (1983). "Academic Work". *Review of Educational Psychology, 53*(2), 159–199.

DOYLE, W. (1985). Effective secondary classroom practices. In R. M. J. KYLE (ed.), *Reaching for Excellence: An Effective Schools Sourcebook.* Washington, D.C.: U.S. Government Printing Office.

DUBE, W. D. (1983). *Expressionists and Expressionism.* NY: Skira, Rizzoli.

DUBERMAN, M. (1972). *Black Mountain.* NY: Dutton.

DUNN, N. E. (1981). Children's achievement at school-entry age as a function of mothers' and fathers' teaching sets. *The Elementary School Journal, 81,* 245–253.

DUVIGNAUD, J. (1972). *The Sociology of Art*. London: Paladin.

ECKER, D. W. *Defining behavioral objectives for aesthetic education*. St. Ann, MO: CEM-REL.

ECKER, D. W. (1967). Justifying aesthetic judgments. *Art Education, 20*(5), 5–8.

ECKER, D. W., and KAELIN, E. F. (1958). Aesthetics in public school art teaching. *College Art Journal, 17*(4), 382–391.

ECKER, D. W., and KAELIN, E. F. (1972). The limits of aesthetic inquiry: A guide to educational research. In L. G. THOMAS (ed.), *Philosophical Redirection of Educational Research* (pp. 258–286). 71st Yearbook of the National Society for the Study of Education, Pt. 1. Chicago: University of Chicago Press.

EFLAND, A. (1976). The school art style: A functional analysis. *Studies in Art Education, 17*(2), 37–44.

EFLAND, A. D. (1987). Curriculum antecedents of discipline-based art education. *The Journal of Aesthetic Education, 21*(2), 57–94.

EISNER, E. W. (1966). The development of information and attitude toward art at the secondary and college levels. *Studies in Art Education, 8*(1), 43–51.

EISNER, E. W. (1969). Teaching the humanities: Is a new era possible? *Educational Leadership, 26*(7), 561–564.

EISNER, E. W. (1972). *Educating Artistic Vision*. NY: McMillan.

EISNER, E. W. (1976). *The Arts, Human Development and Education*. Berkeley, CA: McCutchan.

EISNER, E. W. (ed.), (1978). *Reading, the Arts, and the Creation of Meaning*. Reston, VA.: National Art Education Association.

EISNER, E. W. (1982). *Cognition and Curriculum*. NY: Longman.

EISNER, E. W. (1984). Alternative approaches to curriculum development. *Studies in Art Education, 25*(4), 259–264.

EISNER, E. W. (1985). *The Art of Educational Evaluation: A Personal View*. Philadelphia: The Falmer Press.

EISNER, E. W. (1987). The role of discipline-based art education in America's schools. *Art Education, 40*(5), 6–27.

EISNER, E. W. & ECKER, D. W. (1966). *Readings in Art Education*. Waltham, MA: Blaisdell.

ELBOW, P. (1981). *Writing with Power: Techniques for Mastering the Writing Process*. NY: Oxford University Press.

ELSEN, A. E. (1972). *Purposes of Art*. New York: Holt, Rinehart and Winston.

ERICKSON, M. (1977). Uses of art history in art education. *Studies in Art Education, 18*(3), 22–29.

ERICKSON, M. (1983). Teaching art history as an inquiry process. *Art Education, 36*(5), 28–31.

ERICKSON, M. and KATTER, E. (1981). *How Do You Do Art History?* Kutztown, PA: MELD.

ERICKSON, M. and KATTER, E. (1981). *Artifacts,* Kutztown, PA: MELD.

ERICKSON, E. H. (1958). *Young Man Luther: A Study in Psychoanalysis and History.* NY: Norton.

ETZIONI, A. (1984). *Self-discipline, Schools, and the Business Community.* Final Report to the U.S. Chamber of Commerce, Washington, D.C. ERIC Document No. ED 249–335.

FEATHERSTONE, H. (February 1985). Homework. *The Harvard Education Letter.*

FEINSTEIN, H. (1982). Meaning and visual metaphor. *Studies in Art Education, 23*(2), 45–55.

FEINSTEIN, H. (1982). Art means values. *Art Education, 35*(5), 13–15.

FEINSTEIN, H. (1983). The therapeutic trap in metaphoric interpretation. *Art Education, 36*(4), 30–33.

FEINSTEIN, H. (1984). The metaphoric interpretation of paintings: Effects of the clustering strategy and relaxed attention exercises. *Studies in Art Education, 25*(2), 77–83.

FEINSTEIN, H. (1989). The art response guide: How to read art for meaning, a primer for art criticism. *Art Education, 42*(3), 43–53.

FELDMAN, E. B. (1965). The nature of the aesthetic experience. In J. HAUSMAN (ed.), *Report of the Commission on Art Education* (pp. 35–46). Washington, D.C.: National Art Education Association.

FELDMAN, E. B. (1966). Research as the verification of aesthetics. In R. SMITH (ed.), *Aesthetics and Criticism in Art Education* (pp. 56–61). Chicago: Rand McNally.

FELDMAN, E. B. (1967). *Art As Image and Idea.* Englewood Cliffs, NJ: Prentice-Hall.

FELDMAN, E. B. (1970). *Becoming Human through Art: Aesthetic Experience in the School.* Englewood Cliffs, NJ: Prentice-Hall.

FELDMAN, E. B. (1973). The teacher as model critic. *Journal of Aesthetic Education, 7*(1), 50–57.

FELDMAN, E. B. (1981). *Varieties of Visual Experience.* Englewood Cliffs, NJ: Prentice-Hall.

FELDMAN, E. B. (1985). *Thinking about Art.* Englewood Cliffs, NJ: Prentice-Hall.

FELDMAN, D. H. (1987). Developmental psychology and art education: Two fields at the crossroads. *The Journal of Aesthetic Education, 21*(2), 243–259.

FESTINGER, L. A. (1957). *A Theory of Cognitive-Dissonance.* Evanston, IL: Row, Peterson.

FICHNER-RATHUS, L. (1986). *Understanding Art.* Englewood Cliffs, NJ: Prentice-Hall.

FIELDING, G. D., and SCHALOCK, H. D. (1985). *Promoting the Professional Development of Teachers and Administrators.* Eugene, OR: ERIC Clearinghouse on Educational Management.

FINCH, C. (1968). *Pop Art.* NY: Dutton.

FINE, E. H. (1978). *Women and Art: A History of Women Painters and Sculptors from the Renaissance to the 20th Century.* Montclair, NJ: Allanheld & Schram.

FINN, C. E., Jr. (1984). Toward strategic independence: Nine Commandments for enhancing school effectiveness. *Phi Delta Kappan, 65*(8), 513–524.

FINN, C. E., Jr., RAVITCH, D., and ROBERTS, P. (Eds.) (1985). *Challenges to the Humanities.* NY: Holmes and Meier.

FITZGERALD, F. (1979). *America Revised: History School Books in the Twentieth Century.* Boston: Atlantic Little-Brown.

FLEMING, W. (1974). *Art and Ideas.* NY: Holt, Rinehart, and Winston.

FORSETH, S. D. (1976). The effects of art activities on attitude and achievement in fourth-grade children pertinent to the learning of mathematics and art. (Doctoral dissertation, University of Minnesota). *Dissertation Abstracts International, 37,* 7590A.

FOSTER, H. (1983). *The Anti-Aesthetic: Essays on Postmodern Culture.* Port Townsend, WA: Bay Press.

FOUCAULT, M. (1973). *The Order of Things.* NY: Vintage Books.

FOX, H. (1987). *Avante-Garde in the Eighties.* Los Angeles: Los Angeles County Museum of Art.

FRANENA, W. K. (1965). *Three Historical Philosophies of Education: Aristotle, Kant, and Dewey.* Glenview, IL: Scott, Foresman.

FREUD, S. (1959). *Beyond the Pleasure Principle.* NY: Bantam Books.

FREUD, S. (1964). *Leonardo da Vinci and a Memory of His Childhood.* NY: Norton.

FRIEDLANDER, M. (1932). *On Art and Connoisseurship.* Translated by T. BORENVI. Oxford: Bruno Cassirieu.

FRY, E. (1981). *Cubism.* NY: Norton.

FRY, R. (1920). *Vision and Design.* London.

FRY, R. (1927). *Cezanne: A Study of His Development.* London: L. and V. Woolf.

GABLIK, S. (1984). *Has Modernism Failed?.* New York: Thames and Hudson.

GAGNE, R. (1977). *The Conditions of Learning.* NY: Holt, Rinehart, and Winston.

GALVEZ-HJORNEVIK, C. (January-February 1986). Mentoring among teachers: A review of the literature. *Journal of Teacher Education,* 6–11.

GARDNER, H. (1973). *The Arts and Human Development: A Psychological Study of the Artistic Process.* NY: Wiley.

GARDNER, H. (1980). *Artful scribbles: The significance of children's drawings.* NY: Basic Books.

GARDNER, H. (1983). Artistic intelligences. *Art Education, 36*(2), 47–49.

GARDNER, H. and WINNER, E. (1976). How children learn...three stages of understanding art. *Psychology Today, 9,* 42–43.

GEAHIGAN, G. (1980). Metacritical inquiry in art education. *Studies in Art Education, 21*(3), 54–67.

GENTNER, D., and STEVENS, A. L. (eds.) (1983). *Mental Models.* Hillsdale, NJ: Erlbaum Associates.

GETZELS, J. W., & CSIKZENTMIHALYI, M. (1976). *The Creative Vision: A Longitudinal Study of Problem Finding in Art.* NY: Wiley.

GETZELS, J. W., and DILLON, J. T. (1973). The nature of giftedness and the education of the gifted. In R. M. W. TRAVERS (ed.), *Second Handbook of Research on Teaching* (pp. 689–731). Chicago: Rand McNally.

GILBERT, R. & MCCARTER, W. (1988). *Living With Art.* NY: Knopf.

GILHORN, C. (1970). Pop pedagogy: Looking at the coke bottle. In M. FISHWICK and R. BROWN (eds.), *Icons of Popular Culture.* Bowling Green, OH: Bowling Green University Press.

GILLIATT, M. (1980). The effects of habituation, the Feldman-Mittler methodology, and studio activities on expanding art preferences of elementary students. *Studies in Art Education, 21*(2), 43–49.

GINSBURG, A., and HANSON, S. (1985). *Values and Educational Success Among Disadvantaged Students.* Final Report to the U.S. Department of Education, Washington, D.C.

GLIDEWELL, J., et al. (1983). Professional support systems: The teaching profession. In A. NADLER, J. FISHER, and B. DePAULO (eds.), *Applied Research in Help-Seeking and Reactions to Aid.* NY: Academic Press.

GODFREY, T. (1986). *The New Image: Painting in the 1980's.* NY: Abbeville Press.

GOLDBERG, M. (1958). Recent research on the talented. *Teachers' College Record, 60*(3), 150–163.

GOLDSMITH, A. H. (1982). Codes of discipline: Developments, dimensions, directions. *Education and Urban Society* (pp. 185–195). ERIC Document No. EJ 260932.

GOLDSTEIN, E., SAUNDERS, R., KOWALCHUK, J. D., & KATZ, T. H. *Understanding and Creating Art, Books I & II.* Dallas: Garrard Publishing Co.

GOLLECK, R. (1987). *Der Blaue Reiter.* NY: teNeues Press.

GOLLOB, H. F. and DITTES, J. E. (1965). Effects of manipulated self-esteem on persuasability depending on threat and complexity of communication. *Journal of Personality and Social Psychology, 2,* 195–201.

GOMBRICH, E. H. (1960–61). *Art and Illusion.* NY: Pantheon Books.

GOMBRICH, E. H. (1983). *The Story of Art* (13th ed.). NY: Praeger.

GOOD, T. L. (1982). How teachers' expectations affect results. *American Education, 18*(10), 25–32.

GOOD, T. L., and BROPHY, J. E. (1984). *Looking in Classrooms* (3rd ed). NY: Harper and Row.

GOODMAN, N. (1976). *Languages of Art: An Approach to a Theory of Symbols.* Indianapolis: Hackett.

GOODMAN, N. (1984). *Of Mind and Other Matters.* Cambridge: Harvard University Press.

GOWAN, J., and DEMOS, G. D. (1964). *The Education and Guidance of the Ablest.* Springfield, IL: Charles C. Thomas.

GOWANS, A. (1974). Popular arts and historic artifact: New principles for studying history in art. In J. M. N. FISHWICK, (ed.), *Popular Architecture.* Bowling Green, OH: Bowling Green Popular Press, pp. 88–105.

GRANT, G. (1981). The character of education and the education of character. *Daedalus, 110*(3), 135–149.

GRANT, G. (1985). Schools that make an imprint: Creating a strong positive ethos. In J. H. BUNZEL (ed.), *Challenge to American Schools: The Case for Standards and Values,* (pp. 127–143). NY: Oxford University Press.

GRAVES, D. H. (1983). *Writing: Teachers and Children at Work.* Exeter, NH: Heinemann Educational Books.

GRAY, J. U. (1987). A seventy-five percent solution for the success of DBAE. *Art Education, 40*(5), 54–57.

GRAY, S. T. (1984). How to create a successful school/community partnership. *Phi Delta Kappan, 65*(6), 405–409.

GRAY, W. A., and GRAY, M. M. (November 1985). Synthesis of research on mentoring beginning teachers. *Educational Leadership, 37*–43.

GREENE, M. (1981). Aesthetic literacy in general education. In J. F. SOLTIS (ed.), *Philosophy and Education* (pp. 115–141). 80th Yearbook of the National Society for the Study of Education, Pt. 1, Chicago: University of Chicago Press.

GREER, W. D. (1982). A structure of discipline concepts for DBAE. *Studies in Art Education, 28*(4), 227–233.

GREER, W. D. (1984). A discipline-based view of art education: Approaching art as a subject of study. *Studies in Art Education, 25*(4), 212–218.

GRIGSBY, J. E. (1977). *Art and Ethnics: Background for Teaching Youth in a Pluralistic Society.* Dubuque: Wm. C. Brown.

GROSSMAN, E. (1984). Program planning for the visual arts. *Art Education, 37*(3), 6–10.

HAGAMAN, S. (1988). Philosophical aesthetics in the art class: A look toward implementation. *Art Education, 41*(3), 18–22.

HALDANE, J. J. (1983). Art's perspective on value. *Art Education, 36*(1), 8–9.

HALL, J. B. (1978). Undergraduate elementary education major's attitude towards the teaching of art. (Doctoral dissertation, University of Alabama). *Dissertation Abstracts International, 27,* 2029A.

HALLORAN, J. D. (1967). *Attitude Formation and Change.* Westport, Conn.: Greenwood Press, Publishers.

HAMBLEN, K. A. (1984). An art criticism questioning strategy within the framework of Bloom's taxonomy. *Studies in Art Education, 26*(1), 41–50.

HAMBLEN, K. A. (1984). Artistic perception as a function of learned expectations. *Art Education, 37*(3), 20–26.

HAMBLEN, K. A. (1985). Developing aesthetic literacy through contested concepts. *Art Education, 38*(5), 19–24.

HAMBLEN, K. A. (1987). What general education can tell us about evaluation in art. *Studies in Art Education, 28*(4), 246–250.

HAMBLEN, K. A. (1987). An examination of discipline-based art education issues. *Studies in Art Education, 28*(2), 68–78.

HAMBLEN, K. A. (1988). Approaches to aesthetics in art education: A critical theory perspective. *Studies in Art Education, 29*(2), 81–90.

HANSON, S., and GINSBURG, A. (1985). *Gaining Ground: Values and High School Success.* Final Report to the U.S. Department of Education, Washington, D.C.

HARARI, O., and COVINGTON, M. V. (1981). Reactions to achievement behavior from a teacher and student perspective: A developmental analysis. *American Educational Research Journal, 18*(1), 15–28.

HARDIMAN, G. W. and ZERNICH, T. (1981). *Foundations for Curriculum Development and Evaluation in Art Education.* Champaign, IL: Stipes.

HARRIS, M. E. (1987). *The Art of Black Mountain College.* MIT Press.

HASELBERGER, H. (1961). Methods of studying ethnographic art. *Current Anthropology, 2*, 341–384.

HASTIE, R. and SCHMIDT, C. *Encounters With Art.* NY: McGraw-Hill.

HAUSER, A. (1982). *The Sociology of Art* (K. Northcott, trans.). Chicago: University of Chicago.

HAUSMAN, J. (ed.). (1965). *Report of the Commission on Art Education.* Washington, DC: National Art Education Association.

HAWLEY, W., and ROSENHOLTZ, S. with GOODSTEIN, H. and HASSELBRING, T. (1984). Good schools: What research says about improving student achievement. *Peabody Journal of Education, 61*(4).

HAYES-ROTH, B., and GOLDIN, S. E. (1980). *Individual Differences in Planning Processes.* Santa Monica, CA: The Rand Corp.

HEATH, S. B. (1983). *Ways with Words: Language, Life and Work in Communities and Classrooms.* NY: Cambridge University Press.

HEIDT, A. H. (1986). Creating art appreciation activities. *Art Education, 39*(1), 23–28.

HENRI, R. (1958). *The Art Spirit.* Philadelphia: Lippincott.

HEWETT, G. J., and RUSH, J. C. Finding buried treasures: Aesthetic scanning with children. *Art Education, 40*(1), 41–45.

HIRSCH, E. D. (1983). Cultural Literacy. *The American Scholar, 52,* 159–169.

HIRSCH, E. D. (1985). Cultural literacy and the schools. *American Educator, 74,* 8–15.

HIRSCH, E. D. (1987). *Cultural Literacy: What Every American Needs to Know.* Boston: Houghton Mifflin.

HITLER, A. (1943). *Mein Kampf* (R. MATHEIM, trans.). Boston: Houghton Mifflin.

HOBBS, J. A. (1985). *Art in Context.* Orlando, FL: Harcourt Brace Jovanovich.

HOBBS, J. A. (1984). Popular art vs. fine art. *Art Education, 37*(3), 11–15.

HOFSTADTER, A. (1965). *Truth and Art.* NY: Columbia University Press.

HOLLINGSWORTH, P. L. (1983). The combined effect of mere exposure, counterattitudinal advocacy, and art criticism methodology on upper elementary and junior high students' affect towards works of art. *Studies in Art Education,* 24(2), 101–110.

HOROWITZ, F. A. (1985). *More Than You See: A Guide to Art.* NY: Harcourt Brace Jovanovich.

HORTAS, C. R. (1984). Foreign languages and humane learning. In C. E. FINN, D. RAVITCH, and R. T. FANCHER (eds.), *Against Mediocrity: The Humanities in America's High Schools.* NY: Holmes and Meier.

HOSPERS, J. (1982). *Understanding the Arts.* Englewood Cliffs, NJ: Prentice-Hall.

HOVLAND, C. I., CAMPBELL, E. H., & BROCK, T. (1957). The effects of "commitment" on opinion change following communication. In C. I. HOVLAND (ed.), *Order of Presentation in Persuasion.* New Haven, Conn.: Yale University Press.

HOVLAND, C. I., JANIS, I. L., and KELLEY, H. H. (1953). *Communication and Persuasion.* New Haven, CT: Yale University Press.

HOWARD, V. A. (1971). Harvard project zero: A fresh look at art education. *Journal of Aesthetic Education, 5*(1), 61–73.

HUBBARD, G. (1969). *Art in the High School.* Belmont, Ca: Wadsworth.

HUGHES, R. (1980). *The Shock of the New.* NY: Knopf.

HUMES, A. (1981). *The Composing Process: A Summary of the Research.* Austin, TX: Southwest Regional Laboratory ERIC Document No. ED 222925.

HUNTER, M. and GEE, K. (1988). Art educators: Escalate your teaching skills (Part I). *NAEA Advisory.* Reston, VA: National Art Education Association.

HUNTER, M. and GEE, K. (1988). Art appreciation/art history lesson (Part II). *NAEA Advisory.* Reston, VA: National Art Education Association.

HUNTER, M. and GEE, K. (1988). Studio art lesson (Part III). *NAEA Advisory.* Reston, VA: National Art Education Association.

HURWITZ, A. (1983). *The Gifted and Talented in Art: A Guide to Program Planning.* Worcester, MA: Davis.

HURWITZ, A. (1986). *Teaching Art History: What Forms Can it Take?* Harrisburg, Penn.: Pennsylvania State Dept. of Education, Pennsylvania's Symposium II on Art Education. (ERIC Document Preproduction Service, ED 287 759).

HURWITZ, A. and MADEJA, S. S. (1977). *The Joyous Vision: Source Book.* Englewood Cliffs, NJ: Prentice-Hall.

INSKO, C. A. (1964). Primacy vs. recency in persuasion as a function of the timing of arguments and measures. *Journal of Abnormal and Social Psychology, 69,* 381–391.

IRVINE, H. (1984). An art centered art curriculum. *Art Education, 37*(3), 16–19.

JAMISON, D., SUPPES, P., and WELLS, S. (1974). The effectiveness of alternative instructional media: A survey. *Review of Educational Research, 44*(1), 1–67.

JANSON, H. W. (1962). *History of Art.* Englewood Cliffs, NJ: Prentice-Hall.

JOHANSEN, P. (1979). An art appreciation teaching model for visual aesthetic education. *Studies in Art Education, 20*(3), 4–5.

JOHNSON, H. M. (1986). *How Do I Love Me? (2nd edition).* Salem, WI: Sheffield.

JOHNSON, M. (ed.). (1981). *Philosophical Perspectives on Metaphor.* Minneapolis: University of Minnesota Press.

JOHNSON, S. (1985). *One Minute for Myself.* NY: Morrow.

JUNG, C. (ed.) (1964). *Man and His Symbols.* NY: Doubleday.

KATTER, E. (1988). An approach to art games: Playing and planning. *Art Education, 41*(3), 46–54.

KATTER, E. (1986). *Art History Instruction: From History to Practice.* Harrisburg, Penn.: Pennsylvania State Dept. of Education, Pennsylvania's Symposium II on Art Education. (ERIC Document Reproduction Service, ED 287 759).

KAUFMAN, I. (1963). Art education: A discipline? *Studies in Art Education, 4*(2), 15–23.

KEITH, T. Z. (1982). Time spent on homework and high school grades: A large-sample path analysis. *Journal of Educational Psychology, 74*(2), 248–253.

KELLOGG, R. (1969). *Analyzing Children's Art.* Palo Alto, CA: National Press Books.

KELLOUGH, R. and KIM, E. (1972). *A Resource Guide for Secondary Teaching.* NY: MacMillan Pub. Co. Inc.

KELLY, J. J. (1970). *The Sculptural Idea.* Minneapolis: Burgess.

KEPES, G. (1965). *Education of Vision.* NY: Braziller.

KEPES, G. (1944). *Language of Vision.* Chicago: Theobold.

KERN, E. J. (1987). Antecedents of discipline-based art education: State departments of education curriculum documents. *The Journal of Aesthetic Education, 21*(2), 35–57.

KERN, E. J. (1984). The aesthetic education curriculum program and curriculum reform. *Studies in Art Education, 25*(4), 219–225.

KIMBALL, S. B. (1972). Social and cultural congruences in American civilization. *Journal of Aesthetic Education, 6*(1–2), 39–52.

KLEINBAUER, W. E. (1971). *Modern Perspectives in Western Art History.* NY: Holt, Rinehart, and Winston.

KLEINBAUER, W. E. (1987). Art history in discipline-based art education. *The Journal of Aesthetic Education, 21*(2), 205–216.

KNOBLER, N. (1980). *The Visual Dialogue* (3rd ed.). NY: Henry Holt.

KOESTLER, A. (1949). *Insight and Outlook.* NY: MacMillan.

KOESTLER, A. (1964). *The Act of Creation.* London: Hutchinson.

KOROSCIK, J. S. (1982). The effects of prior knowledge, presentation time, and task demands on visual art processing. *Studies in Art Education, 23*(3), 13–22.

KOROSCIK, J. S. (1984). Cognition in viewing and talking about art. *Theory Into Practice, 23*(4), 330–333.

KRAMER, H. (1973). *The Age of the Avante-Garde.* NY: Farrar, Straus & Giroux.

KRATHWOHL, D. R., BLOOM, B. S. and MASIA, B. B. (1964). *Taxonomy of Educational Objectives: Handbook II: Affective Domain.* NY: McKay.

KRUPP, J. (Spring 1987). Mentoring: A means by which teachers become staff developers. *Journal of Staff Development,* 12–15.

KUHN, M. (1984). Restructuring the future of art education curricula. *Studies in Art Education, 25*(4), 271–275.

KULIK, J. A., and KULIK, C. C. (1984). Synthesis of research on effects of accelerated instruction. *Educational Leadership, 42*(2), 84–89.

KURLANSKY, M. J. (1977). Pop goes the culture. *Change, 9*(6), 36–39.

KURTZ, B. (1987). *Visual Imagination.* Englewood Cliffs, NJ: Prentice-Hall.

LACHAPELLE, J. R. (1983). Creativity research: Its sociological and educational limitations. *Studies in Art Education, 24*(2), 131–139.

LACHAPELLE, J. R. (1984). The sociology of art and art education: A relationship reconsidered. *Studies in Art Education, 26*(1), 34–40.

LAKOFF, G. & JOHNSON, M. (1980). *Metaphors We Live By.* Chicago: University of Chicago Press.

LANDAU, J. (1986). Looking, thinking, and learning: Visual literacy for children. *Art Education, 39*(1), 17–21.

LANGER, S. (1953). *Feeling and Form.* NY: Scribner's.

LANGER, S. (1957). *Problems in Art.* NY: Scribner's.

LANIER, V. (1976). *Essays in Art Education: The Development of One Point of View* (2nd ed.). NY: MSS Educational Publishing.

LANIER, V. (1981). Aesthetic literacy as the product of art education. In *The Product of a Process* (pp. 115–121). *Proceedings of the 24th INSEA World Congress, Rotterdam, 1981.* Amsterdam: De Trommel.

LANIER, V. (1981). Popularization without misrepresentation: Curriculum content for aesthetic literacy. *Art Education, 34*(6), 5–12.

LANIER, V. (1984). Eight guidelines for selecting art curriculum content. *Studies in Art Education, 25*(4), 232–238.

LANIER, V. (1987). A*R*T*, a friendly alternative to DBAE. *Art Education, 40*(5), 46–53.

LANKFORD, E. L. (1992). *Aesthetics: Issues and Inquiry.* Reston, VA: National Art Education Association.

LANKFORD, E. L. (1984). A phenomenological methodology for art criticism. *Studies in Art Education, 25*(3), 151–158.

LANKFORD, E. L. (1986). Making sense of aesthetics. *Studies in Art Education, 28*(1), 48–52.

LANSING, K. M. (1976). *Art, Artists, and Art Education.* Dubuque: Dendal-Hunt.

LANSING, K. M., and RICHARDS, A. E. (1981). *The Elementary Teacher's Art Handbook.* NY: Holt, Rinehart, and Winston.

LEE, S. (1982). *A History of Far Eastern Art.* NY: Abrams.

LEHMAN, D. L. (1970). *Role Playing and Teacher Education: Manual for Developing Innovative Teachers.* Washington, DC: Commission on Undergraduate Education in the Biological Sciences.

LEVINE, A. (1980). *When Dreams and Heroes Died: A Portrait of Today's College Student.* San Francisco: Jossey-Bass.

LINDER, D. E., COOPER, J., and JONES, E. E. (1967). Decision freedom as a determinant of the role of incentive magnitude in attitude change. *Journal of personality and Social Psychology, 6,* 245–254.

LINDERMAN, E. (1980). *Teaching Secondary School Art.* Dubuque: Wm. C. Brown.

LIPMAN, M. (1967). *What Happens in Art.* NY: Appleton-Century-Crofts.

LITTLE, J. W. (1983). Norms of collegiality and experimentation: Workplace conditions of school success. *American Educational Research Journal, 19*(3), 325–340.

LOGAN, F. M. (1975). Update '75: Growth in American art education. *Studies in Art Education, 17*(1), 7–16.

LORTIE, D. (1975). *Schoolteacher: A Sociological Study.* Chicago: University of Chicago Press.

LOWENFELD, V. (1947). *Creative and mental growth.* New York: MacMillan.

LOWENFELD, V. and BRITTAIN, L. (1982). *Creative and Mental Growth,* (7th ed.). NY: MacMillan.

LOWENTHAL, D. (1985). *The Past is a Foreign Country.* Cambridge: Cambridge University Press.

LOWIN, A. (1967). Approach and avoidance: Alternative modes of selective exposure to information. *Journal of Personality and Social Psychology, 6,* 1–9.

LUCIE-SMITH, E. (1982). *Art in the Seventies,* Ithaca: Cornell University Press.

LUCIE-SMITH, E. (1985). *Movements in Art Since 1945.* NY: Norton.

LUMSDAINE, A. A., and JANIS, I. L. (1953). Resistance to "counter-propaganda" produced by one-sided and two-sided "propaganda" presentations. *Public Opinion Quarterly, 17,* 311–318.

MacGregor, N. (1970). Concepts of criticism: Implications for art education. *Studies in Art Education, 11*(2), 27–33.

MacQueen, J. (1970). *Allegory.* London: Methuen.

Madeja, S. S. (1971). Aesthetic education: An area of study. *Art Education, 24*(8), 16–19.

Madeja, S. S. (1973). *All the Arts for Every Child.* NY: JDR 3rd Fund, Inc.

Madeja, S. S. (ed). (1978). *The Arts, Cognition, and Basic Skills.* St. Louis: CEMREL.

Madeja, S. S. (1980). The art curriculum: Sins of omission. *Art Education, 33*(6), 24–26.

Madeja, S. S., and Onuska, S. (1977). *Through the Arts to the Aesthetic: The CEMREL Aesthetic Education Curriculum.* St. Louis: CEMREL, Inc.

Mager, R. F. and Pipe, P. (1970). *Analyzing Performance Problems.* Belmont, CA: Fearon.

Mager, R. F. (1984). *Preparing Instructional Objectives* (2nd ed.). Belmont, CA: David S. Lake.

Margolis, J. (1962). *Philosophy Looks at the Arts.* NY: Scribner's.

Mason, J. (1983). An examination of reading instruction in third and fourth grades. *The Reading Teacher, 36*(9), 906–913.

McCarthy, M. J. (1978). *Introducing Art History: A Guide for Teachers.* Toronto: Ontario Institute for Studies in Education.

McFarlane, J. (1978). The mind of modernism. In M. Bradbury and J. McFarlane (eds.), *Modernism 1890-1930* (pp. 71–93). NJ: Humanities.

McFee, J. K. (1971). *Preparation for Art* (2nd ed.). Belmont, CA: Wadsworth.

McFee, J. K. (1984). An analysis of the goal, structure, and social context of the 1965 Penn State seminar and the 1983 Getty Institute for Educators on the Visual Arts. *Studies in Art Education, 25*(4), 276–281.

McFee, J. K. & Degge, R. M. (1977). *Art Culture and Environment: A Catalyst for Teaching.* Belmont, Ca: Wadsworth Pub. Co.

McGuire, W. J. (1961). Resistance to persuasion conferred by active and passive prior refutation of the same and alternative counter-arguments. *Journal of Abnormal and Social Psychology, 63,* 329–332.

McLuhan, M. (1967). *The Medium is the Message.* NY: Ballantine.

McShine, K. (1987). *Berlin art 1961–1987.* NY: teNeues.

Michael, J. A. (1980). Studio art experience: The heart of art education. *Art Education, 33*(2), 15–19.

Miller, J. L. (1980). A study of attitudes of school board presidents, superintendents, and elementary and secondary principals in Missouri school districts concerning visual arts education and the perception of those attitudes by art teachers. (Doctoral dissertation, University of Kansas). *Dissertation Abstracts International, 41,* 4942A.

Miller, N. and Campbell, D. T. (1959). Recency and primacy in persuasion as a function of the timing of speeches and measurements. *Journal of Abnormal and Social Psychology, 59,* 1–9.

MILLS, J. (1966). Opinion change as a function of the communicator's desire to influence and liking for the audience. *Journal of Experimental Social Psychology, 2,* 152–159.

MILLS, J. and JELLISON, J. M. (1968). Effect on opinion change of similarity between the communicator and the audience he addressed. *Journal of Personality and Social Psychology, 9,* 153–159.

MITTLER, G. A. (1972). Attitude modification towards works of art. *Studies in Art Education, 13*(2), 58.

MITTLER, G. A. (1976). An instructional strategy designed to overcome the adverse effects of established students attitudes towards works of art. *Studies in Art Education, 17*(3), 13–31.

MITTLER, G. A. (1980). Learning to look/looking to learn: A proposed approach to art appreciation at the secondary level. *Art Education, 33*(3), 17–21.

MITTLER, G. A. (1986). *Art in Focus.* Peoria: Bennett & McKnight.

MOFFATT, J. F. (1969). Art history as a pedagogical science. *Art Education, 22*(3), 24–28.

MOHAN, M. (1972). *Peer Tutoring as a Technique for Teaching the Unmotivated.* Fredonia, NY: State University of New York Teacher Education Research Center. ERIC Document No. ED 061154.

MORINE-DERSHIMER, G. (1983). Instructional strategy and the creation of classroom status. *American Educational Research Journal, 20*(4), 645–661.

MORRIS, J. W. and STUCKHARDT, M. H. (1977). Art attitude: Conceptualization and implication. *Studies in Art Education, 19*(1), 21–28.

MORRIS, V. C., and others (1984). *Principals in Action: The Reality of Managing Schools.* Columbus, OH: Merrill.

MULLER, G. (1973). *The New Avant-Garde.* NY: Praeger.

MUKERJEE, R. (1959). *The Social Function of Art.* NY: Philosophical Library.

MUNZ, P. (1977). *The Shapes of Time: A New Look at the Philosophy of History.* Middletown, CT: Wesleyan University Press.

NAGLE, J. (1980). *The Responsive Arts.* Sherman Oaks, CA: Alfred.

NAISBITT, J. (1984). *Megatrends.* NY: Warner Books.

National Academy of Science, National Academy of Engineering, Institute of Medicine, and Committee on Science, Engineering and Public Policy. (1984). *High Schools and the Changing Workplace: The Employer's View.* Washington, D.C.: National Academy Press.

National Advisory Council on Vocational Education. (1984). *Conference Summary: Vocational Education and Training Policy for Today and Tomorrow.* Washington, D.C.

National Art Education Association. (1968). *The Essentials of a Quality School Art Program.* Reston, VA: Author.

National Assessment for Educational Progress (1981). *Art and Young Americans, 1974-79: Results from the Second National Art Assessment.* Denver, CO: Author.

National Center for Education Statistics. (1983). *School District Survey of Academic Requirements and Achievement.* Washington, D.C.: U.S. Department of Education, Fast Response Survey Systems, ERIC Document No. ED 238097.

National Endowment for the Arts. (1988). *Toward Civilization: Overview from a Report on Arts Education.* Washington, D.C.: Author.

NATRIELLO, G. (1984). Teachers' perceptions of the frequency of evaluation and assessments of their effort and effectiveness. *American Educational Research Journal, 21*(3), 579–595.

NATRIELLO, G., and DORNBUSCH, S. M. (1981). Pitfalls in the evaluation of teachers by principals. *Administrator's Notebook, 29*(6), 1–4.

NEALE, J. L. (1973). An examination of an inservice course to effect change in teacher's attitudes toward teaching art: A study conducted in economically poor areas of Chicago. (Doctoral dissertation, New York University). *Dissertation Abstracts International, 34,* 4064A.

NERET, G. (1986). *The Art of the Twenties.* NY: Rizzoli.

NICKERSON, C., LOLLIS, C., and PORTER, E. *Miraculous Me!* Seattle, WA: CHEF.

NORBERG-SCHULTZ, C. (1975). *Meaning in Western Architecture.* NY: Praeger.

OCVIRK, O. G. (1975). *Art Fundamentals.* Dubuque: Wm. C. Brown.

O'HARE, D. (1976). Individual differences in perceived similarity and preference for visual art: A multidimensional scaling analysis. *Perception & Psychophysics, 20*(6), 445–452.

O'HARE, D. (1979). Multidimensional scaling representations and individual differences in concept learning of artistic style. *British Journal of Psychology, 70,* 219–230.

PACKARD, S. (1984). Contemporary reform and the contents of curricula. *Studies in Art Education, 25*(4), 265–270.

PALLAS, A. M., and ALEXANDER, K. L. (1983). Sex differences in quantitative SAT performance: New evidence on the differential coursework hypothesis. *American Educational Research Journal, 20*(2), 165–182.

PANOFSKY, E. (1955). *Meaning in the Visual Arts.* Chicago: University of Chicago Press.

PANOFSKY, E. (1962). *Studies in Iconology: Humanistic themes in the art of the Renaissance* (rev. ed.). NY: Harper & Row.

PANOFSKY, E. (1968). *Idea: A Concept in Art Theory.* NY: Harper & Row.

PAPAGEORGIS, D. & MCGUIRE, W. J. (1962). Effectiveness of forewarning in developing resistance to persuasion. *Public Opinion Quarterly, 26,* 24–34.

PAPPAS, G. (ed.). (1970). *Concepts in Art and Education.* London: MacMillan.

PARKS, M. E. (1986). An analysis of attitude recognition, formation, and change concepts in selected art education textbooks. *Studies in Art Education, 27*(4), 198–208.

PARKS, M. E. (1988). How does the work mean? *Art Education, 41*(3), 55–61.

PARKS, M. E. (1989). Art education in a post-modern age. *Art Education, 42*(2), 10–13.

PARKS, M. E. (1990, April) Identifying art content for curriculum development. Paper presented at the annual convention of the National Art Education Association, Kansas, City, MO.

PARSONS, M. J. (1976). A suggestion concerning the development of aesthetic experience in children. *Journal of Aesthetics and Art Criticism, 34*(3), 305–314.

PARSONS, M. J. (1987). Talk about a painting: a cognitive developmental analysis. *The Journal of Aesthetic Education, 21*(1), 37–55.

PARSONS, M.; JOHNSTON, M.; and DURHAM, R. (1978). Developmental stages of children's aesthetic responses. *Journal of Aesthetic Education,* 83–104.

PASTON, H. S. (1973). *Learning to Teach Art.* Lincoln, NE: Professional Educators.

PAZIENZA, J. (1986). *Investigating the Discipline of Art History.* Harrisburg, Penn.: Pennsylvania State Dept. of Education, Pennsylvania's Symposium II on Art Education. (ERIC Document Reproduction Service, ED 287 759).

PEPPER, S. (1945). *The Basis of Criticism in the Arts.* Cambridge: Harvard University Press.

PERFETTI, C. A., and LESGOLD, A. M. (1979). Coding and comprehension in skilled reading and implications for reading instruction. In L. B. RESNICK and P. A. WEAVER (eds.), *Theory and Practice of Early Reading, vol. 1* (pp. 57–84). Hillsdale, NJ: Erlbaum Associates.

PETERSON, K., and WILSON, J. J. (1976). *Women Artists: Recognition and Reappraisal from Early Middle Ages to the Twentieth Century.* NY: Harper & Row.

PHENIX, P. H. (1964). *Realms of Meaning.* NY: McGraw-Hill.

PHI DELTA KAPPA. (1980). *Why Do Some Urban Schools Succeed? The Phi Delta Kappa Study of Exceptional Urban Elementary Schools.* Bloomington, IN: Phi Delta Kappa.

PHIPPS, R. and WINK, R. (1987). *Invitation to the Gallery: An Introduction to Art.* Dubuque: Wm. C. Brown.

PIAGET, J. (1954). *The Construction of Reality in the Child.* NY: Basic Books.

PIAGET, J. (1969). *The Language and Thought of the Child.* NY: World Publishing.

PIAGET, J. (1977). *The Development of Thought: Equilibration of Cognitive Structure.* NY: Viking Press.

PLUMMER, G. S. (1974). *Children's Art Judgment.* Dubuque: Wm. C. Brown.

POGGIOLI, R. (1968). *The Theory of the Avant-Garde* (G. Fitzgerald, Trans.). Cambridge, MA: Belknap.

POINTON, M. (1980). *History of Art: A Students' Handbook.* London: Allen & Unwin.

POPOWICZ, L. A. (1975). Interdisciplinary approach to biology integrated with art: a vehicle for changing attitudes toward science. (Doctoral Dissertation, Boston College). *Dissertation Abstracts International, 35,* 7143A.

PREBLE, D., and PREBLE, S. (1985). *Artforms.* New York: Harper & Row.

PROWN, J. (1982). Mind in matter: An introduction to material culture theory and method. *Winterhur Portfolio, 17,* 1–19.

PUM, R. J. (1971). *Differential characteristics of art-teaching majors and elementary education majors in college: As measured by selected attitude, value, and personality factors.* (Unpublished doctoral dissertation, Ball State University).

PURDY, D., EITZEN, D. S., and HUFNAGEL, R. (1982). Are athletes students? The educational attainment of college athletes. *Social Problems, 29*(4), 439–448.

PURKEY, S., and SMITH, M. (1983). Effective schools: A Review. *The Elementary School Journal, 83*(4), 427–452.

RADER, M., and JESSUP, B. (1976). *Art and Human Values.* Englewood Cliffs, NJ: Prentice-Hall.

RAVITCH, D. (November 17, 1985). Decline and fall of teaching history. *New York Times Magazine,* pp. 50–52; 101; 117.

RAVITCH, D. (1985). From history to social studies. In *The Schools We Deserve: Reflections on the Educational Crisis of Our Times* (pp. 112–132). NY: Basic Books.

READ, H. (1968). *A Concise History of Modern Painting.* NY: Praeger.

READ, H. (1968). *The Meaning of Art.* Boston: Faber & Faber.

READ, H. (1967). *Art and Alienation: The Role of the Artist in Society.* New York: Horizon Press.

READ, H. (19??). *Art and Society.* New York: Pantheon Books.

REASONER, R. *Building Self-Esteem: A Comprehensive Program.* Santa Cruz, CA: Educational and Training Services, Inc.

REDFIELD, D. L., and ROUSSEAU, E. W. (1981). A meta-analysis of experimental research on teacher questioning behavior. *Review of Educational Research, 51*(2), 237–245.

REID, L. A. (1973). Aesthetics and aesthetic education. In D. FIELD & J. NEWICK (eds.), *The Study of Education and Art* (pp. 164–186). Boston: Routledge & Kegan Paul.

RESNICK, D. B., and RESNICK, L. B. (1977). The nature of literacy: An historical exploration. *Harvard Educational Review, 47*(5), 370–385.

RICE, D. (1986). *The Uses and Abuses of Art History.* Harrisburg, PA: Pennsylvania State Dept. of Education, Pennsylvania's Symposium II on Art Education. (ERIC Document Reproduction Service, ED 287 759).

RICH, D. K. (1985). *The Forgotten Factor in School Success—The Family.* Washington, D.C.: Home and School Institute.

RICHTER, H. (1985). *DaDa: Art & Anti-Art.* NY: Norton.

RISATTI, H. (1987). Art criticism in discipline-based art education. *The Journal of Aesthetic Education, 21*(2), 217–226.

ROBINS, C. (1984). *The Pluralist Era: American Art 1968–1981.* New York: Harper & Row.

ROHLEN, T. P. (1983). *Japan's High Schools.* Berkeley: University of California Press.

RORSCHACH, E., and WHITNEY, R. (1986). Relearning to teach: Peer observation as a means of professional development. *American Educator, 10*(4), 38–44.

ROSE, B. (1975). *America Art Since 1900.* NY: Praeger.

ROSE, B. (1975). *Readings in American Art: 1900–1975.* NY: Praeger.

ROSENBERG, H. (1976). *Art on the Edge: Creators and Situation.* NY: MacMillan.

ROSENSHINE, B. (1983). Teaching functions in instructional programs. *Elementary School Journal, 83*(4), 335–351.

ROSENSTIEL, A. K.; MORISON, P.; SILVERMAN, J.; and GARDNER, H. (1978). Critical judgment: A developmental study. *The Journal of Aesthetic Education, 12*(4), 95–107.

ROSKILL, M. (1976). *What is Art History?* NY: Harper & Row.

ROSS, M. (1985). *The Aesthetic in Education.* Elmsford, NY: Pergamon.

ROTTERS, E. (1982). *Berlin 1910–1933.* NY: Rizzoli.

RUDENSTINE, A. (1981). *Russian Avant-Garde: The George Costakis Collection.* NY: Abrams.

RUSH, J. C. (1987). Interlocking images: The conceptual core of a discipline-based art lesson. *Studies in Art Education, 28*(4), 206–220.

RUSH, J. C., and LOVANO-KERR, J. (1982). Aesthetic education research, teaching art, and Harvard Project Zero: Some observations. *Journal of Aesthetic Education, 16*(4), 81–91.

RUSSELL, J. (1965). *Seurat.* London: Thames & Hudson.

RUSSELL, J. (1981). *The Meanings of Modern Art.* New York: Harper & Row.

RUSSELL, R. (1986). The aesthetician as a model in learning about art. *Studies in Art Education, 27*(4), 186–197.

RUTTER, M. (1983). School effects on pupil progress: Research findings and policy implications. In L. S. SHULMAN and G. SYKES (eds.), *Handbook of Teaching and Policy* (pp. 3–41). NY: Longman.

SAVUTO, B. J. (1977). High school student attitudes and perceptions of crafts as education in Nassau County, Long Island. (Doctoral dissertation, Columbia University Teachers College). *Dissertation Abstracts International, 38,* 3884A.

SAWYER, R. (1962, Revised Edition). *The Way of Storytelling.* NY: Viking Press.

SEGAL, J., CHIPMAN, S., and GLASER, R. (1985). *Thinking and Learning Skills, Vol. I: Relating Instruction to Research.* Hillsdale, NJ: Erlbaum Associates.

SCHAPIRO, M. (1953). The apples of Cezanne: An essay on the meaning of still-life. *Art News Annual.*

SCHAPIRO, M. (1952). *Paul Cezanne*. NY: Abrams.

SCHINELLER, J. A. (1975). *Art/Search and Self-Discovery*. Worcester, MA: Davis.

SCHULTZ, L. (1980). A studio curriculum for art education. *Art Education, 33*(6), 10–15.

SCOTT, W. A. (1957). Attitude change through reward of verbal behavior. *Journal of Abnormal and Social Psychology, 55*, 72–75.

SEVIGNY, M. J. (1987). Discipline-based art education and teacher education. *The Journal of Aesthetic Education, 21*(2), 95–128.

SHERRILL, C. (1979). *Creative Arts for the Severely Handicapped (2nd ed.)*. Springfield, IL.: CHARLES C. THOMAS.

SHOR, I., and FREIRE, P. (1987). What is the "dialogical method" of teaching? *Journal of Education, 169*(3), 11–31.

SILBERMAN, A. (1968). Introduction: A definition of the sociology of art. *International Social Science Journal, 20*, 567–588.

SIMPSON, C. R. (1981). *SOHO: The Artist in the City*. Chicago: University of Chicago.

SINATRA, R. (1986). *Visual Literacy: Connections to Thinking, Reading and Writing*. Springfield, IL.: CHARLES C. THOMAS.

SKINNER, B. F. (1938). *The Behavior of Organisms*. NY: Appleton.

SKINNER, B. F. (1968). *The Technology of Teaching*. NY: Appleton.

SKINNER, B. F. (1969). *Contingencies of Reinforcement: A Theoretical Analysis*. NY: Appleton.

SMITH, C. R. (1983). *Learning Disabilities: The Interaction of the Learner, Task, and Setting*. Boston: Little, Brown.

SMITH, R. A. (Ed.). (1966). *Aesthetics and Criticism in Art Education*. Chicago: Rand McNally.

SMITH, R. A. (1979). Concepts, concept learning, and art education. *Review of Research in Visual Arts Education, 11*, 7–15.

SMITH, R. A. (1984). From aesthetic criticism to humanistic understanding: A practical illustration. *Studies in Art Education, 25*(4), 238–244.

SMITH, R. A. (1986). *Excellence in Art Education: Ideas and Initiatives*. Reston, VA: National Art Education Association.

SMITH, R. A. (1987). The changing image of art education: theoretical antecedents of discipline-based art education. *The Journal of Aesthetic Education, 21*(2), 3–34.

SPADY, W. (1971). Status, achievement, and motivation in the American high school. *School Review, 79*(3), 379–403.

SPRATT, F. Art production in discipline-based art education. *The Journal of Aesthetic Education, 21*(2), 197–204.

STALLINGS, J. (1980). Allocated academic learning time revisited, or beyond time on task. *Educational Researcher, 9*(11), 11–16.

STERNBERG, R. J. (1987). Teaching critical thinking: Eight easy ways to fail before you begin. *Phi Delta Kappan, 68*(6), 456–459.

STIPEK, D. (1981). Children's perceptions of their own and their classmates' ability. *Journal of Educational Psychology, 73*(3), 404–410.

STOKROCKI, M. (Spring, 1989). Suggestions for teaching art to at-risk students. *NAEA Advisory*, Reston, VA: National Art Education Association.

STOKROCKI, M. (1988). Teaching art to students of minority cultures. *Journal of Multi-Cultural and Cross-Cultural Research in Art Education, 6*(1), 99–111.

STOKROCKI, M. (1986). A portrait of an effective elementary art teacher. *Studies in Art Education, 27*(2), 81–93.

SUGGS, M. S. (1976). Phenomenological analysis, art studio production, and task order effects on student aesthetic attitude, art studio production, and aspective preception of paintings. (Doctoral dissertation, University of Maryland). *Dissertation Abstracts International, 37,* 3353A.

TAUNTON, M. (1982). Aesthetic responses of young children to the visual arts: A review of the literature. *Journal of Aesthetic Education, 16*(3), 93–109.

THERNSTROM, S. (1985). The humanities and our cultural Challenge. In C. E. FINN, D. RAVITCH, and P. ROBERTS (eds.), *Challenges to the Humanities*. NY: Holmes and Meier.

TILGHMAN, B. (1973). *Language and Aesthetics*. Lawrence, KS: University Press of Kansas.

TOFFLER, A. (1970). *Future Shock*. NY: Random House.

TOMPKINS, C. (1975). *Report on Post-Modern Art*. NY: Viking Press.

TSUGAWA, A. (1968). The nature of the aesthetic and human values. *Art Education, 21*(8), 11–20.

TYE, K. A., and TYE, B. B. (1984). Teacher isolation and school reform. *Phi Delta Kappan, 65*(5), 319–322.

UHLIN, D. M. (1979). *Art for the Exceptional Children (2nd ed.)*. Dubuque: Wm. C. Brown.

U. S. Department of Education. (1986). *What Works: Research about Teaching and Learning*. Washington, D. C.: Author.

VIRDEN, P. (1972). The social determinants of aesthetic styles. *British Journal of Aesthetics, 12*(2), 175–185.

WAGNER, L. A. (November 1985). Ambiguities and possibilities in California's mentor teacher program. *Educational Leadership, 23*–29.

WALBERG, H. J. (1969). A portrait of the artist and scientist as a young man. *Exceptional Children, 36*(1), 5–11.

WALBERG, H. J. (1983). Scientific literacy and economic productivity in international perspective. *Daedalus, 112*(2), 1–28.

WALBERG, H. J. (1984). Families as partners in educational productivity. *Phi Delta Kappan, 65*(6), 397–400.

WALBERG, H. J. (1984). Improving the productivity of America's schools. *Educational Leadership, 41*(8), 19–27.

WALBERG, H. J. (1984). What makes schooling effective? A synthesis and a critique of three national studies. *Contemporary Education: A Journal of Reviews, 1*(1), 22–34.

WALBERG, H. J. (1985). Homework's powerful effects on learning. *Educational Leadership, 42*(7), 76–79.

WALBERG, H. J., and SHANAHAN, T. (1983). High school effects on individual students. *Educational Researcher, 12*(7), 4–9.

WALSTER, E.; ARONSON, E.; and ABRAHAMS, D. (1966). On increasing the persuasiveness of a low prestige communicator. *Journal of Experimental Social Psychology, 2,* 325–342.

WEINER, B. (1979). A theory of motivation for some classroom experiences. *Journal of Educational Psychology, 71,* 3–25.

WEINSTEIN, R. Et al. (1982). Student perceptions of differential teacher treatment in open and traditional classrooms. *Journal of Educational Psychology, 74,* 678–692.

WEITZ, M. (1976). Art: Who needs it? *Journal of Aesthetic Education, 10*(1), 19–27.

WELTY, W. M. (July/August, 1989). Discussion method teaching: How to make it work. *Change, 21,* 41–49.

WERHANE, P. H. (1984). *Philosophical Issues in Art.* Englewood Cliffs, NJ: Prentice-Hall.

WHITESEL, L. S. (1975). Scale construction for the measurement of women art students' career commitments. *Studies in Art Education, 17*(1), 47–53.

WHITFORD, F. (1983). *Bauhaus.* NY: Norton.

WILLINGHAM, W. W. (1985). *Success in College: The Role of Personal Qualities and Academic Ability.* NY: The College Board.

WILSON, B. (1971). Evaluation of learning in art education. In B. BLOOM, T. J. HASTINGS, and G. F. MADEUS (eds.), *Handbook of Formative and Summative Evaluation of Student Learning* (pp. 449–458). NY: McGraw-Hill.

WILSON, B. (1986). *Of Trivial Facts and Speculative Inquiry: Philosophical Quandaries About Teaching Art History in the Schools.* Harrisburg, PA: Pennsylvania State Dept. of Education, Pennsylvania's Symposium II on Art Education. (ERIC Document Preproduction Services, ED 287 759).

WILSON, B. (1988). *Art Education, Civilization and the 21st Century: A Researcher's Reflections on the National Endowment for the Arts' Report to Congress.* Reston, VA: National Art Education Association.

WILSON, J. (1967). *Language and the Pursuit of Truth.* London: Cambridge University Press.

WINNER, E. (1982). *Invented Worlds: The Psychology of the Arts.* Cambridge: Harvard University Press.

WISE, A. E., and others (1984). *Teacher Evaluation: A Study of Effective Practices.* Santa Monica, CA: Rand Corporation. ERIC Document No. ED 246559.

WOLFFLIN, H. (1932) (reprint 1950). *Principles of Art History.* NY: Dover.

WRIGHT, F. L. (1960). *Writings and Buildings.* DAUFMAN, E. and RAEBURN, B. (eds.). NY: Horizon.

ZELENSKY, P. and FISHER, M. P. (1988). *The Art of Seeing.* Englewood Cliffs, NJ: Prentice-Hall.

ZEMSKY, R., and MEYERSON, M. (1986). *The Training Impulse.* NY: McGraw-Hill.

SUBJECT BIBLIOGRAPHIES

ART EDUCATION AND EXCEPTIONALITIES

Anderson, F. E. (1978). *Art for All the Children: A Creative Sourcebook for the Impaired Child.* Springfield, IL: Charles C. Thomas.

Anderson, F. E. and Morreau, L. (1984). *Individualized education programs in art: Benefits or Burden?* Art Education, 37(6), 10–14.

Art Educators of New Jersey. (1984). *Insights—Art in Special Education: Educating the Handicapped Through Art* (3rd ed.). NJ: Author.

Blandy, D. (1985). Review of art and mainstreaming: Art instruction for exceptional children in regular school classes. *Studies in Art Education*, 26(3), 189–190.

Bloom, B. S. (ed.). (1985). *Developing Talent in Young People.* NY: Ballantine Books.

Bloom, B. S., and Sosniak, L. A. (November 1981). Talent development vs. schooling. *Educational Leadership*, 39(2), 86–94.

Clark, B. (1983). *Growing up gifted* (2nd ed). Columbus, OH: C. E. Merrill.

Clark, G. A. and Zimmerman, E. (1984). *Educating artistically talented students.* Syracuse, NY: Syracuse University Press.

Clements, C. B. and Clements, R. D. (1984). *Arts and Mainstreaming: Art Instruction for Exceptional Children in Regular School Classes.* Springfield, IL.: Charles C. Thomas.

Cohn, S. J., George, W. C., and Stanley, J. C. (Eds.). (1979). Educational acceleration of intellectually talented youths: Prolonged discussion by a varied group of professionals. In W. C. George, S. J. Cohn, and J. E. Stanley (Eds.), *Educating the Gifted: Acceleration and Enrichment*, (pp. 183–238). Baltimore: Johns Hopkins University Press.

Copeland, B. (1984). Mainstreaming art for the handicapped: Resources for teacher preparation. *Art Education*, 37(6), 22–23.

Dallis, C. (1975). The effects of a black-oriented teaching strategy on attitude change, aesthetic taste, and cognitive learning in art appreciation. (doctoral dissertation, University of Georgia). *Dissertation Abstracts International*, 36, 5648A.

Getzels, J. W., and Dillon, J. T. (1973). The nature of giftedness and the education of the gifted. In R. M. W. Travers (Ed.), *Second Handbook of Research on Teaching*, (pp. 689–731). Chicago: Rand McNally.

Ginsburg, A., and Hanson, S. (1985). *Values and Educational Success Among Disadvantaged Students.* Final Report to the U.S. Department of Education, Washington, D.C.

Goldberg, M. (1958). Recent research on the talented. *Teachers' College Record*, 60(3), 150–163.

Gowan, J., and Demos, G. D. (1964). *The Education and Guidance of the Ablest.* Springfield, IL: Charles C. Thomas.

Grigsby, J. E. (1977). *Art and Ethnics: Background for Teaching Youth in a Pluralistic Society.* Dubuque: Wm. C. Brown.

Hortas, C. R. (1984). Foreign languages and humane learning. In C. E. Finn, D. Ravitch, and R. T. Fancher (eds.), *Against Mediocrity: The Humanities in America's High Schools.* NY: Holmes and Meier.

Hurwitz, A. (1983). *The Gifted and Talented in Art: A Guide to Program Planning.* Worcester, MA: Davis.

Kulik, J. A., and Kulik, C. C. (1984). Synthesis of research on effects of accelerated instruction. *Educational Leadership*, 42(2), 84–89.

Lanier, V. (1984). Eight guidelines for selecting art curriculum content. *Studies in Art Education*, 25(4), 232–238.

Madeja, S. S. (1973). *All the Arts for Every Child.* NY: JDR 3rd Fund, Inc.

Nickerson, C., Lollis, C., and Porter, E. *Miraculous Me!* Seattle, WA: CHEF.

Phi Delta Kappa. (1980). *Why Do Some Urban Schools Succeed?* The Phi Delta Kappa Study of Exceptional Urban Elementary Schools. Bloomington, IN: Phi Delta Kappa.

Reasoner, R. *Building Self-Esteem: A Comprehensive Program*. Santa Cruz, CA: Educational and Training Services, Inc.

Sherrill, C. (1979). *Creative Arts for the Severely Handicapped* (2nd ed.). Springfield, IL.: Charles C. Thomas.

Smith, C. R. (1983). *Learning Disabilities: The Interaction of the Learner, Task, and Setting*. Boston: Little, Brown.

Stokrocki, M. (Spring, 1989). Suggestions for teaching art to at-risk students. *NAEA Advisory*, Reston, VA: National Art Education Association.

Stokrocki, M. (1988). Teaching art to students of minority cultures. *Journal of Multi-Cultural and Cross-Cultural Research in Art Education*, 6(1), 99–111.

Uhlin, D. M. (1979). *Art for the Exceptional Children* (2nd ed.). Dubuque: Wm. C. Brown.

ART EDUCATION—GENERAL

Adams, R. L. (1980). A survey of attitudes of Alabama primary teachers toward selected concepts of Viktor Lowenfeld's teachings regarding art education. (doctoral dissertation, The Florida State University). *Dissertation Abstracts International*, 41, 3843A.

Anderson, F. E. and Morreau, L. (1984). Individualized education programs in art: Benefits or Burden? *Art Education*, 37(6), 10–14.

Art Education, (1983, March), 36(2). Art and the mind (Special issue).

Beittel, K. R. (1973). *Alternatives for art education research: Inquiry into the making of art*. Dubuque: Wm. C. Brown.

Chapman, L. H. (1985). Curriculum development as process and product. *Studies in Art Education*, 26(4), 206–211.

Chapman, L. H. (1978). *Approaches to art in education*. NY: Harcourt Brace Jovanovich.

Chapman, L. H. (1982). *Instant Art, Instant Culture: The Unspoken Policy for American Schools*. NY: Teachers College Press.

Cook, J. M. (1977). Measurement of affective art objectives. *School Arts*, 77(2), 14–17.

Davis, D. J. *Behavioral emphasis in art education*. Reston, VA: National Art Education Association.

Davis, D. J. (1966). The effects of two methods of teaching art upon creative thinking, art attitudes, and aesthetic quality of art products in beginning college art students. (Doctoral dissertation, University of Minnesota). *Dissertation Abstracts International*, 27, 2272A.

DiLeo, J. H. (1970). *Young children and their drawings*. NY: Bruner-Mazel.

Dobbs, S. M. (1974). Research and reason: Recent literature and ideas in American art education. *Curriculum Theory Network*, 4(2–3), 169–191.

Dobbs, S. M. (1979). *Art Education and Back to Basics*. Reston, VA: National Art Education Association.

Efland, A. (1976). The school art style: A functional analysis. *Studies in Art Education*, 17(2), 37–44.

Eisner, E. W. (1966). The development of information and attitude toward art at the secondary and college levels. *Studies in Art Education*, 8(1), 43–51.

Eisner, E. W. (1969). Teaching the humanities: Is a new era possible? *Educational Leadership*, 26(7), 561–564.

Eisner, E. W. (1972). *Educating Artistic Vision*. NY: McMillan.

Eisner, E. W. (1976). *The Arts, Human Development and Education*. Berkeley, CA: McCutchan.

Eisner, E. W. (1982). *Cognition and Curriculum*. NY: Longman.

Eisner, E. W. (1984). Alternative approaches to curriculum development. *Studies in Art Education*, 25(4), 259–264.

Eisner, E. W. (1985). *The Art of Educational Evaluation: A Personal View*. Philadelphia: The Falmer Press.

Eisner, E. W., and Ecker, D. W. (1966). *Readings in Art Education*. Waltham, MA: Blaisdell.

Feldman, E. B. (1970). *Becoming Human Through Art: Aesthetic Experience in the School*. Englewood Cliffs, NJ: Prentice-Hall.

Feldman, D. H. (1987). Developmental psychology and art education: Two fields at the crossroads. *The Journal of Aesthetic Education*, 21(2), 243–259.

Gardner, H. (1973). *The Arts and Human Development: A Psychological Study of the Artistic Process*. NY: Wiley.

Gardner, H. (1980). *Artful scribbles: The significance of children's drawings*. NY: Basic Books.

Getzels, J. W., and Csikzentmihalyi, M. (1976). *The Creative Vision: A Longitudinal Study of Problem Finding in Art*. NY: Wiley.

Grossman, E. (1984). Program planning for the visual arts. *Art Education*, 37(3), 6–10.

Hall, J. B. (1978). Undergraduate elementary education major's attitude towards the teaching of art. (Doctoral dissertation, University of Alabama). *Dissertation Abstracts International*, 27, 2029A.

Hamblen, K. A. (1987). What general education can tell us about evaluation in art. *Studies in Art Education*, 28(4), 246–250.

Hardiman, G. W., and Zernich, T. (19??). *Foundations for Curriculum Development and Evaluation in Art Education*. Champaign, IL: Stipes.

Hausman, J. (Ed.). (1965). *Report of the Commission on Art Education*. Washington, DC: National Art Education Association.

Howard, V. A. (1971). Harvard project zero: A fresh look at art education. *Journal of Aesthetic Education,* 5(1), 61–73.

Hubbard, G. (1969). *Art in the High School.* Belmont, CA: Wadsworth.

Hunter, M., and Gee, K. (1988). Art educators: Escalate your teaching skills (Part I). *NAEA Advisory.* Reston, VA: National Art Education Association.

Hunter, M., and Gee, K. (1988). Art appreciation/art history lesson (Part II). *NAEA Advisory.* Reston, VA: National Art Education Association.

Hunter, M., and Gee, K. (1988). Studio art lesson (Part III). *NAEA Advisory.* Reston, VA: National Art Education Association.

Kellogg, R. (1969). *Analyzing Children's Art.* Palo Alto, CA: National Press Books.

LaChapelle, J. R. (1983). Creativity research: Its sociological and educational limitations. *Studies in Art Education,* 24(2), 131–139.

Lanier, V. (1976). *Essays in Art Education: The Development of One Point of View* (2nd ed.). NY: MSS Educational Publishing.

Lanier, V. (1984). Eight guidelines for selecting art curriculum content. *Studies in Art Education,* 25(4), 232–238.

Lansing, K. M. (1976). *Art, Artists, and Art Education.* Dubuque: Dendal-Hunt.

Lansing, K. M., & Richards, A. E. (1981). *The Elementary Teacher's Art Handbook.* NY: Holt, Rinehart, and Winston.

Linderman, E. (1980). *Teaching Secondary School Art.* Dubuque: Wm. C. Brown.

Logan, F. M. (1975). Update '75: Growth in American art education. *Studies in Art Education,* 17(1), 7–16.

Lowenfeld, V. & Brittain, L. (1987). *Creative and Mental Growth,* (8th ed.). NY: MacMillan.

Madeja, S. S. (ed). (1978). *The Arts, Cognition, and Basic Skills.* St. Louis: CEMREL.

Madeja, S. S. (1980). The art curriculum: Sins of omission. *Art Education,* 33(6), 24–26.

McFee, J. K. (1971). *Preparation for Art* (2nd ed.). Belmont, CA: Wadsworth.

McFee, J. K., and Degge, R. M. (1977). *Art Culture and Environment: A Catalyst for Teaching.* Belmont, CA: Wadsworth.

Michael, J. A. (1980). Studio art experience: The heart of art education. *Art Education,* 33(2), 15–19.

Miller, J. L. (1980). A study of attitudes of school board presidents, superintendents, and elementary and secondary principals in Missouri school districts concerning visual arts education and the perception of those attitudes by art teachers. (Doctoral dissertation, University of Kansas). *Dissertation Abstracts International,* 41, 4942A.

Mittler, G. A. (1972). Attitude modification towards works of art. *Studies in Art Education,* 13(2), 58.

Mittler, G. A. (1976). An instructional strategy designed to overcome the adverse effects of established students attitudes towards works of art. *Studies in Art Education*, 17(3), 13–31.

Morris, J. W. and Stuckhardt, M. H. (1977). Art attitude: Conceptualization and implication. *Studies in Art Education*, 19(1), 21–28.

National Art Education Association. (1968). *The Essentials of a Quality School Art Program*. Reston, VA: Author.

National Assessment for Educational Progress (1981). *Art and Young Americans, 1974–79: Results from the Second National Art Assessment*. Denver, CO: Author.

Neale, J. L. (1973). An examination of an inservice course to effect change in teacher's attitudes toward teaching art: A study conducted in economically poor areas of Chicago. (Doctoral dissertation, New York University). *Dissertation Abstracts International, 34*, 4064A.

Pappas, G. (ed.). (1970). *Concepts in Art and Education*. London: MacMillan.

Parks, M. E. (1986). An analysis of attitude recognition, formation, and change concepts in selected art education textbooks. *Studies in Art Education*, 27(4), 198–208.

Paston, H. S. (1973). *Learning to Teach Art*. Lincoln, NE: Professional Educators.

Pum, R. J. (1971). *Differential characteristics of art-teaching majors and elementary education majors in college: As measured by selected attitude, value, and personality factors.* (Unpublished doctoral dissertation, Ball State University.)

Savuto, B. J. (1977). *High school student attitudes and perceptions of crafts as education in Nassau County, Long Island.* (Doctoral dissertation, Columbia University Teachers College). Dissertation Abstracts International, 38, 3884A.

Schultz, L. (1980). A studio curriculum for art education. *Art Education*, 33(6), 10–15.

Smith, R. A. (1979). Concepts, concept learning, and art education. *Review of Research in Visual Arts Education*, 11, 7–15.

Stokrocki, M. (1986). A portrait of an effective elementary art teacher. *Studies in Art Education*, 27(2), 81–93.

Weitz, M. (1976). Art: Who needs it? *Journal of Aesthetic Education*, 10(1), 19–27.

Whitesel, L. S. (1975). Scale construction for the measurement of women art students' career commitments. *Studies in Art Education*, 17(1), 47–53.

Wilson, B. (1971). Evaluation of learning in art education. In B. Bloom, T. J. Hastings, and G. F. Madeus (Eds.), *Handbook of Formative and Summative Evaluation of Student Learning* (pp. 449–458). NY: McGraw-Hill.

Winner, E. (1982). *Invented Worlds: The Psychology of the Arts*. Cambridge: Harvard University Press.

AUTHENTIC ASSESSMENT BIBLIOGRAPHY

Brandt, R. (1987). On assessment in the arts: A conversation with Howard Gardner. *Educational Leadership*, 45(4), 30–34.

Campbell, J. (1992). Laser disk portfolio: Total child assessment. *Educational Leadership*, 49(8), 69–70.

Gardner, H., and Grunbaum, J. (1986). *The assessment of artistic thinking: Comments on the national assessment of educational progress in the arts.* Cambridge, MA: National Assessment of Student Achievement. (ERIC Document Reproduction Service No. ED 279 677).

Gitomer, D., Grosh, S., and Price, K. (1992). Portfolio culture in arts education. *Art Education*, 45(1), 7–15.

Gomez, M., Grave, E., and Bloch, M. (1991). Reassessing portfolio assessment: Rhetoric and reality. *Language Arts*, 68, 620–627.

Hamblen, K. A. (1987). What general education can tell us about evaluation in art. *Studies in Art Education*, 28(4), 246–250.

Hansen, J. (1992). Literacy portfolios: Helping students know themselves. *Educational Leadership*, 49(8), 66–68.

Hausman, J. (1992). On the use of portfolios in evaluation. *Art Education*, 45(1), 4–5.

Lamme, L., and Hysmith, C. (1991). One school's adventure into portfolio assessment. *Language Arts*, 68, 629–640.

Maeroff, G. (1991). Assessing alternative assessment. *Phi Delta Kappan*, 73(4), 272–281.

Magee, L. J., and Price, K. R. (1992). Propel: Visual arts in Pittsburgh. *School Arts*, 91(8), 42–45.

Silver, H. F., and Strong, R. (1992). *Challenge and Response: Authentic Achievement as a Strategy for In-Depth Learning.* ???, NJ: Hanson Silver Strong and Associates.

Wiggins, G. (1989). A true test: Toward more authentic and equitable assessment. *Phi Delta Kappan*, 703–712.

Wiggins, G. (1992). Creating tests worth taking. *Educational Leadership*, 49(8), 26–33.

Wolf, D. P. (1987). Opening up assessment. *Educational Leadership*, 45(4), 24–29.

Wolf, D. P., and Pistone, N. (1991). *Taking Full Measure: Rethinking Assessment Through the Arts.* New York: The College Board.

DISCIPLINE-BASED ART EDUCATION

Anderson, T. (1986). Talking about art with children: From theory to practice. *Art Education*, 39(1), 5–8.

Barkan, M. (1962). The visual arts in secondary-school education. *School Review*, 70(4).

Barkan, M. (1962). Transition in art education: Changing conceptions of curriculum and theory. *Art Education*, 15(7), 12–18.

Barkan, M. (1963). Is there a discipline of art education? *Studies in Art Education*, 4(2), 4–9.

Barkan, M. (1966). Prospects for change in the teaching of art. *Art Education*, 19(8), 4–8.

Barnet, S. (1985). *A short guide to writing about art* (2nd ed.). Boston: Little, Brown.

Broudy, H. S. (1985). Curriculum validity in art education. *Studies in art education,* 26(4). 212–215.

Chalmers, F. G. (1987). Beyond current conceptions of Discipline-based art education. *Art Education,* 40(5), 58–61.

Chapman, L. H. (1985). Curriculum development as process and product. *Studies in Art Education,* 26(4), 206–211.

Clark, G. A., Day, M. D., and Greer, W. D. (1987). Discipline-based art education: Becoming students of art. *The Journal of Aesthetic Education,* 21(2), 129–193.

Cohen, E. G., and Benton, J. (1988). Making groupwork work. *American Educator,* 12(3), 10–17.

Day, M. D. (1985). Evaluating student achievement in discipline-based art programs. *Studies in Art Education,* 26(4), 232–240.

Day, M. D. (1987). Discipline-based art education in secondary classrooms. *Studies in Art Education,* 28(4), 234–242.

Day, M., and others. (1984). *Art history, art criticism, and art production.* Santa Monica, CA: The Rand Corp.

DiBlasio, M. K. (1985). Continuing the translation: Further delineation of the DBAE format. *Studies in Art Education,* 26(4), 197–205.

DiBlasio, M. K. (1987). Reflections on the theory of discipline-based art education. *Studies in Art Education,* 28(4), 221–6.

Dobbs, S. M. (1974). Research and reason: Recent literature and ideas in American art education. *Curriculum Theory Network,* 4(2–3), 169–191.

Dobbs, S. M. (1979). *Art Education and Back to Basics.* Reston, VA: National Art Education Association.

Dobbs, S. M. (ed.). (1988). *Research readings for discipline-based art education: A journey beyond creating.* Reston, VA: National Art Education Association.

Douglas, N. J., Schwartz, J. B., and Taylor, J. B. (1981). The relationship of cognitive style of young children and their modes of responding to paintings. *Studies in Art Education,* 22(3), 24–31.

Efland, A. (1976). The school art style: A functional analysis. *Studies in Art Education,* 17(2), 37–44.

Efland, A. D. (1987). Curriculum antecedents of discipline-based art education. *The Journal of Aesthetic Education,* 21(2), 57–94.

Eisner, E. W. (1966). The development of information and attitude toward art at the secondary and college levels. *Studies in Art Education,* 8(1), 43–51.

Eisner, E. W. (1984). Alternative approaches to curriculum development. *Studies in Art Education,* 25(4), 259–264.

Eisner, E. W. (1987). The role of discipline-based art education in America's schools. *Art Education,* 40(5), 6–27.

Feldman, E. B. (1967). *Art as Image and Idea*. Englewood Cliffs, NJ: Prentice-Hall.

Feldman, E. B. (1970). *Becoming Human Through Art: Aesthetic Experience in the School*. Englewood Cliffs, NJ: Prentice-Hall.

Gardner, H. (1973). *The Arts and Human Development: A Psychological Study of the Artistic Process*. NY: J. Wiley.

Gardner, H. (1980). *Artful scribbles: The significance of children's drawings*. NY: Basic Books.

Gardner, H. (1983). Artistic intelligences. *Art Education*, 36(2), 47–49.

Gardner, H. and Winner, E. (1976). How children learn…three stages of understanding art. *Psychology Today*, 9, 42–43.

Gilliatt, M. (1980). The effects of habituation, the Feldman-Mittler methodology, and studio activities on expanding art preferences of elementary students. *Studies in Art Education*, 21(2), 43–49.

Goldstein, E. Saunders R., Kowalchuk, J. D., and Katz, T. H. (1986) *Understanding and Creating Art, Books I & II*. Dallas: Garrard.

Gray, J. U. (1987). A seventy-five percent solution for the success of DBAE. *Art Education*, 40(5), 54–57.

Greer, W. D. (1982). A structure of discipline concepts for DBAE. *Studies in Art Education*, 28(4), 227–233.

Greer, W. D. (1984). A discipline-based view of art education: Approaching art as a subject of study. *Studies in Art Education*, 25(4), 212–218.

Grossman, E. (1984). Program planning for the visual arts. *Art Education*, 37(3), 6–10.

Hamblen, K. A. (1987). An examination of discipline-based art education issues. *Studies in Art Education*, 28(2), 68–78.

Hamblen, K. A. (1987). What general education can tell us about evaluation in art. *Studies in Art Education*, 28(4), 246–250.

Heidt, A. H. (1986). Creating art appreciation activities. *Art Education*, 39(1), 23–28.

Hurwitz, A. and Madeja, S. S. (1977). *The Joyous Vision: Source Book*. Englewood Cliffs, NJ: Prentice-Hall.

Irvine, H. (1984). An art centered art curriculum. *Art Education*, 37(3), 16–19.

Kaufman, I. (1963). Art education: A discipline? *Studies in Art Education*, 4(2), 15–23.

Kern, E. J. (1987). Antecedents of discipline-based art education: State departments of education curriculum documents. *The Journal of Aesthetic Education*, 21(2), 35–57.

Koroscik, J. S. (1982). The effects of prior knowledge, presentation time, and task demands on visual art processing. *Studies in Art Education*, 23(3), 13–22.

Koroscik, J. S. (1984). Cognition in viewing and talking about art. *Theory Into Practice*, 23(4), 330–333.

Krathwohl, D. R., Bloom, B. S. and Masia, B. B. (1964). *Taxonomy of Educational Objectives: Handbook II: Affective Domain*. NY: McKay.

Kuhn, M. (1984). Restructuring the future of art education curricula. *Studies in Art Education*, 25(4), 271–275.

Lanier, V. (1984). Eight guidelines for selecting art curriculum content. *Studies in Art Education*, 25(4), 232–238.

Lanier, V. (1987). A*R*T*, a friendly alternative to DBAE. *Art Education*, 40(5), 46–53.

Madeja, S. S. (1980). The art curriculum: Sins of omission. *Art Education*, 33(6), 24–26.

McFee, J. K. (1984). An analysis of the goal, structure, and social context of the 1965 Penn State seminar and the 1983 Getty Institute for Educators on the Visual Arts. *Studies in Art Education*, 25(4), 276–281.

Mittler, G. A. (1972). Attitude modification towards works of art. *Studies in Art Education*, 13(2), 58.

Mittler, G. A. (1976). An instructional strategy designed to overcome the adverse effects of established students' attitudes towards works of art. *Studies in Art Education*, 17(3), 13–31.

Mittler, G. A. (1980). Learning to look/looking to learn: A proposed approach to art appreciation at the secondary level. *Art Education*, 33(3), 17–21.

Mittler, G. A. (1986). *Art in Focus*. Peoria: Bennett & McKnight.

National Art Education Association. (1968). *The Essentials of a Quality School Art Program*. Reston, VA: Author.

National Assessment for Educational Progress (1981). *Art and Young Americans, 1974–79: Results from the Second National Art Assessment*. Denver, CO: Author.

National Endowment for the Arts. (1988). *Toward Civilization: Overview from a Report on Arts Education*. Washington, D.C.: Author.

Packard, S. (1984). Contemporary reform and the contents of curricula. *Studies in Art Education*, 25(4), 265–270.

Parks, M. E. (1988). How does the work mean? *Art Education*, 41(3), 55–61.

Parks, M. E. (1990, April). *Identifying art content for curriculum development*. Paper presented at the annual convention of the National Art Education Association, Kansas City, MO.

Parsons, M. J. (1987). Talk about a painting: a cognitive developmental analysis. *The Journal of Aesthetic Education*, 21(1), 37–55.

Parsons, M., Johnston, M. and Durham, R. (1978). Developmental stages of children's aesthetic responses. *Journal of Aesthetic Education*, 83–104.

Rorschach, E., and Whitney, R. (1986). Relearning to teach: Peer observation as a means of professional development. *American Educator*, 10(4), 38–44.

Rush, J. C. (1987). Interlocking images: The conceptual core of a discipline-based art lesson. *Studies in Art Education*, 28(4), 206–220.

Sevigny, M. J. (1987). Discipline-based art education and teacher education. *The Journal of Aesthetic Education*, 21(2), 95–128.

Shor, I., and Freire, P. (1987). What is the "dialogical method" of teaching? *Journal of Education*, 169(3), 11–31.

Smith, R. A. (1986). *Excellence in Art Education: Ideas and Initiatives*. Reston, VA: National Art Education Association.

Smith, R. A. (1987). The changing image of art education: theoretical antecedents of discipline-based art education. *The Journal of Aesthetic Education*, 21(2), 3–34.

Spratt, F. Art production in discipline-based art education. *The Journal of Aesthetic Education*, 21(2), 197–204.

Suggs, M. S. (1976). *Phenomenological analysis, art studio production, and task order effects on student aesthetic attitude, art studio production, and aspective preception of paintings*. (Doctoral dissertation, University of Maryland). Dissertation Abstracts International, 37, 3353A.

Welty, W. M. (July/August, 1989). Discussion method teaching: How to make it work. *Change*, 21, 41–49.

Wilson, B. (1988). *Art Education, Civilization and the 21st Century: A Researcher's Reflections on the National Endowment for the Arts' Report to Congress*. Reston, VA: National Art Education Association.

GENERAL EDUCATION BIBLIOGRAPHY

Adler, M. J. (1982). *The Paideia Proposal: An Educational Manifesto*. New York: MacMillan.

Alexander, C. N., Jr., and Campbell, E. Q. (1964). Peer influences on adolescent educational aspirations and attainments. *American Sociological Review*, 29, 568–575.

Alloway, L. (1975). *Topics in America Since 1945*. NY: Norton.

Allington, R. L. (1984). Oral reading. In P. D. Pearson (ed.) *Handbook of Reading Research*, (pp. 829–864). NY: Longman.

Anderson, R. C., Soiro, R. J., and Montague, W. (1977). *Schooling and the Acquisition of Knowledge*. Hillsdale, NJ: Erlbaum Associates.

Anderson, R. C., and others. (1985). *Becoming a Nation of Readers: The Report of the Commission on Reading*. Urbana, IL: University of Illinois, Center for the Study of Reading.

Applebee, A. N. (1978). *The Child's Concept of Story: Ages Two to Seventeen*. Chicago: University of Chicago Press.

Applebee, A. N. (1984). *Contexts for Learning to Write: Studies of Secondary School Instruction*. Norwood, NJ: Ablex.

Ausubel, D., Novak, J. D., & Hanesian, H. (1978). *Educational Psychology: A Cognitive view* (2nd ed.). NY: Holt, Rinehart, and Winston.

Baker, A., and Greene, E. (1977). *Storytelling: Art and Technique*. NY: Bowker.

Basualdo, S. M., and Basualdo, E. A. (1980). *Models to prevent and deal with disruptive behavior(s) in the classroom: A review of the literature*. ERIC Document No. ED 202812.

Becker, H. J., and Epstein, J. (1982). Parent involvement: A survey of teacher practices. *The Elementary School Journal*, 83(2), 85–102.

Berliner, D. (1983). The executive functions of teaching. *The Instructor*, 93(2), 28–40.

Berliner, D. (1984). The half-full glass: A review of research on teaching. In P. L. Hosford (ed.), *Using What We Know About Teaching*. Alexandria, VA: Association for Supervision and Curriculum Development.

Berliner, D., and Rosenshine, B. (1976). *The Acquisition of Knowledge in the Classroom*. San Francisco: Far West Laboratory for Educational Research and Development.

Bettelheim, B. (1975). *The Uses of Enchantment: The Meaning and Importance of Fairy Tales*. NY: Knopf.

Bird, T., and Little, J. W. (1985). *Instructional Leadership in Eight Secondary Schools. Final Report to the U.S. Department of Education*, National Institute of Education, Boulder, CO: Center for Action Research.

Bloom, A. (1987). *The Closing of the American Mind*. NY: Simon and Schuster.

Bloom, B. S. (Ed.). (1985). *Developing Talent in Young People*. NY: Ballantine Books.

Bloom, B. S., Englehart, M. D., Furts, E. J., Hill, W. H., and Krathwohl, D. R. (eds.). (1956). *Taxonomy of Educational Objectives: The Classification of Educational Goals. Handbook I: Cognitive Domain*. NY: David McKay.

Bloom, B. S., and Sosniak, L. A. (November 1981). Talent development vs. schooling. *Educational Leadership*, 39(2), 86–94.

Bossert, S. (1985). Effective elementary schools. In R. Kyle (Ed.), *Reaching for Excellence: An Effective Schools Sourcebook*. (pp. 39–53). Washington, D.C.: U.S. Government Printing Office.

Braddock, J. H., II. (1981). Race, athletics, and educational attainment. *Youth and Society*, 12(3), 335–350.

Branford, J. D. (1979). *Human Cognition: Learning, Understanding, and Remembering*. Belmont, CA: Wadsworth.

Brodinsky, B. (1980). *Student discipline: Problems and solutions. AASA Critical Issues Report*. Arlington, VA: American Association of School Administrators. ERIC Document No. ED 198206.

Brookover, W. B., and others. (1979). *School Systems and Student Achievement: Schools Make a Difference*. NY: Praeger.

Brophy, J. (1979). Teacher behavior and its effects. *Journal of Educational Psychology*, 71(6), 733–750.

Brophy, J. E. (1981). Teacher praise: A functional analysis. *Review of Education Research*, 51, 5–32.

Brophy, J., and Evertson, C. M. (1976). *Learning from Teaching: A Developmental Perspective*. Boston, MA: Allyn and Bacon.

Brown, A. L., and Smiley, S. S. (1978). The development of strategies for studying texts. *Child Development*, 49, 1076–1088.

Bruner, J. (1977). *The Process of Education* (with new preface). Cambridge: Harvard University Press. (first published 1960).

Burnstein, E., Stotland, E., and Zander, A. (1961). A similarity to a model and self-evaluation. *Journal of Abnormal and Social Psychology*, 62, 257–264.

Canfield, J. *Self-esteem in the classroom: A curriculum guide*. Pacific Palisades, CA: Self-Esteem Seminars.

Canfield, J., and Wells, H. 100 *Ways to enhance self-concept in the classroom*. Santa Cruz, CA: Educational and Training Services, Inc.

Carnine, D. R., Gersten, R., and Green, S. (1982). The principal as instructional leader: A second look. *Educational Leadership*, 40(3), 47–50.

Cattermole, J., and Robinson, N. (1985). Effective Home/School/Communications—From the Parents' Perspective. *Phi Delta Kappan*, 67(1), 48–50.

Center for Public Resources. (1982). *Basic Skills in the U.S. Work Force: The Contrasting Perceptions of Business, Labor, and Public Education*. NY: Author.

Chall, J. S. (1983). *Learning to Read: The Great Debate (2nd ed.)*. NY: McGraw-Hill.

Chall, J., Conard, S., and Harris, S. (1977). *An Analysis of Textbooks in Relation to Declining SAT Scores*. NY: College Entrance Examination Board. Brown, A. L., and Smiley, S. S. (1978).

Chomsky, C. (1972). Stages in language development and reading exposure. *Harvard Educational Review*, 42, 1–33.

Clark, B. (1983). *Growing up gifted* (2nd ed). Columbus, OH: C. E. Merrill.

Cohen, E. G. & Benton, J. (1988). Making groupwork work. *American Educator*, 12(3), 10–17.

Cohn, S. J., George, W. C., and Stanley, J. C. (eds.). (1979). Educational acceleration of intellectually talented youths: Prolonged discussion by a varied group of professionals. In W. C. George, S. J. Cohn, and J. E. Stanley (eds.), *Educating the Gifted: Acceleration and Enrichment*, (pp. 183–238). Baltimore: Johns Hopkins University Press.

Coleman, J. S., Hoffer, T., and Kilgore, S. (1982). *High School Achievement: Public, Catholic and Private Schools Compared*. NY: Basic Books.

Committee for Economic Development. (1985). *Investing in Our Children: Businesses and the Public Schools: A Statement*. New York and Washington, D.C.: Author.

Cook, E. (1969). The Ordinary and the Fabulous: *An Introduction to Myths, Legends and Fairy Tales for Teachers and Storytellers.* Cambridge and NY: Cambridge University Press.

Corcoran, T. (1985). Effective secondary schools. In R. Kyle (Ed.), *Reaching for Excellence: An Effective Schools Sourcebook,* (pp. 71–97). Washington, D.C.: U.S. Government Printing Office.

Craik, F. I. M., and Watkins, M. J. (1973). The role of rehearsal in short-term memory. *Journal of Verbal Learning and Verbal Behavior,* 12, 599–607.

Devin-Sheehan, L., Feldman, R. S., and Allen, V. L. (1976). Research on children tutoring children: A critical Review. *Review of Educational Research,* 46(3), 355–385.

DiPrete, T. A. (1981). *Discipline, Order, and Student Behavior in American High Schools.* Chicago: National Opinion Research Center. ERIC Document No. ED 224137.

Doyle, W. (1983). "Academic Work." *Review of Educational Psychology,* 53(2), 159–199.

Doyle, W. (1985). Effective secondary classroom practices. In R. M. J. Kyle (ed.), *Reaching for Excellence: An Effective Schools Sourcebook.* Washington, D.C.: U.S. Government Printing Office.

Dunn, N. E. (1981). Children's achievement at school-entry age as a function of mothers' and fathers' teaching sets. *The Elementary School Journal,* 81, 245–253.

Elbow, P. (1981). *Writing with Power: Techniques for Mastering the Writing Process.* NY: Oxford University Press.

Etzioni, A. (1984). *Self-discipline, Schools, and the Business Community. Final Report to the U.S. Chamber of Commerce, Washington, D.C.* ERIC Document No. ED 249–335.

Featherstone, H. (February 1985). Homework. *The Harvard Education Letter.*

Fielding, G. D., and Schalock, H. D. (1985). *Promoting the Professional Development of Teachers and Administrators.* Eugene, OR: ERIC Clearinghouse on Educational Management.

Finn, C. E., Jr. (1984). Toward strategic independence: Nine Commandments for enhancing school effectiveness. *Phi Delta Kappan,* 65(8), 513–524.

Finn, C. E., Jr., Ravitch, D., and Roberts, P. (Eds.) (1985). *Challenges to the Humanities.* NY: Holmes and Meier.

Fitzgerald, F. (1979). *America Revised: History School Books in the Twentieth Century.* Boston: Atlantic Little-Brown.

Franena, W. K. (1965). *Three Historical Philosophies of Education: Aristotle, Kant, and Dewey.* Glenview, IL: Scott, Foresman.

Gagne, R. (1977). *The Conditions of Learning.* NY: Holt, Rinehart, and Winston.

Galvez-Hjornevik, C. (January-February 1986). Mentoring among teachers: A review of the literature. *Journal of Teacher Education,* 6–11.

Ginsburg, A., and Hanson, S. (1985). *Values and Educational Success Among Disadvantaged Students.* Final Report to the U.S. Department of Education, Washington, D.C.

Glidewell, J., and others. (1983). Professional support systems: The teaching profession. In A. Nadler, J. Fisher, and B. DePaulo (Eds.), *Applied Research in Help-Seeking and Reactions to Aid.* NY: Academic Press.

Goldsmith, A. H. (1982). Codes of discipline: Developments, dimensions, directions. *Education and Urban Society* (pp. 185–195). ERIC Document No. EJ 260932.

Good, T. L. (1982). How teachers' expectations affect results. *American Education,* 18(10), 25–32.

Good, T. L., and Brophy, J. E. (1984). *Looking in Classrooms* (3rd ed.). NY: Harper & Row.

Goodman, N. (1984). *Of Mind and Other Matters.* Cambridge: Harvard University Press.

Grant, G. (1981). The character of education and the education of character. *Daedalus,* 110(3), 135–149.

Grant, G. (1985). Schools that make an imprint: Creating a strong positive ethos. In J. H. Bunzel (ed.), *Challenge to American Schools: The Case for Standards and Values,* (pp. 127–143). NY: Oxford University Press.

Graves, D. H. (1983). *Writing: Teachers and Children at Work.* Exeter, NH: Heinemann Educational Books.

Gray, S. T. (1984). How to create a successful school/community partnership. *Phi Delta Kappan,* 65(6), 405–409.

Gray, W. A., & Gray, M. M. (November 1985). Synthesis of research on mentoring beginning teachers. *Educational Leadership,* 37–43.

Hanson, S., and Ginsburg, A. (1985). *Gaining Ground: Values and High School Success.* Final Report to the U.S. Department of Education, Washington, D.C.

Harari, O., and Covington, M. V. (1981). Reactions to achievement behavior from a teacher and student perspective: A developmental analysis. *American Educational Research Journal,* 18(1), 15–28.

Hawley, W., and Rosenholtz, S. with Goodstein, H. and Hasselbring, T. (1984). Good schools: What research says about improving student achievement. *Peabody Journal of Education,* 61(4).

Hayes-Roth, B., and Goldin, S. E. (1980). *Individual Differences in Planning Processes.* Santa Monica, CA: The Rand Corp.

Heath, S. B. (1983). *Ways with Words: Language, Life and Work in Communities and Classrooms.* NY: Cambridge University Press.

Hirsch, E. D. (1983). Cultural Literacy. *The American Scholar,* 52, 159–169.

Hirsch, E. D. (1985). Cultural literacy and the schools. *American Educator*, 74, 8–15.

Hirsch, E. D. (1987). *Cultural Literacy: What Every American Needs to Know*. Boston: Houghton Mifflin.

Hortas, C. R. (1984). Foreign languages and humane learning. In C. E. Finn, D. Ravitch, and R. T. Fancher (eds.), *Against Mediocrity: The Humanities in America's High Schools*. NY: Holmes and Meier.

Humes, A. (1981). *The Composing Process: A Summary of the Research*. Austin, TX: Southwest Regional Laboratory ERIC Document No. ED 222925.

Jamison, D., Suppes, P., and Wells, S. (1974). The effectiveness of alternative instructional media: A survey. *Review of Educational Research*, 44(1), 1–67.

Johnson, H. M. (1986). *How Do I Love Me?* (2nd edition). Salem, WI: Sheffield.

Johnson, S. (1985). *One Minute for Myself*. NY: Morrow.

Keith, T. Z. (1982). Time spent on homework and high school grades: A large-sample path analysis. *Journal of Educational Psychology*, 74(2), 248–253.

Kellough, R., and Kim, E. (1972). *A Resource Guide for Secondary Teaching*. NY: MacMillan.

Krathwohl, D. R.; Bloom, B. S. and Masia, B. B. (1964). *Taxonomy of Educational Objectives: Handbook II: Affective Domain*. NY: McKay.

Krupp, J. (Spring 1987). Mentoring: A means by which teachers become staff developers. *Journal of Staff Development*, 12–15.

Kulik, J. A., and Kulik, C. C. (1984). Synthesis of research on effects of accelerated instruction. *Educational Leadership*, 42(2), 84–89.

Lehman, D. L. (1970). *Role Playing and Teacher Education: Manual for Developing Innovative Teachers*. Washington, DC: Commission on Undergraduate Education in the Biological Sciences.

Levine, A. (1980). *When Dreams and Heroes Died: A Portrait of Today's College Student*. San Francisco: Jossey-Bass, Inc.

Little, J. W. (1983). Norms of collegiality and experimentation: Workplace conditions of school success. *American Educational Research Journal*, 19(3), 325–340.

Lortie, D. (1975). *Schoolteacher: A Sociological Study*. Chicago: University of Chicago Press.

Mager, R. F. & Pipe, P. (1970). *Analyzing Performance Problems*. Belmont, CA: Fearon.

Mager, R. F. (1984). *Preparing Instructional Objectives* (2nd ed.). Belmont, CA: David S. Lake.

Mason, J. (1983). An examination of reading instruction in third and fourth grades. *The Reading Teacher*, 36(9), 906–913.

Mohan, M. (1972). *Peer Tutoring as a Technique for Teaching the Unmotivated*. Fredonia, NY: State University of New York Teacher Education Research Center. ERIC Document No. ED 061154.

Morine-Dershimer, G. (1983). Instructional strategy and the creation of classroom status. *American Educational Research Journal*, 20(4), 645–661.

National Academy of Science, National Academy of Engineering, Institute of Medicine, and Committee on Science, Engineering and Public Policy. (1984). *High Schools and the Changing Workplace: The Employer's View*. Washington, D.C.: National Academy Press.

National Advisory Council on Vocational Education. (1984). *Conference Summary: Vocational Education and Training Policy for Today and Tomorrow*. Washington, D.C.: Author.

National Center for Education Statistics. (1983). *School District Survey of Academic Requirements and Achievement*. Washington, D.C.: U.S. Department of Education, Fast Response Survey Systems, ERIC Document No. ED 238097.

Natriello, G. (1984). Teachers' perceptions of the frequency of evaluation and assessments of their effort and effectiveness. *American Educational Research Journal*, 21(3), 579–595.

Natriello, G., and Dornbusch, S. M. (1981). Pitfalls in the evaluation of teachers by principals. *Administrator's Notebook*, 29(6), 1–4.

Nickerson, C., Lollis, C., & Porter, E. *Miraculous Me!* Seattle, WA: CHEF.

Pallas, A. M., and Alexander, K. L. (1983). Sex differences in quantitative SAT performance: New evidence on the differential coursework hypothesis. *American Educational Research Journal*, 20(2), 165–182.

Perfetti, C. A., and Lesgold, A. M. (1979). Coding and comprehension in skilled reading and implications for reading instruction. In L. B. Resnick and P. A. Weaver (eds.), *Theory and Practice of Early Reading*, vol. 1 (pp. 57–84). Hillsdale, NJ: Erlbaum Associates.

Phi Delta Kappa. (1980). *Why Do Some Urban Schools Succeed? The Phi Delta Kappa Study of Exceptional Urban Elementary Schools*. Bloomington, IN: Phi Delta Kappa.

Piaget, J. (1954). *The Construction of Reality in the Child*. NY: Basic Books.

Piaget, J. (1969). *The Language and Thought of the Child*. NY: World.

Piaget, J. (1977). *The Development of Thought: Equilibration of Cognitive Structure*. NY: Viking Press.

Purdy, D., Eitzen, D. S., and Hufnagel, R. (1982). Are athletes students? The educational attainment of college athletes. *Social Problems*, 29(4), 439–448.

Purkey, S., and Smith, M. (1983). Effective schools: A Review. *The Elementary School Journal*, 83(4), 427–452.

Reasoner, R. *Building Self-Esteem: A Comprehensive Program*. Santa Cruz, CA: Educational and Training Services, Inc.

Redfield, D. L., and Rousseau, E. W. (1981). A meta-analysis of experimental research on teacher questioning behavior. *Review of Educational Research*, 51(2), 237–245.

Rich, D. K. (1985). *The Forgotten Factor in School Success—The Family*. Washington, D.C.: Home and School Institute.

Rohlen, T. P. (1983). *Japan's High Schools*. Berkeley, CA: University of California Press.

Rorschach, E., and Whitney, R. (1986). Relearning to teach: Peer observation as a means of professional development. *American Educator*, 10(4), 38–44.

Rosenshine, B. (1983). Teaching functions in instructional programs. *Elementary School Journal*, 83(4), 335–351.

Rutter, M. (1983). School effects on pupil progress: Research findings and policy implications. In L. S. Shulman and G. Sykes (eds.), *Handbook of Teaching and Policy* (pp. 3–41). NY: Longman.

Sawyer, R. (1962, Revised Edition). *The Way of Storytelling*. NY: The Viking Press.

Segal, J., Chipman, S., and Glaser, R. (1985). *Thinking and Learning Skills, Vol. I: Relating Instruction to Research*. Hillsdale, NJ: Erlbaum Associates.

Shor, I., and Freire, P. (1987). What is the "dialogical method" of teaching? *Journal of Education*, 169(3), 11–31.

Spady, W. (1971). Status, achievement, and motivation in the American high school. *School Review*, 79(3), 379–403.

Stallings, J. (1980). Allocated academic learning time revisited, or beyond time on task. *Educational Researcher*, 9(11), 11–16.

Sternberg, R. J. (1987). Teaching critical thinking: Eight easy ways to fail before you begin. *Phi Delta Kappan*, 68(6), 456–459.

Stipek, D. (1981). Children's perceptions of their own and their classmates' ability. *Journal of Educational Psychology*, 73(3), 404–410.

Thernstrom, S. (1985). The humanities and our cultural Challenge. In C. E. Finn, D. Ravitch, and P. Roberts (eds.), *Challenges to the Humanities*. NY: Holmes and Meier.

Tye, K. A., and Tye, B. B. (1984). Teacher isolation and school reform. *Phi Delta Kappan*, 65(5), 319–322.

U.S. Department of Education. (1986). *What Works: Research About Teaching and Learning*. Washington, D.C.: Author.

Wagner, L. A. (November 1985). Ambiguities and possibilities in California's mentor teacher program. *Educational Leadership*, 23–29.

Walberg, H. J. (1983). Scientific literacy and economic productivity in international perspective. *Daedalus*, 112(2), 1–28.

Walberg, H. J. (1984). Families as partners in educational productivity. *Phi Delta Kappan*, 65(6), 397–400.

Walberg, H. J. (1984). Improving the productivity of America's schools. *Educational Leadership*, 41(8), 19–27.

Walberg, H. J. (1984). What makes schooling effective? A synthesis and a critique of three national studies. *Contemporary Education: A Journal of Reviews*, 1(1), 22–34.

Walberg, H. J. (1985). Homework's powerful effects on learning. *Educational Leadership*, 42(7), 76–79.

Walberg, H. J., and Shanahan, T. (1983). High school effects on individual students. *Educational Researcher*, 12(7), 4–9.

Weiner, B. (1979). A theory of motivation for some classroom experiences. *Journal of Educational Psychology*, 71, 3–25.

Weinstein, R., and others. (1982). Student perceptions of differential teacher treatment in open and traditional classrooms. *Journal of Educational Psychology*, 74, 678–692.

Welty, W. M. (July/August, 1989). Discussion method teaching: How to make it work. *Change*, 21, 41–49.

Willingham, W. W. (1985). *Success in College: The Role of Personal Qualities and Academic Ability*. NY: The College Board.

Wise, A. E., and others. (1984). *Teacher Evaluation: A Study of Effective Practices*. Santa Monica, CA: Rand Corporation. ERIC Document No. ED 246559.

Zemsky, R., and Meyerson, M. (1986). *The Training Impulse*. NY: McGraw-Hill.

INTEGRATING ART WITH OTHER ACADEMIC SUBJECTS ───────

Adams, D. & Fuchs, M. (1985). The fusion of artistic and scientific thinking. *Art Education*, 38(6), 22–24.

Baker, A., and Greene, E. (1977). *Storytelling: Art and Technique*. NY: Bowker.

Barnet, S. (1985). *A short guide to writing about art* (2nd ed.). Boston: Little, Brown.

Bettelheim, B. (1975). *The Uses of Enchantment: The Meaning and Importance of Fairy Tales*. NY: Knopf.

Broude, N. and Garrard, M. D. (1982). *Feminism and Art History: Questioning the Litany*. NY: Harper & Row.

Chalmers, G. (1973). The study of art in a cultural context. *Journal of Aesthetics and Art Criticism*, 32(2), 249–256.

Chalmers, G. (1974). A cultural foundation for education in the arts. *Art Education*, 27(1), 21–25.

Chalmers, G. (1978). Teaching and studying art history: Some anthropological and sociological considerations. *Studies in Art Education*, 20(1), 18–25.

Cook, E. (1969). *The Ordinary and the Fabulous: An Introduction to Myths, Legends and Fairy Tales for Teachers and Storytellers*. Cambridge and New York: Cambridge University Press.

Corwin, S. (1990). Art as a tool for learning American history: A preliminary report of a study at National Arts Education Research Center New York University. *THE NYSATA BULLETIN*, 40(1), 23–26.

Deinhard, H. (1975). Reflections on art history and sociology of art. *Art Journal*, 35(1), 20–32.

Derylak, R. (1989). *Enhancing Art Learning Based on Social Studies Curriculum Objectives*. (Unpublished Graduate Project, State University College at Buffalo.)

Duvignaud, J. (1972). *The Sociology of Art*. London: Paladin.

Eisner, E. W. (1969). Teaching the humanities: Is a new era possible? *Educational Leadership*, 26(7), 561–564.

Eisner, E. W. (ed.), (1978). *Reading, the Arts, and the Creation of Meaning*. Reston, VA.: National Art Education Association.

Feinstein, H. (1982). Meaning and visual metaphor. *Studies in Art Education*, 23(2), 45–55.

Feldman, E. B. (1981). *Varieties of Visual Experience*. Englewood Cliffs, NJ: Prentice-Hall.

Fitzgerald, F. (1979). *America Revised: History School Books in the Twentieth Century*. Boston: Atlantic Little-Brown.

Forseth, S. D. (1976). The effects of art activities on attitude and achievement in fourth-grade children pertinent to the learning of mathematics and art. (Doctoral dissertation, University of Minnesota). *Dissertation Abstracts International*, 37, 7590A.

Getzels, J. W., and Csikzentmihalyi, M. (1976). *The Creative Vision: A Longitudinal Study of Problem Finding in Art*. NY: Wiley.

Gilhorn, C. (1970). Pop pedagogy: Looking at the coke bottle. In M. Fishwick and R. Brown (Eds.), *Icons of Popular Culture*. Bowling Green, OH: Bowling Green University Press.

Goodman, N. (1976). *Languages of Art: An Approach to a Theory of Symbols*. Indianapolis: Hackett.

Gowans, A. (1974). Popular arts and historic artifact: New principles for studying history in art. In J. M. N. Fishwick, (ed.), *Popular Architecture*. Bowling Green: Bowling Green Popular Press, 88–105.

Graves, D. H. (1983). *Writing: Teachers and Children at Work*. Exeter, NH: Heinemann Educational Books.

Greene, M. (1981). Aesthetic literacy in general education. In J. F. Soltis (ed.), *Philosophy and Education* (pp. 115–141). 80th Yearbook of the National Society for the Study of Education, Pt. 1, Chicago: University of Chicago Press.

Heath, S. B. (1983). *Ways with Words: Language, Life and Work in Communities and Classrooms*. NY: Cambridge University Press.

Heidt, A. H. (1986). Creating art appreciation activities. *Art Education*, 39(1), 23–28.

Hirsch, E. D. (1983). Cultural Literacy. *The American Scholar*, 52, 159–169.

Hirsch, E. D. (1985). Cultural literacy and the schools. *American Educator*, 74, 8–15.

Hirsch, E. D. (1987). *Cultural Literacy: What Every American Needs to Know*. Boston: Houghton Mifflin.

Hitler, A. (1943). *Mein Kampf* (translated by R. Matheim). Boston: Houghton Mifflin.

Hobbs, A. (1985). *Art in Context*. Orlando, FL: Harcourt Brace Jovanovich.

Hobbs, J. A. (1984). Popular art vs. fine art. *Art Education*, 37(3), 11–15.

Hortas, C. R. (1984). Foreign languages and humane learning. In C. E. Finn, D. Ravitch, and R. T. Fancher (eds.), *Against Mediocrity: The Humanities in America's High Schools*. NY: Holmes and Meier.

Humes, A. (1981). *The Composing Process: A Summary of the Research*. Austin, TX: Southwest Regional Laboratory ERIC Document No. ED 222925.

Johnson, M. (Ed.). (1981). *Philosophical Perspectives on Metaphor*. Minneapolis: The University of Minnesota Press.

Kimball, S. B. (1972). Social and cultural congruences in American civilization. *Journal of Aesthetic Education*, 6(1–2), 39–52.

Kleinbauer, W. E. (1971). *Modern Perspectives in Western Art History*. NY: Holt, Rinehart, and Winston.

Kurlansky, M. J. (1977). Pop goes the culture. *Change*, 9(6), 36–39.

LaChapelle, J. R. (1984). The sociology of art and art education: A relationship reconsidered. *Studies in Art Education*, 26(1), 34–40.

Lakoff, G. & Johnson, M. (1980). *Metaphors We Live By*. Chicago: The University of Chicago Press.

Lee, S. (1982). *A History of Far Eastern Art*. NY: Abrams.

MacQueen, J. (1970). *Allegory*. London: Methuen.

McFee, J. K., and Degge, R. M. (1977). *Art Culture and Environment: A Catalyst for Teaching*. Belmont, CA: Wadsworth.

McLuhan, M. (1967). *The Medium is the Message*. NY: Ballantine.

Moffatt, J. F. (1969). Art history as a pedagogical science. *Art Education*, 22(3), 24–28.

Mukerjee, R. (1959). *The Social Function of Art*. NY: Philosophical Library.

Nagle, J. (1980). *The Responsive Arts*. Sherman Oaks, CA: Alfred.

Naisbitt, J. (1984). *Megatrends*. NY: Warner Books.

Panofsky, E. (1955). *Meaning in the Visual Arts*. Chicago: University of Chicago Press.

Panofsky, E. (1962). *Studies in Iconology: Humanistic themes in the art of the Renaissance* (rev. ed.). NY: Harper & Row.

Panofsky, E. (1968). Idea: *A Concept in Art Theory*. NY: Harper & Row.

Parks, M. E. (1989). Art education in a post-modern age. *Art Education*, 42(2), 10–13.

Phenix, P. H. (1964). *Realms of Meaning*. NY: McGraw-Hill.

Popowicz, L. A. (1975). Interdisciplinary approach to biology integrated with art: a vehicle for changing attitudes toward science. (Doctoral Dissertation, Boston College). *Dissertation Abstracts International*, 35, 7143A.

Prown, J. (1982). Mind in matter: An introduction to material culture theory and method. *Winterhur Portfolio*, 17, 1–19.

Ravitch, D. (1985). *From history to social studies. In The Schools We Deserve: Reflections on the Educational Crisis of Our Times* (pp. 112–132). NY: Basic Books.

Read, H. (1967). *Art and Alienation: The Role of the Artist in Society.* New York: Horizon Press.

Read, H. (19??). *Art and Society.* New York: Pantheon Books.

Resnick, D. B., and Resnick, L. B. (1977). The nature of literacy: An historical exploration. *Harvard Educational Review*, 47(5), 370–385.

Sawyer, R. (1962, Revised Edition). *The Way of Storytelling.* NY: The Viking Press.

Schineller, J. A. (1975). *Art/Search and Self-Discovery.* Worcester, MA: Davis.

Silberman, A. (1968). Introduction: A definition of the sociology of art. *International Social Science Journal*, 20, 567–588.

Sinatra, R. (1986). *Visual Literacy: Connections to Thinking, Reading and Writing.* Springfield, IL: Charles C. Thomas.

Smith, R. A. (1984). From aesthetic criticism to humanistic understanding: A practical illustration. *Studies in Art Education*, 25(4), 238–244.

Thernstrom, S. (1985). The humanities and our cultural Challenge. In C. E. Finn, D. Ravitch, and P. Roberts (eds.), *Challenges to the Humanities.* NY: Holmes and Meier.

Tilghman, B. (1973). *Language and Aesthetics.* Lawrence, KS: University Press of Kansas.

Toffler, A. (1970). *Future Shock.* NY: Random House.

Tsugawa, A. (1968). The nature of the aesthetic and human values. *Art Education*, 21(8), 11–20.

Walberg, H. J. (1969). A portrait of the artist and scientist as a young man. *Exceptional Children*, 36(1), 5–11.

PSYCHOLOGY AND ART EDUCATION _____

Arnheim, R. (1962). *Picasso's Guernica: The Genesis of a Painting.* Berkeley and Los Angeles: University of California Press.

Arnheim, R. (1969). *Visual Thinking.* Berkeley: University of California Press.

Arnheim, R. (1983). Perceiving, thinking, forming. *Art Education*, 36(2), 9–11.

Aronson, E. (1966). The psychology of insufficient justification: An analysis of some conflicting data. In S. Feldman (ed.), *Cognitive Consistency*. NY: Academic Press, pp. 115–133.

Aronson, E., and Golden, B. W. (1962). The effect of relevant and irrelevant aspects of communicator credibility on opinion change. *Journal of Personality*, 30, 135–146.

Art Education, (1983, March), 36(2). *Art and the mind* (Special issue).

Ausubel, D., Novak, J. D., & Hanesian, H. (1978). *Educational Psychology: A Cognitive view* (2nd ed.). NY: Holt, Rinehart, and Winston.

Berger, J. (1972). *Ways of seeing*. London: BBC and Penguin Books.

Berscheid, E. & Walster, E. (1969). Attitude change. In J. Mills (ed.), *Experimental Social Psychology*, Toronto: The MacMillan Company, pp. 121–232.

Bettelheim, B. (1975). *The Uses of Enchantment: The Meaning and Importance of Fairy Tales*. NY: Knopf.

Branford, J. D. (1979). *Human Cognition: Learning, Understanding, and Remembering*. Belmont, CA: Wadsworth.

Brophy, J. (1979). Teacher behavior and its effects. *Journal of Educational Psychology*, 71(6), 733–750.

Brophy, J. E. (1981). Teacher praise: A functional analysis. *Review of Education Research*, 51, 5–32.

Brophy, J., and Evertson, C. M. (1976). *Learning from Teaching: A Developmental Perspective*. Boston, MA: Allyn and Bacon.

Burnstein, E.; Stotland, E., and Zander, A. (1961). A similarity to a model and self-evaluation. *Journal of Abnormal and Social Psychology*, 62, 257–264.

Canfield, J. *Self-esteem in the classroom: A curriculum guide*. Pacific Palisades, CA: Self-Esteem Seminars.

Canfield, J., and Wells, H. *100 Ways to enhance self-concept in the classroom*. Santa Cruz, CA: Educational and Training Services, Inc.

Cook, J. M. (1977). Measurement of affective art objectives. *School Arts*, 77(2), 14–17.

Craik, F. I. M., and Watkins, M. J. (1973). The role of rehearsal in short-term memory. *Journal of Verbal Learning and Verbal Behavior*, 12, 599–607.

Eisner, E. W. (1976). *The Arts, Human Development and Education*. Berkeley: McCutchan.

Eisner, E. W. (1982). *Cognition and Curriculum*. NY: Longman.

Feldman, D. H. (1987). Developmental psychology and art education: Two fields at the crossroads. *The Journal of Aesthetic Education*, 21(2), 243–259.

Festinger, L. A. (1957). *A Theory of Cognitive-Dissonance*. Evanston, IL.: Row, Peterson.

Gagne, R. (1977). *The Conditions of Learning*. NY: Holt, Rinehart, and Winston.

Gardner, H. (1973). *The Arts and Human Development: A Psychological Study of the Artistic Process*. NY: Wiley.

Gardner, H. (1980). *Artful scribbles: The significance of children's drawings*. NY: Basic Books.

Gardner, H. (1983). Artistic intelligences. *Art Education*, 36(2), 47–49.

Gardner, H. and Winner, E. (1976). How children learn…three stages of understanding art. *Psychology Today*, 9, 42–43.

Gentner, D., and Stevens, A. L. (eds.) (1983). *Mental Models*. Hillsdale, NJ: Erlbaum Associates.

Gollob, H. F., and Dittes, J. E. (1965). Effects of manipulated self-esteem on persuasability depending on threat and complexity of communication. *Journal of Personality and Social Psychology*, 2, 195–201.

Goodman, N. (1984). *Of Mind and Other Matters*. Cambridge: Harvard University Press.

Halloran, J. D. (1967). *Attitude Formation and Change*. Westport, CT: Greenwood Press.

Hovland, C. I.; Campbell, E. H.; and Brock, T. (1957). The effects of "commitment" on opinion change following communication. In C. I. Hovland (ed.). *Order of Presentation in Persuasion*. New Haven: Yale University Press.

Hovland, C. I.; Janis, I. L.; and Kelley, H. H. (1953). *Communication and Persuasion*. New Haven: Yale University Press.

Insko, C. A. (1964). Primacy vs. recency in persuasion as a function of the timing of arguments and measures. *Journal of Abnormal and Social Psychology*, 69, 381–391.

Jung, C. (ed.) (1964). *Man and His Symbols*. NY: Doubleday.

Koestler, A. (1949). *Insight and Outlook*. NY: MacMillan.

Koestler, A. (1964). *The Act of Creation*. London: Hutchinson.

Krathwohl, D. R.; Bloom, B. S. and Masia, B. B. (1964). *Taxonomy of Educational Objectives: Handbook II: Affective Domain*. NY: McKay.

Linder, D. E.; Cooper, J.; and Jones, E. E. (1967). Decision freedom as a determinant of the role of incentive magnitude in attitude change. *Journal of Personality and Social Psychology*, 6, 245–254.

Lowin, A. (1967). Approach and avoidance: Alternative modes of selective exposure to information. *Journal of Personality and Social Psychology*, 6, 1–9.

Lumsdaine, A. A., and Janis, I. L. (1953). Resistance to "counter-propaganda" produced by one-sided and two-sided "propaganda" presentations. *Public Opinion Quarterly*, 17, 311–318.

Madeja, S. S. (ed). (1978). *The Arts, Cognition, and Basic Skills*. St. Louis: CEMREL.

McGuire, W. J. (1961). Resistance to persuasion conferred by active and passive prior refutation of the same and alternative counter-arguments. *Journal of Abnormal and Social Psychology*, 63, 329–332.

Miller, N., and Campbell, D. T. (1959). Recency and primacy in persuasion as a function of the timing of speeches and measurements. *Journal of Abnormal and Social Psychology*, 59, 1–9.

Mills, J. (1966). Opinion change as a function of the communicator's desire to influence and liking for the audience. *Journal of Experimental Social Psychology*, 2, 152–159.

Mills, J. & Jellison, J. M. (1968). Effect on opinion change of similarity between the communicator and the audience he addressed. *Journal of Personality and Social Psychology*, 9, 153–159.

O'Hare, D. (1976). Individual differences in perceived similarity and preference for visual art: A multidimensional scaling analysis. *Perception & Psychophysics*, 20(6), 445–452.

O'Hare, D. (1979). Multidimensional scaling representations and individual differences in concept learning of artistic style. *British Journal of Psychology*, 70, 219–230.

Papageorgis, D., and McGuire, W. J. (1962). Effectiveness of forewarning in developing resistance to persuasion. *Public Opinion Quarterly*, 26, 24–34.

Piaget, J. (1954). *The Construction of Reality in the Child*. NY: Basic Books.

Piaget, J. (1969). *The Language and Thought of the Child*. NY: World.

Piaget, J. (1977). *The Development of Thought: Equilibration of Cognitive Structure*. NY: Viking Press.

Scott, W. A. (1957). Attitude change through reward of verbal behavior. *Journal of Abnormal and Social Psychology*, 55, 72–75.

Skinner, B. F. (1938). *The Behavior of Organisms*. NY: Appleton.

Skinner, B. F. (1968). *The Technology of Teaching*. NY: Appleton.

Skinner, B. F. (1969). *Contingencies of Reinforcement: A Theoretical Analysis*. NY: Appleton.

Walster, E.; Aronson, E.; and Abrahams, D. (1966). On increasing the persuasiveness of a low prestige communicator. *Journal of Experimental Social Psychology*, 2, 325–342.

Weiner, B. (1979). A theory of motivation for some classroom experiences. *Journal of Educational Psychology*, 71, 3–25.

Weinstein, R. Et al. (1982). Student perceptions of differential teacher treatment in open and traditional classrooms. *Journal of Educational Psychology*, 74, 678–692.

Winner, E. (1982). *Invented Worlds: The Psychology of the Arts*. Cambridge: Harvard University Press.

TEACHING ART HISTORY

Ackerman, J. (1973). Toward a new social theory of art. *New Literary History*, 4, 315–330.

Ackerman, J., and Carpenter, T. (1963). *Art and Archaeology*. Englewood Cliffs, NJ: Prentice-Hall.

Alloway, L. (1975). *Topics in America Since 1945*. NY: Norton.

Anderson, T. (1985). Toward a socially defined curriculum. *Art Education*, 38(5), 16–18.

Auping, M. (1987). *Abstract Expressionism*. NY: Abrams.

Baigell, M. (1974). *The American scene: Paintings of the 1930's*: NY: Praeger.

Barr, A. (1966). *Vincent van Gogh*. NY: Arno Press.

Battcock, G. (1968). *Minimal Art*. NY: Dutton.

Battcock, G. (1966). *The new art: A critical anthology*. NY: Dutton.

Baxandall, M. (1985). *Patterns of Intention: On the Historical Explanation of Pictures*. New Haven: Yale University Press.

Bayer, H., and Gropius, W. (1976). *Bauhaus 1919–1928*. Boston: New York Graphic Society.

Bersson, R. (1986). Why art education lacks social relevance: A contextual analysis. *Art Education*, 39(4), 41–45.

Boorstein, D. (1973). *The Americans: The Democratic Experience*. NY: Vintage Books.

Broude, N. and Garrard, M. D. (1982). *Feminism and Art History: Questioning the Litany*. NY: Harper & Row.

Chalmers, G. (1973). The study of art in a cultural context. *Journal of Aesthetics and Art Criticism*, 32(2), 249–256.

Chalmers, G. (1974). A cultural foundation for education in the arts. *Art Education*, 27(1), 21–25.

Chalmers, G. (1978). Teaching and studying art history: Some anthropological and sociological considerations. *Studies in Art Education*, 20(1), 18–25.

Chalmers, F. G. (1987). Beyond current conceptions of Discipline-based art education. *Art Education*, 40(5), 58–61.

Cleaver, D. G. (1985). *Art: An Introduction* (4th ed.). NY: Harcourt Brace Jovanovich.

Coke, V. D. (1975). *100 Years of Photographic History*. Albuquerque: U. of New Mexico Press.

Cole, D. (1973). *From Tipi to Sky Scraper: History of Women in Architecture*. Boston: Boston Press.

Collingwood, R. G. (1956). *The Idea of History*. Oxford: Oxford University Press.

Copplestone, T. (1983). *Art in Society: A Guide to the Visual Arts*. Englewood Cliffs, NJ: Prentice-Hall.

Davis, D. (1977). *ArtCulture*. NY: Harper & Row.

Day, M. D. (1969). The compatibility of art history and studio art activity in the junior high school art program. *Studies in Art Education*, 10(2), 57–65.

Deinhard, H. (1975). Reflections on art history and sociology of art. *Art Journal*, 35(1), 20–32.

Dube, W. D. (1983). *Expressionists and Expressionism*. NY: Skira, Rizzoli.

Duberman, M. (1972). *Black Mountain*. NY: Dutton.

Duvignaud, J. (1972). *The Sociology of Art*. London: Paladin.

Elsen, A. E. (1972). *Purposes of Art*. New York: Holt, Rinehart, and Winston.

Erickson, M. (1977). Uses of art history in art education. *Studies in Art Education*, 18(3), 22–29.

Erickson, M. (1983). Teaching art history as an inquiry process. *Art Education*, 36(5), 28–31.

Erickson, M. and Katter, E. (1981). *How Do You Do Art History?* Kutztown, PA: MELD.

Erickson, M. and Katter, E. (1981). *Artifacts*, Kutztown, PA: MELD.

Erikson, E. H. (1958). *Young Man Luther: A Study in Psychoanalysis and History*. NY: Norton.

Feldman, E. B. (1981). *Varieties of Visual Experience*. Englewood Cliffs, NJ: Prentice-Hall.

Feldman, E. B. (1985). *Thinking About Art*. Englewood Cliffs, NJ: Prentice-Hall.

Fichner-Rathus, L. (1986). *Understanding Art*. Englewood Cliffs, NJ: Prentice-Hall.

Finch, C. (1968). *Pop Art*. NY: Dutton.

Fine, E. H. (1978). *Women and Art: A History of Women Painters and Sculptors from the Renaissance to the 20th Century*. Montclair, NJ: Allanheld & Schram.

Fitzgerald, F. (1979). *America Revised: History School Books in the Twentieth Century*. Boston: Atlantic Little-Brown.

Fleming, W. (1974). *Art and Ideas*. NY: Holt, Rinehart, and Winston.

Foster, H. (1983). *The Anti-Aesthetic: Essays on Postmodern Culture*. Port Townsend, WA: Bay Press.

Fox, H. (1987). *Avante-Garde in the Eighties*. Los Angeles: Los Angeles County Museum of Art.

Fry, E. (1981). *Cubism*. NY: W. Norton.

Fry, R. (1920). *Vision and Design*. London.

Fry, R. (1927). *Cezanne: A Study of His Development*. London: L. and V. Woolf.

Gilbert, R., and McCarter, W. (1988). *Living With Art*. NY: Knopf.

Gilhorn, C. (1970). Pop pedagogy: Looking at the coke bottle. In M. Fishwick and R. Brown (eds.), *Icons of Popular Culture*. Bowling Green, OH: Bowling Green University Press.

Godfrey, T. (1986). *The New Image: Painting in the 1980's*. NY: Abbeville Press.

Goldstein, E; Saunders, R.; Kowalchuk, J. D.; and Katz, T. H. *Understanding and Creating Art, Books I & II*. Dallas: Garrard.

Golleck, R. (1987). *Der Blaue Reiter*. NY: teNeues Press.

Gombrich, E. H. (1983). *The Story of Art* (13th ed.). NY: Praeger.

Gowans, A. (1974). Popular arts and historic artifact: New principles for studying history in art. In J. M. N. Fishwick, (ed.), *Popular Architecture*. Bowling Green, OH: Bowling Green Popular Press, 88–105.

Harris, M. E. (1987). *The Art of Black Mountain College*. MIT Press.

Haselberger, H. (1961). Methods of studying ethnographic art. *Current Anthropology*, 2, 341–384.

Hastie, R., and Schmidt, C. *Encounters With Art*. NY: McGraw-Hill.

Hauser, A. (1982). *The Sociology of Art* (K. Northcott, trans.). Chicago: University of Chicago.

Hirsch, E. D. (1983). Cultural Literacy. *The American Scholar*, 52, 159–169.

Hirsch, E. D. (1985). Cultural literacy and the schools. *American Educator*, 74, 8–15.

Hirsch, E. D. (1987). *Cultural Literacy: What Every American Needs to Know*. Boston: Houghton Mifflin.

Hitler, A. (1943). *Mein Kampf* (R. Matheim, trans.). Boston: Houghton Mifflin.

Hobbs, J. A. (1985). *Art in Context*. Orlando, FL: Harcourt Brace Jovanovich.

Hobbs, J. A. (1984). Popular art vs. fine art. *Art Education*, 37(3), 11–15.

Horowitz, F. A. (1985). *More Than You See: A Guide to Art*. NY: Harcourt Brace Jovanovich.

Hughes, R. (1980). *The Shock of the New*. NY: Knopf.

Hunter, M. & Gee, K. (1988). Art appreciation/art history lesson (Part II). *NAEA Advisory*. Reston, VA: National Art Education Association.

Hurwitz, A. (1986). *Teaching Art History: What Forms Can it Take?* Harrisburg, PA: Pennsylvania State Dept. of Education, Pennsylvania's Symposium II on Art Education. (ERIC Document Preproduction Service, ED 287 759).

Hurwitz, A. and Madeja, S. S. (1977). *The Joyous Vision: Source Book*. Englewood Cliffs, NJ: Prentice-Hall.

Janson, H. W. (1962). *History of Art*. Englewood Cliffs, NJ: Prentice-Hall.

Katter, E. (1988). An approach to art games: Playing and planning. *Art Education*, 41(3), 46–54.

Katter, E. (1986). *Art History Instruction: From History to Practice*. Harrisburg, PA: Pennsylvania State Dept. of Education, Pennsylvania's Symposium II on Art Education. (ERIC Document Reproduction Service, ED 287 759).

Kimball, S. B. (1972). Social and cultural congruences in American civilization. *Journal of Aesthetic Education*, 6(1–2), 39–52.

Kleinbauer, W. E. (1971). *Modern Perspectives in Western Art History*. NY: Holt, Rinehart, and Winston.

Kleinbauer, W. E. (1987). Art history in discipline-based art education. *The Journal of Aesthetic Education*, 21(2), 205–216.

Knobler, N. (1980). *The Visual Dialogue* (3rd ed.). NY: Henry Holt.

Kramer, H. (1973). *The Age of the Avante-Garde*. NY: Farrar, Straus & Giroux.

Kurlansky, M. J. (1977). Pop goes the culture. *Change*, 9(6), 36–39.

Kurtz, B. (1987). *Visual Imagination*. Englewood Cliffs, NJ: Prentice-Hall.

LaChapelle, J. R. (1984). The sociology of art and art education: A relationship reconsidered. *Studies in Art Education*, 26(1), 34–40.

Lee, S. (1982). *A History of Far Eastern Art*. NY: Abrams.

Linderman, E. (1980). *Teaching Secondary School Art*. Dubuque: Wm. C. Brown Co.

Lowenthal, D. (1985). *The Past is a Foreign Country*. Cambridge: Cambridge University Press.

Lucie-Smith, E. (1982). *Art in the Seventies*, Ithaca: Cornell University Press.

Lucie-Smith, E. (1985). *Movements in Art Since 1945*. NY: Norton.

McCarthy, M. J. (1978). *Introducing Art History: A Guide for Teachers*. Toronto: Ontario Institute for Studies in Education.

McFarlane, J. (1978). The mind of modernism. In M. Bradbury and J. McFarlane (eds.), *Modernism 1890–1930* (pp. 71–93). NJ: Humanities.

McFee, J. K. (1971). *Preparation for Art* (2nd ed.). Belmont, CA: Wadsworth.

McFee, J. K. (1984). An analysis of the goal, structure, and social context of the 1965 Penn State seminar and the 1983 Getty Institute for Educators on the Visual Arts. *Studies in Art Education*, 25(4), 276–281.

McFee, J. K., and Degge, R. M. (1977). *Art Culture and Environment: A Catalyst for Teaching*. Belmont, CA: Wadsworth.

McShine, K. (1987). *Berlin art 1961–1987*. NY: teNeues.

Moffatt, J. F. (1969). Art history as a pedagogical science. *Art Education*, 22(3), 24–28.

Muller, G. (1973). *The New Avant-Garde*. NY: Praeger.

Mukerjee, R. (1959). *The Social Function of Art*. NY: Philosophical Library.

Munz, P. (1977). *The Shapes of Time: A New Look at the Philosophy of History*. Middletown, CT: Wesleyan University Press.

Nagle, J. (1980). *The Responsive Arts*. Sherman Oaks, CA: Alfred.

Naisbitt, J. (1984). *Megatrends*. NY: Warner Books.

Neret, G. (1986). *The Art of the Twenties*. NY: Rizzoli.

Norberg-Schultz, C. (1975). *Meaning in Western Architecture*. NY: Praeger.

Ocvirk, O. G. (1975). *Art Fundamentals*. Dubuque: Wm. C. Brown.

Panofsky, E. (1955). *Meaning in the Visual Arts*. Chicago: University of Chicago Press.

Panofsky, E. (1962). *Studies in Iconology: Humanistic themes in the art of the Renaissance* (rev. ed.). NY: Harper & Row.

Parks, M. E. (1989). Art education in a post-modern age. *Art Education,* 42(2), 10–13.

Pazienza, J. (1986). *Investigating the Discipline of Art History.* Harrisburg, PA: Pennsylvania State Dept. of Education, Pennsylvania's Symposium II on Art Education. (ERIC Document Reproduction Service, ED 287 759).

Peterson, K., and Wilson, J. J. (1976). *Women Artists: Recognition and Reappraisal from Early Middle Ages to the Twentieth Century.* NY: Harper & Row.

Phipps, R., and Wink, R. (1987). *Invitation to the Gallery: An Introduction to Art.* Dubuque: Wm. C. Brown.

Pointon, M. (1980). *History of Art: A Students' Handbook.* London: Allen & Unwin.

Preble, D., and Preble, S. (1985). *Artforms.* New York: Harper & Row.

Prown, J. (1982). Mind in matter: An introduction to material culture theory and method. *Winterhur Portfolio,* 17, 1–19.

Ravitch, D. (November 17, 1985). Decline and fall of teaching history. *New York Times Magazine,* pp. 50–52; 101; 117.

Ravitch, D. (1985). *From history to social studies. In The Schools We Deserve: Reflections on the Educational Crisis of Our Times* (pp. 112–132). NY: Basic Books.

Read, H. (1968). *A Concise History of Modern Painting.* NY: Praeger.

Read, H. (1968). *The Meaning of Art.* Boston: Faber & Faber.

Read, H. (1967). *Art and Alienation: The Role of the Artist in Society.* NY: Horizon Press.

Read, H. (19??). *Art and Society.* New York: Pantheon Books.

Rice, D. (1986). *The Uses and Abuses of Art History.* Harrisburg, PA: Pennsylvania State Dept. of Education, Pennsylvania's Symposium II on Art Education. (ERIC Document Reproduction Service, ED 287 759).

Richter, H. (1985). *DaDa: Art & Anti-Art.* NY: Norton.

Robins, C. (1984). *The Pluralist Era: American Art 1968–1981.* NY: Harper & Row.

Rose, B. (1975). *America Art Since 1900.* NY: Praeger.

Rose, B. (1975). *Readings in American Art: 1900–1975.* NY: Praeger.

Roskill, M. (1976). *What is Art History?* NY: Harper & Row.

Rotters, E. (1982). *Berlin 1910–1933.* NY: Rizzoli.

Rudenstine, A. (1981). *Russian Avant-Garde: The George Costakis Collection.* NY: Abrams.

Russell, J. (1965). *Seurat.* London: Thames & Hudson.

Russell, J. (1981). *The Meanings of Modern Art.* New York: Harper & Row.

Schapiro, M. (1952). *Paul Cezanne.* NY: Abrams.

Silberman, A. (1968). *Introduction: A definition of the sociology of art.* International Social Science Journal, 20, 567–588.

Simpson, C. R. (1981). SOHO: *The Artist in the City*. Chicago: University of Chicago Press.

Thernstrom, S. (1985). The humanities and our cultural Challenge. In C. E. Finn, D. Ravitch, and P. Roberts (eds.), *Challenges to the Humanities*. NY: Holmes and Meier.

Toffler, A. (1970). *Future Shock*. NY: Random House.

Tompkins, C. (1975). *Report on Post-Modern Art*. NY: Viking Press.

Whitford, F. (1983). *Bauhaus*. NY: Norton.

Wilson, B. (1986). *Of Trivial Facts and Speculative Inquiry: Philosophical Quandaries About Teaching Art History in the Schools*. Harrisburg, PA: Pennsylvania State Dept. of Education, Pennsylvania's Symposium II on Art Education. (ERIC Document Preproduction Services, ED 287 759).

Wolfflin, H. (1932) (reprint 1950). *Principles of Art History*. NY: Dover.

Wright, F. L. (1960). *Writings and Buildings*. Daufman, E., and Raeburn, B. (eds.). NY: Horizon.

Zelensky, P. and Fisher, M. P. (1988). *The Art of Seeing*. Englewood Cliffs, NJ: Prentice-Hall.

TEACHING CRITICISM AND AESTHETICS

Adams, R. L. (1985). Aesthetic dialogue for children: Paradigm and program. *Art Education*, 38(5), p. 12–15.

Anderson, T. (1986). Talking about art with children: From theory to practice. *Art Education*, 39(1), 5–8.

Arnheim, R. (1962). *Picasso's Guernica: The Genesis of a Painting*. Berkeley and Los Angeles: University of California Press.

Arnheim, R. (1969). *Visual Thinking*. Berkeley: University of California Press.

Arnheim, R. (1983). Perceiving, thinking, forming. *Art Education*, 36(2), 9–11.

Bachtel-Nash, A. (1985). Teaching aesthetic perception in the elementary school. *Art Education*, 38(5), 6–11.

Barnet, S. (1985). *A short guide to writing about art* (2nd ed.). Boston: Little, Brown.

Barthes, R. (1972). *Mythologies*. NY: Hill and Wang.

Barthes, R. (1981). *Camera Lucida*. NY: Hill and Wang.

Battcock, G. (1966). *The new art: A critical anthology*. NY: Dutton.

Beardsley, M. C. (1966). *Aesthetics from Classical Greece to the Present: A Short History*. NY: MacMillan.

Beardsley, M. C. (1981). *Aesthetics: Problems in the Philosophy of Criticism* (2nd ed.). Indianapolis: Hackett.

Bell, C. (1914). *Art*. London: Chatto & Windus.

Bell, C. (1922). *Since Cezanne*. London: Chatto & Windus.

Berger, J. (1972). *Ways of seeing*. London: BBC and Penguin Books.

Bird, E. (1979). Aesthetic neutrality and the sociology of art. In M. Barrett, P. Corrigan, A. Kuhn, and J. Wolff (eds.), *Ideology and Cultural Production* (pp. 25–48). NY: St. Martin's Press.

Broude, N., and Garrard, M. D. (1982). *Feminism and Art History: Questioning the Litany*. NY: Harper & Row.

Broudy, H. S. (1966). The structure of knowledge in the arts. In R. A. Smith (ed.), *Aesthetics and Criticism in Art Education: Problems in Defining, Explaining, and Evaluating Art* (pp. 23–45). Chicago: Rand McNally.

Broudy, H. S. (1972). *Enlightened Cherishing: An Essay on Aesthetic Education*. Urbana: University of Illinois Press. Distributed by Kappa Delta Pi, Lafayette, IN.

Broudy, H. S. (1987). Theory and practice in aesthetic education. *Studies in Art Education*, 28(4), 195–197.

Child, I. L. (1970). The problem of objectivity in esthetic value. In G. Pappas (ed.), *Concepts in Art and Education*. NY: MacMillan.

Collier, G. (1972). *Art and the Creative Consciousness*. Englewood Cliffs, NJ: Prentice-Hall.

Collingwood, R. G. (1956). *The Idea of History*. Oxford: Oxford University Press.

Collingwood, R. G. (1958). *Principles of Art*. Oxford: Oxford University Press.

Crawford, D. W. (1987). Aesthetics in discipline-based art education. *The Journal of Aesthetic Education*, 21(2), 227–242.

Cromer, J. (1990). *Criticism: History, Theory and Practice of Art Criticism in Art Education*. Reston, VA: National Art Education Association.

Dallis, C. (1975). *The effects of a black-oriented teaching strategy on attitude change, aesthetic taste, and cognitive learning in art appreciation*. (Doctoral dissertation, University of Georgia). Dissertation Abstracts International, 36, 5648A.

Danto, A. C. (1981). *The Transfiguration of the Commonplace*. Cambridge, MA: Harvard University.

Dewey, J. (1934). *Art As Experience*. NY: Capricorn Books, Putnam's.

Dickie, G. (1971). *Aesthetics: An Introduction*. Indianapolis: Bobbs-Merrill.

Dickie, G., and Sclafani, R. (Eds.) (1977). *Aesthetics: A Critical Anthology*. NY: St. Martin's Press.

Douglas, N. J.; Schwartz, J. B.; and Taylor, J. B. (1981). The relationship of cognitive style of young children and their modes of responding to paintings. *Studies in Art Education*, 22(3), 24–31.

Ecker, D. W. *Defining behavioral objectives for aesthetic education*. St. Ann, MO: CEM-REL.

Ecker, D. W. (1967). Justifying aesthetic judgments. *Art Education*, 20(5), 5–8.

Ecker, D. W., and Kaelin, E. F. (1958). Aesthetics in public school art teaching. *College Art Journal*, 17(4), 382–391.

Ecker, D. W., and Kaelin, E. F. (1972). The limits of aesthetic inquiry: A guide to educational research. In L. G. Thomas (ed.), *Philosophical Redirection of Educational Research* (pp. 258–286). 71st Yearbook of the National Society for the Study of Education, Pt. 1. Chicago: University of Chicago Press.

Feinstein, H. (1982). Meaning and visual metaphor. *Studies in Art Education*, 23(2), 45–55.

Feinstein, H. (1982). Art means values. *Art Education*, 35(5), 13–15.

Feinstein, H. (1983). The therapeutic trap in metaphoric interpretation. *Art Education*, 36(4), 30–33.

Feinstein, H. (1984). The metaphoric interpretation of paintings: Effects of the clustering strategy and relaxed attention exercises. *Studies in Art Education*, 25(2), 77–83.

Feinstein, H. (1989). The art response guide: How to read art for meaning, a primer for art criticism. *Art Education*, 42(3), 43–53.

Feldman, E. B. (1965). The nature of the aesthetic experience. In J. Hausman (ed.), *Report of the Commission on Art Education* (pp. 35–46). Washington, D.C.: National Art Education Association.

Feldman, E. B. (1966). Research as the verification of aesthetics. In R. Smith (ed.), *Aesthetics and Criticism in Art Education* (pp. 56–61). Chicago: Rand McNally.

Feldman, E. B. (1967). *Art As Image and Idea*. Englewood Cliffs, NJ: Prentice-Hall.

Feldman, E. B. (1970). *Becoming Human through Art: Aesthetic Experience in the School*. Englewood Cliffs, NJ: Prentice-Hall.

Feldman, E. B. (1973). The teacher as model critic. *Journal of Aesthetic Education*, 7(1), 50–57.

Feldman, E. B. (1985). *Thinking About Art*. Englewood Cliffs, NJ: Prentice-Hall.

Foster, H. (1983). *The Anti-Aesthetic: Essays on Postmodern Culture*. Port Townsend, WA: Bay Press.

Foucault, M. (1973). *The Order of Things*. NY: Vintage Books.

Friedlander, M. (1932). *On Art and Connoisseurship* (T. Borenvi, trans.) Oxford: Bruno Cassirieu.

Fry, R. (1920). *Vision and Design*. London.

Fry, R. (1927). *Cezanne: A Study of His Development*. London: L. and V. Woolf.

Gablik, S. (1984). *Has Modernism Failed?*. New York: Thames and Hudson.

Gardner, H. (1973). *The Arts and Human Development: A Psychological Study of the Artistic Process*. NY: Wiley.

Gardner, H. (1980). *Artful scribbles: The significance of children's drawings*. NY: Basic Books.

Gardner, H. (1983). Artistic intelligences. *Art Education*, 36(2), 47–49.

Gardner, H. and Winner, E. (1976). How children learn…three stages of understanding art. *Psychology Today*, 9, 42–43.

Geahigan, G. (1980). Metacritical inquiry in art education. *Studies in Art Education*, 21(3), 54–67.

Gilliatt, M. (1980). The effects of habituation, the Feldman-Mittler methodology, and studio activities on expanding art preferences of elementary students. *Studies in Art Education*, 21(2), 43–49.

Gombrich, E. H. (1960–61). *Art and Illusion*. NY: Pantheon Books.

Goodman, N. (1976). *Languages of Art: An Approach to a Theory of Symbols*. Indianapolis: Hackett.

Greene, M. (1981). Aesthetic literacy in general education. In J. F. Soltis (ed.), *Philosophy and Education* (pp. 115–141). 80th Yearbook of the National Society for the Study of Education, Pt. 1, Chicago: University of Chicago Press.

Hagaman, S. (1988). Philosophical aesthetics in the art class: A look toward implementation. *Art Education*, 41(3), 18–22.

Haldane, J. J. (1983). Art's perspective on value. *Art Education*, 36(1), 8–9.

Hamblen, K. A. (1984). An art criticism questioning strategy within the framework of Bloom's taxonomy. *Studies in Art Education*, 26(1), 41–50.

Hamblen, K. A. (1984). Artistic perception as a function of learned expectations. *Art Education*, 37(3), p. 20–26.

Hamblen, K. A. (1985). Developing aesthetic literacy through contested concepts. *Art Education*, 38(5), 19–24.

Hamblen, K. A. (1988). Approaches to aesthetics in art education: A critical theory perspective. *Studies in Art Education*, 29(2), 81–90.

Heidt, A. H. (1986). Creating art appreciation activities. *Art Education*, 39(1), 23–28.

Henri, R. (1958). *The Art Spirit*. Philadelphia: Lippincott.

Hewett, G. J. & Rush, J. C. Finding buried treasures: Aesthetic scanning with children. *Art Education*, 40(1), 41–45.

Hobbs, J. A. (1985). *Art in Context*. Orlando, FL: Harcourt Brace Jovanovich.

Hobbs, J. A. (1984). Popular art vs. fine art. *Art Education*, 37(3), 11–15.

Hofstadter, A. (1965). *Truth and Art*. NY: Columbia University Press.

Hollingsworth, P. L. (1983). The combined effect of mere exposure, counterattitudinal advocacy, and art criticism methodology on upper elementary and junior high students' affect towards works of art. *Studies in Art Education*, 24(2), 101–110.

Horowitz, F. A. (1985). *More Than You See: A Guide to Art*. NY: Harcourt Brace Jovanovich.

Hospers, J. (1982). *Understanding the Arts*. Englewood Cliffs, NJ: Prentice-Hall.

Hurwitz, A. and Madeja, S. S. (1977). *The Joyous Vision: Source Book*. Englewood Cliffs, NJ: Prencitce-Hall.

Johansen, P. (1979). An art appreciation teaching model for visual aesthetic education. *Studies in Art Education*, 20(3), 4–5.

Johnson, M. (Ed.). (1981). *Philosophical Perspectives on Metaphor*. Minneapolis: The University of Minnesota Press.

Jung, C. (ed.) (1964). *Man and His Symbols*. NY: Doubleday.

Katter, E. (1988). An approach to art games: Playing and planning. *Art Education*, 41(3), 46–54.

Kelly, J. J. (1970). *The Sculptural Idea*. Minneapolis: Burgess.

Kepes, G. (1965). *Education of Vision*. NY: Braziller.

Kepes, G. (1944). *Language of Vision*. Chicago: Theobold.

Kern, E. J. (1984). The aesthetic education curriculum program and curriculum reform. *Studies in Art Education*, 25(4), 219–225.

Koestler, A. (1949). *Insight and Outlook*. NY: MacMillan.

Koestler, A. (1964). *The Act of Creation*. London: Hutchinson.

Koroscik, J. S. (1982). The effects of prior knowledge, presentation time, and task demands on visual art processing. *Studies in Art Education*, 23(3), 13–22.

Koroscik, J. S. (1984). Cognition in viewing and talking about art. *Theory into Practice*, 23(4), 330–333.

Kramer, H. (1973). *The Age of the Avante-Garde*. NY: Farrar, Straus & Giroux.

Kurlansky, M. J. (1977). Pop goes the culture. *Change*, 9(6), 36–39.

Lakoff, G. & Johnson, M. (1980). *Metaphors We Live By*. Chicago: University of Chicago Press.

Landau, J. (1986). Looking, thinking, and learning: Visual literacy for children. *Art Education*, 39(1), 17–21.

Langer, S. (1953). *Feeling and Form*. NY: Scribner's.

Langer, S. (1957). *Problems in Art*. NY: Scribner's.

Lanier, V. (1976). *Essays in Art Education: The Development of One Point of View* (2nd ed.). NY: MSS Educational Publishing.

Lanier, V. (1981). *Aesthetic literacy as the product of art education. In The Product of a Process* (pp. 115–121). Proceedings of the 24th INSEA World Congress, Rotterdam, 1981. Amsterdam: De Trommel.

Lanier, V. (1981). Popularization without misrepresentation: Curriculum content for aesthetic literacy. *Art Education*, 34(6), 5–12.

Lankford, E. L. (1992). *Aesthetics: Issues and Inquiry*. Reston, VA.: National Art Education Association.

Lankford, E. L. (1984). A phenomenological methodology for art criticism. *Studies in Art Education*, 25(3), 151–158.

Lankford, E. L. (1986). Making sense of aesthetics. *Studies in Art Education*, 28(1), 48–52.

Lipman, M. (1967). *What Happens in Art*. NY: Appleton-Century-Crofts.

MacGregor, N. (1970). Concepts of criticism: Implications for art education. *Studies in Art Education*, 11(2), 27–33.

MacQueen, J. (1970). *Allegory*. London: Methuen.

Madeja, S. S. (1971). Aesthetic education: An area of study. *Art Education*, 24(8), 16–19.

Madeja, S. S., and Onuska, S. (1977). *Through the Arts to the Aesthetic*: The CEMREL Aesthetic Education Curriculum. St. Louis: CEMREL.

Margolis, J. (1962). *Philosophy Looks at the Arts*. NY: Scribner's.

McFarlane, J. (1978). The mind of modernism. In M. Bradbury and J. McFarlane (eds.), *Modernism 1890–1930* (pp. 71–93). NJ: Humanities.

McLuhan, M. (1967). *The Medium Is the Message*. NY: Ballantine.

Mittler, G. A. (1972). Attitude modification towards works of art. *Studies in Art Education*, 13(2), 58.

Mittler, G. A. (1976). An instructional strategy designed to overcome the adverse effects of established students attitudes towards works of art. *Studies in Art Education*, 17(3), 13–31.

Mittler, G. A. (1980). Learning to look/looking to learn: A proposed approach to art appreciation at the secondary level. *Art Education*, 33(3), 17–21.

Mittler, G. A. (1986). *Art in Focus*. Peoria: Bennett & McKnight.

Morris, J. W. and Stuckhardt, M. H. (1977). Art attitude: Conceptualization and implication. *Studies in Art Education*, 19(1), 21–28.

Muller, G. (1973). *The New Avant-Garde*. NY: Praeger.

Mukerjee, R. (1959). *The Social Function of Art*. NY: Philosophical Library.

Munz, P. (1977). *The Shapes of Time: A New Look at the Philosophy of History*. Middletown, CT: Wesleyan University Press.

Panofsky, E. (1955). *Meaning in the Visual Arts*. Chicago: University of Chicago Press.

Panofsky, E. (1962). *Studies in Iconology: Humanistic themes in the art of the Renaissance* (rev. ed.). NY: Harper & Row.

Panofsky, E. (1968). *Idea: A Concept in Art Theory*. NY: Harper & Row.

Parks, M. E. (1988). How does the work mean? *Art Education*, 41(3), 55–61.

Parsons, M. J. (1976). A suggestion concerning the development of aesthetic experience in children. *Journal of Aesthetics and Art Criticism*, 34(3), 305–314.

Parsons, M. J. (1987). Talk about a painting: a cognitive developmental analysis. *The Journal of Aesthetic Education*, 21(1), 37–55.

Parsons, M.; Johnston, M.; and Durham, R. (1978). Developmental stages of children's aesthetic responses. *Journal of Aesthetic Education*, 83–104.

Pepper, S. (1945). *The Basis of Criticism in the Arts*. Cambridge: Harvard University Press.

Phenix, P. H. (1964). *Realms of Meaning*. NY: McGraw-Hill.

Plummer, G. S. (1974). *Children's Art Judgment*. Dubuque: Wm. C. Brown.

Poggioli, R. (1968). *The Theory of the Avant-Garde* (G. Fitzgerald, trans.). Cambridge, MA: Belknap.

Prown, J. (1982). Mind in matter: An introduction to material culture theory and method. *Winterhur Portfolio*, 17, 1–19.

Rader, M., and Jessup, B. (1976). *Art and Human Values*. Englewood Cliffs, NJ: Prentice-Hall.

Read, H. (1968). *The Meaning of Art*. Boston: Faber & Faber.

Read, H. (1967). *Art and Alienation: The Role of the Artist in Society*. New York: Horizon Press.

Read, H. (19??). *Art and Society*. New York: Pantheon Books.

Reid, L. A. (1973). Aesthetics and aesthetic education. In D. Field and J. Newick (eds.), *The Study of Education and Art* (pp. 164–186). Boston: Routledge & Kegan Paul.

Risatti, H. (1987). Art criticism in discipline-based art education. *The Journal of Aesthetic Education*, 21(2), 217–226.

Rosenberg, H. (1976). *Art on the Edge: Creators and Situation*. NY: MacMillan.

Rosenstiel, A. K.; Morison, P.; Silverman, J.; and Gardner, H. (1978). Critical judgment: A developmental study. *The Journal of Aesthetic Education*, 12(4), 95–107. Dissertation Abstracts International, 37, 3353A.

Taunton, M. (1982). Aesthetic responses of young children to the visual arts: A review of the literature. *Journal of Aesthetic Education*, 16(3), 93–109.

Thernstrom, S. (1985). The humanities and our cultural Challenge. In C. E. Finn, D. Ravitch, and P. Roberts (eds.), *Challenges to the Humanities*. NY: Holmes and Meier.

Tilghman, B. (1973). *Language and Aesthetics*. Lawrence, KS: University Press of Kansas.

Toffler, A. (1970). *Future Shock*. NY: Random House.

Tompkins, C. (1975). *Report on Post-Modern Art*. NY: Viking Press.

Tsugawa, A. (1968). The nature of the aesthetic and human values. *Art Education*, 21(8), 11–20.

Virden, P. (1972). The social determinants of aesthetic styles. *British Journal of Aesthetics*, 12(2), 175–185.

Weitz, M. (1976). Art: Who needs it? *Journal of Aesthetic Education*, 10(1), 19–27.

Welty, W. M. (July/August, 1989). Discussion method teaching: How to make it work. *Change*, 21, 41–49.

Werhane, P. H. (1984). *Philosophical Issues in Art*. Englewood Cliffs, NJ: Prentice-Hall.

Wilson, B. (1988). *Art Education, Civilization and the 21st Century: A Researcher's Reflections on the National Endowment for the Arts' Report to Congress*. Reston, VA: National Art Education Association.

Wilson, J. (1967). *Language and the Pursuit of Truth*. London: Cambridge University Press.

Winner, E. (1982). *Invented Worlds: The Psychology of the Arts*. Cambridge: Harvard University Press.

INDEX